POWERPLAY

THE NEW RULES OF GLOBAL INFLUENCE

PK SRIVASTAVA

Made with ♥ on the Notion Press Platform
www.notionpress.com

Dedicated to My Parents

Late Satyendra Prasad And

Late Usha Srivastava

Contents

Foreword *vii*

Prologue *ix*

Preface *xi*

Acknowledgements *xiii*

1. The Shifting Foundations Of Global Geopolitics 1
2. Multipolarity And Power Shifts 5
3. Regional Conflicts And Alliances 13

Case Studies In Multipolar Practice

4. China's Belt And Road Initiative (BRI): Strategy Or Hegemony? 31
5. Russia-Ukraine War: Reshaping The European Security Order 41

Case Study 1

Case Study 2

Case Study 3

6. India-Pakistan Relations After The Pahalgam Attack: Escalation, Diplomacy, And Global Consequences 67
7. Energy Geopolitics And Resource Competition: Old Battles, New Frontiers 84
8. Geo-Economics And Trade Wars 93
9. Climate Change And Environmental Geopolitics 103
10. U.S.-India-China Strategic Triangle: Cooperation, Competition, And Containment 107
11. Artificial Intelligence And The Future Of Geopolitical Power 112
12. Space Geopolitics – The New Strategic Frontier 127

Case Study A: Starlink In The Ukraine War

Case Study B: China's Orbital Logistics And The Tiangong Space Station

13. Digital Sovereignty And The Politics Of Data 139
14. Global Health Geopolitics Post-COVID-19 148
15. Maritime Geopolitics And The Blue Economy 161

Contents

16. Religion, Ideology, And Civilizational Politics 170
17. Strategic Culture And National Identity In Foreign Policy 178
18. The Global South And The Quest For Strategic Autonomy 189
19. India's Strategic Rise In The Emerging Global Order 200
20. Gendered Perspectives In Global Power And Security 215
21. Displacement, Migration, And The Weaponization Of Borders 223
22. Reimagining Global Order In A Fragmented World 238

Author's Reflection 247

Gratitude 251

Foreword

We are witnessing a profound transformation in the global order-one where the traditional anchors of power are no longer limited to military strength or economic supremacy. In today's world, influence is being redefined by technological innovation, information dominance, cultural resonance, and the agility to adapt to fluid geopolitical realities.

Powerplay: The New Rules of Global Influence is a timely and insightful work that captures the essence of this shift. What makes this book particularly compelling is the intellectual depth and clarity with which the author, Punit K Srivastava, dissects these emerging paradigms. A postgraduate in Political Science and International Relations, Punit brings both scholarly rigour and real-world relevance to his analysis. His understanding of the nuanced interplay between statecraft, strategy, and soft power lends this book a rare combination of accessibility and academic richness.

Through incisive commentary and a wide array of contemporary case studies, Punit explores how power is acquired, negotiated, and projected in an increasingly multipolar world. From the recalibration of global institutions and the return of great power rivalry, to the influence of non-state actors and the evolving role of civil society, the book traverses the dynamic terrain of 21st-century geopolitics with admirable precision.

Punit's ingenuity lies not just in identifying trends, but in contextualizing them. He does not merely describe the changing rules of global engagement-he unpacks their implications for policymakers, scholars, and citizens alike. By bridging theory with lived realities, he offers readers a framework to understand the complex choreography of global influence today.

This is more than just a book-it is a thoughtful invitation to rethink power in all its modern forms. I am confident that Powerplay will prove to be an essential companion for anyone seeking to make sense of our rapidly evolving world.

Dr SUDHIR KUMAR
Ex Associate Prof. of Political Science
DAV POSTGRADUATE COLLEGE
AZAMGARH - 276001

Prologue

A World Between Orders

We stand at the threshold of a geopolitical transition that is as uncertain as it is irreversible. The certainties of the 20th century-fixed alliances, bipolar standoffs, a U.S.-anchored world order-have given way to a landscape marked by fragmentation, flux, and fierce competition. This is not merely a redistribution of power among nations; it is a redefinition of what power means, how it is exercised, and who gets to wield it.

The world today is no longer bound by Cold War binaries, nor can it be described by the unipolar triumphalism that followed the collapse of the Soviet Union. Instead, we face a multipolar reality that is uneven and hybrid-where state and non-state actors, democratic and authoritarian regimes, regional coalitions and global corporations, all coexist and contend for influence. Traditional military strength is still vital, but it is now accompanied-if not often supplanted-by economic coercion, digital control, climate diplomacy, and ideological soft power.

From the shifting alignments in the Indo-Pacific to the energy corridors of Eurasia, from the rise of the Global South to the contest over rare earths and data flows, the new theatres' of influence are complex and multidimensional. Conflict has not disappeared-it has migrated. Into cyberspace, into legal interpretations, into supply chains, and even into the narratives we tell about history, identity, and the future.

In this fragmented world, traditional institutions-be they the United Nations, NATO, the World Bank, or the WTO-are struggling to keep pace with emergent realities. They were built for a world that assumed hierarchy, stability, and convergence. Today's world offers none of these assurances. Instead, it demands resilience, reinvention, and a more inclusive architecture of cooperation.

This book-***Powerplay: The New Rules of Global Influence***-is an attempt to decode the anatomy of this evolving world order. It is not a catalogue of current events, but a strategic inquiry into the deeper shifts reshaping global power. Each chapter explores a different axis of influence: military and strategic realignments, climate and energy politics, technological sovereignty, migration and identity, digital borders, economic interdependence, and the rise of alternative governance models.

The goal is not to celebrate or mourn the passing of the old order, but to map the contours of what might come next. For policymakers, scholars, entrepreneurs, and global citizens alike, understanding these dynamics is not optional-it is essential. Because the world that is emerging will not be shaped by default, but by design. And design, in this context, is a function of ideas, institutions, imagination-and above all, influence.

We are in a moment of powerplay. The board is global. The rules are changing. And everyone-whether aware or not-is already a player.

This book is your guide to the game.

Preface

This book began as a set of questions, not conclusions. What happens when the rules of global engagement are no longer agreed upon? When institutions meant to uphold international order are sidelined, circumvented, or weaponized? When power flows not just through borders and armies, but through data, platforms, and values? And most importantly-what comes next?

Over the last decade, I have watched the shifting currents of global politics with growing urgency. From trade wars and strategic decoupling to the eruption of climate conflicts and the recalibration of alliances, the world has entered a period of profound transformation. The anchors that once grounded diplomacy-predictable hierarchies, enduring alliances, institutional trust-have loosened. The global system is still interconnected, but it is no longer coherent.

Powerplay: The New Rules of Global Influence is my effort to make sense of this transformation. It is not a chronicle of decline or triumph, but a call to rethink the architecture of international relations. It argues that while traditional forms of power-military might, economic clout, political alliances-remain relevant, they are now intertwined with newer forces: technological control, narrative legitimacy, ecological sustainability, and normative leadership.

The book draws on case studies and critical moments-from the Indo-Pacific to the Sahel, from the Arctic to cyberspace-to illustrate how influence operates in an age of ambiguity. It is structured to guide the reader through strategic domains, from security and diplomacy to climate, data, identity, and the politics of narrative. Yet, beneath this diversity lies a unifying theme: that we are witnessing not just a power shift, but a paradigm shift.

This is not a solo endeavour. The insights presented here are informed by scholars, diplomats, entrepreneurs, students, and communities across continents who have generously shared their experiences, critiques, and visions. I am particularly indebted to those working at the frontlines of peacebuilding, sustainability, digital equity, and migration justice-whose work often escapes headlines but shapes the real contours of global change.

The intended audience of this book is broad. It includes policy professionals looking to navigate a more contested world, academics seeking interdisciplinary approaches to geopolitics, students imagining alternative futures, and engaged citizens who refuse to accept fatalism as strategy. If this book offers anything, I hope it is a language and lens to decode the present-and a provocation to act with intentionality.

We live in a time of rupture-but also of reinvention. The opportunity lies not in restoring a bygone order, but in co-creating a new one: one where pluralism is strength, cooperation is strategy, and influence is earned not just by might, but by meaning.

This is not the end of global order. It is the beginning of its next draft.

— PK Srivastava

Acknowledgements

As I reflect on the journey that led to the creation of Powerplay: The New Rules of Global Influence, I am overwhelmed with gratitude for the people who have shaped my life, guided my steps, and supported my dreams. This book is not just a product of my efforts, but a testament to the unwavering support and love I have received along the way.

First and foremost, I wish to express my deepest gratitude to my beloved parents, Late Satyendra Prasad and Late Usha Srivastava. Your unconditional love, sacrifices, and teachings have been the foundation of my life. Your strength and wisdom continue to inspire me every day, and I dedicate this work to you. Though you are no longer physically present, your values, love, and guidance live on in everything I do.

To my professional mentors, thank you for your invaluable guidance and steadfast encouragement throughout my journey. Your wisdom and insights have shaped my path and helped me grow with integrity and purpose. I am deeply appreciative of the opportunities you have opened for me and the belief you have shown in my potential.

To my friends, extended family, and loved ones-both near and far-thank you for being my sounding boards, my cheerleaders, and my sources of laughter and strength. Your unwavering belief in me, even during moments of self-doubt, has been invaluable. The love, wisdom, and encouragement you have shared-whether visible or quietly offered-have enriched my journey in countless ways. I am deeply grateful for the joy, camaraderie, and resilience you have brought into my life.

I would also like to express my heartfelt appreciation to Dr. Sudhir Kumar for graciously penning the foreword to this book. Your thoughtful words and generous support have lent this work both honour and credibility, and I am truly humbled by your contribution.

Lastly, to my better half, Shobhna, you have been my unwavering source of strength and understanding. Your belief in me, your patience, and your support through every endeavour have been my greatest blessings. I am forever grateful for your love, companionship, and the joy you bring into my life.

To our children, Aditya and Samriddhi, you both inspire me every day. Aditya, your intelligence, curiosity, and drive make me proud beyond words, while Samriddhi, your creativity, kindness, and vibrant spirit fill our home with warmth and laughter. Together, the three of you make my world complete, and I am truly blessed to have such a wonderful family by my side.

To each of you who have been part of this journey, I offer my heartfelt thanks. Without you, this work would not have been possible.

Punit Srivastava (P.K.)

CHAPTER ONE

The Shifting Foundations of Global Geopolitics

Global geopolitics in the 21st century is experiencing a deep and transformative shift. While familiar elements such as territorial disputes, military posturing, and ideological competition continue to feature prominently, the underlying architecture of global power is evolving in more complex and diffuse ways. The conventional dominance of hard power is now interwoven with newer, less tangible domains-technology, data control, economic interdependence, and climate vulnerability.

Historically, global influence was defined through military strength, imperial reach, and rigid alliance blocs, particularly during the Cold War's bipolar standoff. After the Soviet Union's collapse, the brief period of U.S.-led unipolarity seemed to promise a liberal international order anchored in globalization and democratic norms. However, this order is now fraying.

Today, we are witnessing the erosion of unipolar dominance and the rise of strategic pluralism-a world where multiple powers (state and non-state) exert influence across overlapping spheres. China's techno-authoritarian model, India's civilizational diplomacy, Russia's revisionist strategies, and the Global South's assertive multilateralism are reshaping how power is projected and contested.

Moreover, non-traditional domains such as cyber influence, digital infrastructure, climate diplomacy, and supply chain sovereignty have become central to geopolitical strategy. States are increasingly judged not just by military capability or economic size, but by their ability to shape narratives, control technologies, and navigate systemic disruptions.

In essence, the global order is no longer defined by binary alignments or singular hegemonies. It is multipolar, multidimensional, and volatile-a landscape where power is diffuse, competition is hybrid, and the rules of engagement are constantly evolving.

Key Foundations of This Shift Include:

The 21st-century transformation of global geopolitics is driven by a convergence of structural shifts that challenge the traditional hierarchy of international power. These foundations reflect not just a redistribution of power but a redefinition of how influence is exercised in a fragmented and interdependent world.

1. The Decline of Unipolarity

The post-Cold War era briefly ushered in a unipolar moment, with the United States standing as the uncontested global hegemon. However, the illusion of enduring supremacy faded in the face of military overextension (Iraq, Afghanistan), domestic political polarization, and the 2008 global financial crisis, which exposed systemic vulnerabilities. Washington's ability to unilaterally shape global norms has since waned, giving rise to contestation and regional balancing.

2. The Rise of Multipolarity

Global power is now more diffuse and diversified, with China, India, Brazil, Turkey, and coalitions like BRICS, ASEAN, and the African Union asserting influence across regional and global arenas. These actors promote alternative governance models, challenge Western institutional dominance, and increasingly shape global rules on trade, security, and development—signalling a shift from hegemonic centrality to plural strategic hubs.

3. Hybrid and Asymmetric Threats

The nature of conflict has expanded beyond battlefields. Cyberattacks, disinformation campaigns, pandemic disruptions, and climate-induced crises now constitute key security challenges. These threats are often transnational, non-linear, and low-visibility, involving both state and non-state actors. Influence is increasingly projected through algorithms, energy grids, and information warfare-demanding unconventional defense strategies.

4. Geoeconomic Competition

Global rivalry is now deeply rooted in economic statecraft. Nations compete over supply chain control, critical mineral access, currency dominance, and regulatory influence. Post-COVID disruptions and rising U.S.-China decoupling have pushed countries to "de-risk" economically, leading to industrial reshoring, resource nationalism, and the rise of strategic trade blocs.

5. Fragmentation of Global Governance

Institutions like the UN, WTO, and IMF-pillars of the liberal international order-face crises of legitimacy and effectiveness. They are increasingly seen as slow to adapt and unrepresentative of the Global South. As a result, emerging powers are either calling for deep institutional reform or creating parallel architectures such as the New Development Bank (NDB) and the Asian Infrastructure Investment Bank (AIIB).

6. Identity and Civilizational Politics

Power is also being reshaped by narratives of history, culture, and identity. Civilizational nationalism, historical grievances, and cultural revivalism now drive foreign policy in countries like China (century of humiliation), India (civilizational resurgence), and Russia (Eurasianism). These factors influence everything from alliance preferences to territorial claims, adding a potent ideological dimension to geopolitics.

Implications:

The current geopolitical transformation is not merely about power shifting hands-it reflects a fundamental redefinition of what power entails in the 21st century. Influence is no longer confined to military dominance or economic scale; it now encompasses a state's capacity to shape global narratives, set technological standards, and define the moral and regulatory frameworks that guide international behavior.

In this context, soft power, digital sovereignty, and ecological leadership have become as consequential as hard power. Countries are evaluated by how effectively they control information flows, build resilient innovation ecosystems, and influence multilateral agendas on climate, health, and security.

This introduction reframes geopolitics not as a binary contest (e.g., East vs. West or Global North vs. Global South) but as a fluid interplay of overlapping domains, where state, corporate, and civic actors simultaneously compete and cooperate. It lays the foundation for a deeper inquiry into the new rules of global influence, where power is intersectional, hybrid, and continuously contested.

As the following chapters will illustrate, the global order is not merely shifting-it is undergoing a paradigmatic recalibration in how authority is structured, legitimized, and exercised.

CHAPTER TWO

Multipolarity and Power Shifts

The global order is undergoing a significant transformation from the rigid structures of Cold War bipolarity and the brief dominance of post-Cold War unipolarity to a more fluid and complex multipolar system. In this emerging landscape, power is no longer concentrated in a single superpower but is increasingly distributed across diverse regional and global actors.

Nations like China, India, Russia, Brazil, and Turkey are asserting greater autonomy and influence, not only through economic and military capabilities but by creating alternative institutions, such as the BRICS bloc, AIIB, and regional trade pacts. These actors are also advancing distinct ideological narratives, challenging the liberal norms historically championed by the West.

Multipolarity today is defined by overlapping spheres of influence, dynamic alignments, and issue-based partnerships-reflecting a world where power is contested not just militarily, but across domains like technology, finance, data governance, and climate policy.

This shift signals a decentralization of global governance, where no single power can dictate terms, and cooperation often coexists with rivalry.

Emerging Multipolarity: Current Geopolitical Trends

The emerging multipolar world is characterised not by symmetrical power blocs but by overlapping spheres of influence and regionally concentrated leadership. Several key players are reshaping the global landscape through economic or military power and by creating alternative institutional frameworks and ideological narratives.

China's Strategic Ascent

China's rise stands as the defining axis of 21st-century multipolarity. What was once seen as an emerging economy has now become a comprehensive power, reshaping the balance across economic, geopolitical, and ideological dimensions.

Economic Powerhouse

In economic terms, China has achieved extraordinary scale and global interconnectivity. Its GDP (PPP) has already surpassed that of the U.S., and it is projected to lead even in nominal GDP by the early 2030s (IMF, 2023). As the world's leading exporter and second-largest economy, China has transformed into the engine of global manufacturing, a technological innovator, and a major creditor nation. From rare earth minerals to 5G infrastructure and EV production, Beijing commands critical nodes in global supply chains.

Through initiatives such as the Asian Infrastructure Investment Bank (AIIB) and the Belt and Road Initiative (BRI)-which now involves over 140 countries-China has challenged Western-dominated development models by offering alternative infrastructure financing with fewer political conditions (Hillman, 2021). These platforms project both soft power and dependency, embedding China's economic footprint across Asia, Africa, and parts of Europe and Latin America.

Geostrategic Assertiveness

Militarily, China is pursuing a strategic modernization of the People's Liberation Army (PLA), with massive investments in hypersonic weapons, naval expansion, AI-driven warfare, and cyber capabilities. In the South China Sea, its construction of artificial islands and the militarization of disputed waters reflect a long-term goal of regional dominance and deterrence.

Beijing's growing overseas footprint reinforces this ambition. The establishment of a military base in Djibouti-China's first-and port access agreements in Pakistan (Gwadar), Sri Lanka (Hambantota), and the UAE point to a broader strategic framework known as the "String of Pearls", which refers to a network of Chinese naval and commercial facilities stretching from the South China Sea through the Indian Ocean to the Middle East, designed to secure maritime routes and extend China's strategic influence across critical chokepoints (Holslag, 2015).

The "**String of Pearls**" theory refers to China's strategic effort to expand its influence across the Indian Ocean Region (IOR) through a network of commercial and military bases, port developments, and diplomatic relationships. First articulated in a U.S. Department of Defense report in the early 2000s, the theory suggests that China is seeking to secure its maritime energy routes and assert its presence in key chokepoints stretching from the South China Sea to the Horn of Africa.

Key "pearls" include ports and facilities in Gwadar (Pakistan), Hambantota (Sri Lanka), Chittagong (Bangladesh), and Djibouti, among others-many of which have been developed or financed through Chinese loans and infrastructure projects under the Belt and Road Initiative (BRI). While China maintains these are purely economic ventures, critics argue they could serve dual-use purposes, enhancing China's naval capabilities and strategic reach, particularly vis-à-vis India and the United States.

The theory underscores concerns about a potential Chinese maritime encirclement of India, as well as broader implications for freedom of navigation and regional balance of power in the Indo-Pacific.

These developments mark China's transition from a continental power to a maritime and global strategic actor.

Ideological and Normative Influence

Beyond hard power, China is increasingly engaged in reshaping global narratives. Through the Global Development Initiative (GDI) and the Global Security Initiative (GSI), Beijing promotes a governance model rooted in state sovereignty, non-intervention, and development without liberal conditionalities, offering a counterpoint to Western norms around democracy and human rights.

China also seeks influence in norm-setting institutions, from the UN Human Rights Council to ITU (telecommunications) and standardization bodies, aiming to embed its techno-authoritarian preferences into global governance. Its growing presence in multilateral platforms like BRICS and the Shanghai Cooperation Organisation (SCO) amplifies this influence, positioning China not just as a power within the system, but as a system-shaper.

Opinion:

China's ascent is no longer a forecast-it is a structural reality with far-reaching implications. Through a mix of economic statecraft, military expansion, and ideological projection, Beijing is crafting a model of global power that competes with, rather than integrates into, the Western liberal order. Its rise embodies the essence of contemporary multipolarity: diverse sources of influence converging to redefine the rules, institutions, and centers of global authority.

Russia's Resurgent Posture

Despite grappling with sweeping Western sanctions, technological decoupling, and a shrinking demographic base, Russia has defied expectations of strategic decline by asserting itself as a disruptive yet enduring global player. Far from being confined to the margins of international politics, Russia has leveraged asymmetric tools, regional assertiveness, and strategic recalibration to maintain its relevance in an increasingly multipolar world.

Since the 2008 war in Georgia and the 2014 annexation of Crimea, Moscow has pursued a foreign policy centered on three core imperatives: reasserting dominance in its near abroad, challenging Western-led security and governance frameworks, and expanding influence in under-governed or contested regions. This has been achieved not through economic strength or institutional leadership, but through calibrated disruption, coercive diplomacy, and hybrid warfare.

A turning point came with Russia's decisive intervention in Syria in 2015. By backing the Assad regime militarily and diplomatically, Russia not only shifted the course of the civil war but also reestablished itself as a key power broker in the Middle East-securing long-term basing rights at Tartus and Khmeimim, projecting naval and air power into the Mediterranean, and undermining U.S. influence in the region. This intervention signaled that Russia could punch above its economic weight by exploiting strategic vacuums and by aligning with regimes shunned by the West.

Similarly, Russia's expanding role in Libya, its support for warlords in the Sahel, and its outreach to North African states underscore a broader strategy: to gain leverage over critical chokepoints, migration corridors, and energy routes-thereby converting tactical presence into geopolitical influence (Trenin, 2020).

At the heart of this projection lies hybrid warfare-a strategic toolset that combines military pressure with non-conventional instruments such as disinformation, cyber operations, election interference, and covert military deployments. The Wagner Group, a Kremlin-linked private military company, has become Russia's global arm of plausible deniability. From Mali and Sudan to the Central African Republic and Syria, Wagner operatives secure mining contracts, guard authoritarian regimes, and sow instability in Western spheres of influence-all while maintaining a thin veil of deniability for the Russian state (Sukhankin, 2022).

The ongoing Ukraine war, launched in 2022, has accelerated Russia's strategic pivot away from the West. Isolated from Western markets, financial systems, and technology flows, Moscow has deepened geopolitical, economic, and military ties with China, increased arms and energy trade with Iran, and fostered new partnerships with countries like North Korea and Myanmar. These moves reflect more than reactive adaptation—they illustrate Russia's long-term aim to embed itself in an alternative geopolitical architecture that sidelines Western norms and institutions.

Even in its weakened economic state, Russia continues to exploit the cracks in global governance-navigating sanctions, weaponizing energy exports, and amplifying narratives of Western hypocrisy in forums like BRICS and the SCO. By appealing to anti-colonial sentiment, resource nationalism, and sovereignty discourses, Russia positions itself as a counter-hegemonic force championing a multipolar order-one in which strategic disruption compensates for structural decline.

In summary, Russia's resurgence is not about reclaiming Cold War-era superpower status, but about reinventing its role as a spoiler and broker in a fragmented world. It thrives not by building alliances, but by undermining existing ones; not by economic magnetism, but by coercive influence and geopolitical opportunism. In a multipolar system marked by uncertainty and contestation, Russia's posture is a reminder that relevance need not be symmetrical with strength-and that disruption, when paired with strategic intent, remains a potent form of power.

The Strategic Flexibility of Middle Powers

In an increasingly multipolar and fragmented global order, middle powers such as India, Brazil, Turkey, and Indonesia are leveraging their autonomy and regional influence to pursue flexible, interest-driven foreign policies. Rather than aligning rigidly with any single great power bloc, these states are navigating global competition through strategic hedging, multi-alignment, and issue-based coalitions.

India stands at the forefront of this recalibrated strategic posture-not merely as a middle power, but increasingly as a major global force in its own right. Under the leadership of Prime Minister Narendra Modi, India has institutionalized a doctrine of "multi-alignment" that blends strategic autonomy with assertive global engagement. While strengthening its partnerships with the United States and its allies through platforms like the QUAD, IPEF, and extensive defence cooperation, India has simultaneously maintained deep energy and security ties with Russia, reinforced its commitment to BRICS and the Shanghai Cooperation Organisation (SCO), and played a leading role in forums like IBSA (Pant & Saha, 2022).

India's refusal to align with the Western line on the Russia-Ukraine conflict-evidenced by its abstentions at the United Nations and increased purchases of discounted Russian oil-reflects a confident foreign policy that prioritizes national interests over ideological alignment. This is not a sign of neutrality, but of calibrated influence. Modi's India projects strength through independence, crafting a foreign policy that is neither beholden to the West nor nostalgic for old alliances, but one that actively shapes the global agenda.

Domestically, this ethos is reflected in the Atmanirbhar Bharat (self-reliant India) initiative, which aims to build resilience across key sectors such as defence manufacturing, semiconductors, and green energy, thereby fortifying India's long-term position in global supply chains.

Brazil, under President Lula da Silva, has similarly reasserted its leadership in the Global South by revitalizing CELAC, promoting climate justice, and offering a counter-narrative to Western-led development models. Turkey, straddling Europe and Asia, continues to perform a complex balancing act, shifting between NATO obligations and strategic engagements with Russia, including its mediatory role in the Black Sea Grain Initiative.

Indonesia, meanwhile, used its 2022 G20 presidency to highlight inclusive multilateralism, projecting itself as a pragmatic bridge-builder among global power centers and championing ASEAN centrality.

Together, these actors are redefining what it means to be a middle power. In particular, India's rise signals a broader transformation, where such powers are no longer passive participants in global affairs, but architects of the new rules that will govern the evolving international system.

Opinion:

In essence, these middle powers are no longer passive followers in a great power-dominated world-they are active architects of global norms and institutions. By leveraging strategic flexibility, they protect national interests, assert regional influence, and shape the emerging contours of global governance. At the forefront of this shift is India, which has demonstrated how calibrated multi-alignment, economic resilience, and principled diplomacy can transform a regional actor into a global rule-shaper. India's leadership in forums like the G20, BRICS, and the QUAD exemplifies how middle powers can punch above their weight and drive the agenda in an increasingly multipolar world.

Non-State Actors and Technological Multipolarity

The architecture of global power in the 21st century is no longer shaped solely by sovereign states. Today's multipolarity extends far beyond traditional geopolitics, as non-state actors-especially global technology giants-emerge as influential geopolitical agents. Companies such as Amazon, Apple, Meta, Google, Huawei, Alibaba, and Tencent now possess capacities once reserved for states: controlling critical infrastructure, influencing public discourse, shaping consumer behavior, and setting global data and trade norms.

These tech firms operate across borders, wielding outsized power over digital economies, surveillance infrastructures, and algorithmic governance. In doing so, they have become de facto stakeholders in geopolitical rivalries. Nowhere is this more evident than in the U.S.–China tech contest, which increasingly defines the contours of great power competition in the digital age. The banning of Huawei, semiconductor sanctions against Chinese chipmakers, and the contest over 5G and AI ecosystems reveal how technological dominance has become a key currency of geopolitical power (Segal, 2020).

Simultaneously, cybersecurity, artificial intelligence (AI), and quantum computing have become key domains where the boundaries between state and corporate power are increasingly blurred. Governments now rely on private firms to secure their digital infrastructure, manage data flows, and innovate critical technologies, from AI-enabled weapon systems to vaccine research platforms. This fusion of public and private capabilities challenges conventional notions of sovereignty, accountability, and strategic autonomy.

These developments are not merely technical-they have profound implications for international order and regulatory frameworks. For instance, decisions by a handful of companies about platform governance can shape elections, incite unrest, or suppress dissent. Data sovereignty debates, such as the EU's GDPR regime or India's Digital Personal Data Protection Act, highlight growing efforts by states to reclaim authority over information ecosystems long dominated by transnational firms.

Yet, technological multipolarity does not exist in a geopolitical vacuum. Its implications are most acutely felt in regional arenas, where the ambitions of traditional and emerging powers intersect-and where non-state technological actors increasingly shape the conditions of conflict, commerce, and cooperation.

In regions like the Indo-Pacific, the Middle East, and Sub-Saharan Africa, we are witnessing the convergence of hard power competition with technological influence. Regional actors are not passive observers-they are both agents and arenas of global recalibration. Flashpoints such as the Taiwan Strait, the South China Sea, cyber proxy wars in Eastern Europe, and drone warfare in the Sahel are no longer driven solely by territorial or ideological disputes-they are now deeply entangled with the control and deployment of emerging technologies.

Moreover, these shifts are redefining alliance structures and strategic calculations. Traditional military pacts are being supplemented or even supplanted by tech-driven coalitions, such as the U.S.-led Chip 4 Alliance, the India–Middle East–Europe Economic Corridor (IMEC), and digital infrastructure partnerships between Japan, Australia, and Southeast Asia. As threat perceptions evolve to include cyberattacks, algorithmic manipulation, and data theft, states are reassessing partnerships through a tech-security lens.

In essence, the emergence of non-state actors and technological multipolarity has added new layers to the global power game-layers that are fast-moving, decentralized, and often beyond the direct control of governments. In this new era, power is not only about military might or economic scale-it is about who sets the standards, controls the platforms, and shapes the digital future. As regional theatres become the testing grounds for these dynamics, the need to understand this multidimensional contest-where code meets conflict-has never been more urgent.

CHAPTER THREE

Regional Conflicts and Alliances

The rise of multipolarity is reshaping the global landscape with far-reaching implications for international stability, alliance dynamics, and the architecture of global governance. On one hand, it offers the potential for more inclusive representation and decentralized decision-making, allowing emerging powers and regional actors to play a greater role in shaping global norms and institutions. On the other hand, this diffusion of power introduces greater complexity, fluidity, and strategic uncertainty, as competing interests and shifting alignments make consensus harder to achieve and the risk of miscalculation or fragmentation more pronounced in global affairs.

Realignments and Strategic Alliances

In a multipolar world, alliances are becoming more fluid, functional, and interest-driven, reshaping the traditional notions of bloc politics. Regional conflicts and systemic rivalries have catalyzed new alignments that reflect evolving security concerns, economic interests, and geopolitical aspirations.

The Quadrilateral Security Dialogue (QUAD)-uniting the United States, India, Japan, and Australia-has emerged as a pivotal response to China's growing influence in the Indo-Pacific. While not a formal military alliance, the QUAD champions maritime domain awareness, resilient supply chains, digital connectivity, infrastructure development, and even vaccine diplomacy (Medcalf, 2021). It exemplifies the rise of "coalitions of the willing"-informal but strategic frameworks built around shared concerns rather than treaty obligations.

On the other hand, BRICS has transformed from a loose economic grouping into a platform for systemic challenge and alternative governance. The bloc's recent expansion to include Egypt, Iran, and the UAE signals an effort to broaden its geopolitical footprint and reshape the global financial architecture. Through the New Development Bank (NDB), BRICS provides development finance without Western conditionalities, positioning itself as a counterbalance to institutions like the IMF and World Bank (Armijo & Roberts, 2022).

The Shanghai Cooperation Organisation (SCO), originally focused on counterterrorism, has steadily widened its scope to cover regional security, economic integration, and infrastructure connectivity across Central and South Asia. With members such as China, Russia, India, and Pakistan, and growing observer interest from the Middle East, the SCO functions as a Eurasian security mechanism-serving as a non-Western alternative to NATO, though more decentralized and pragmatic in nature.

These evolving alliances underscore a shift from rigid ideological blocs to flexible, issue-based alignments, shaped by regional priorities and national interests. They reflect how multipolarity fosters both cooperation and contestation, often within the same institutional frameworks.

Global Governance and Institutional Strain

Multipolarity also calls into question the legitimacy and efficiency of the current global governance architecture. Institutions such as the **United Nations Security Council (UNSC)**, **World Trade Organization (WTO)**, and **International Monetary Fund (IMF)** have not kept pace with shifts in global power. The veto structure of the UNSC still reflects post-World War II realities, sidelining rising powers like India, Brazil, and South Africa from permanent membership.

The WTO has also faced gridlocks-especially evident in the paralysis of its dispute resolution mechanism-due to increasing tensions between the U.S., China, and the EU on trade practices, state subsidies, and intellectual property rights (Hopewell, 2021). The IMF's voting shares still overwhelmingly favour developed economies, perpetuating a legitimacy gap in decision-making processes for countries that now contribute a much larger share to global growth.

In response, emerging powers are either pushing for reform or establishing **parallel institutions**, such as regional trade agreements (e.g.,

RCEP, AfCFTA) and sovereign digital currency frameworks (e.g., China's digital yuan, India's e-Rupee), which bypass legacy systems.

Fragmentation and Regionalism

As global consensus becomes harder to achieve, the international system is increasingly marked by fragmentation and the rise of regionalism. With no single hegemon capable of enforcing universal rules, regional blocs and issue-based coalitions have stepped into the vacuum, crafting governance models suited to their unique political, economic, and cultural contexts.

In Africa, the growing influence of the African Union (AU) and the operationalization of the African Continental Free Trade Area (AfCFTA) reflect a drive toward continental integration and indigenous development strategies, reducing reliance on external powers and fostering intra-African trade, infrastructure, and industrial policy.

The European Union (EU), despite internal political rifts, continues to function as a normative power-leading global efforts on climate diplomacy, digital governance, and regulatory standards. Its role in shaping frameworks like the Green Deal and General Data Protection Regulation (GDPR) illustrates how regional actors can influence global norms even in the absence of hard power.

However, this growing regionalization comes with the risk of norm fragmentation. Competing legal and regulatory regimes-in areas such as data privacy, trade compliance, and AI ethics-create overlapping standards that hinder interoperability and global coordination. For instance, the EU's GDPR, China's PIPL, and the U.S.'s state-level privacy laws offer divergent approaches, reflecting not only different values but also competing models of digital sovereignty.

In sum, regionalism offers adaptive governance in a multipolar world, but also introduces new fault lines, where conflicting norms may complicate cooperation and amplify global divides.

Security Dilemmas and Hybrid Conflict

In today's multipolar world, security threats have evolved beyond conventional warfare, becoming increasingly hybrid, decentralized, and multidimensional. State and non-state actors now exploit tools such as cyberattacks, disinformation campaigns, digital espionage, and AI-enabled surveillance to project power and destabilize rivals without crossing traditional thresholds of war.

The Russia-Ukraine conflict exemplifies this shift: alongside tanks and missiles, the battlefield extends to cyber domains, financial systems, and global media narratives. Digital sabotage, infrastructure hacking, and coordinated information warfare have become integral parts of modern conflict strategy (Galeotti, 2022).

Such developments blur the line between war and peace, civilian and combatant, creating dilemmas for traditional security frameworks. For example, NATO's Article 5, designed for kinetic attacks, now faces ambiguity over whether cyber offensives or infrastructure disruption would qualify as grounds for collective defense. In the Indo-Pacific, China's "grey-zone tactics"-including maritime militia swarms, coercive economic actions, and strategic land reclamation-challenge conventional deterrence, forcing rivals to recalibrate their responses (Erickson & Wuthnow, 2016).

Compounding these threats are non-traditional security risks such as climate change, pandemics, and AI-induced instability, which transcend borders and demand cross-sectoral, multilateral coordination. Yet, in a fragmented geopolitical environment, such cooperation is frequently undermined by great power rivalries, as seen during the early COVID-19 response breakdown and repeated deadlocks in global climate negotiations.

Theoretical Reflections: Neorealism and Beyond

The transition from a unipolar to a multipolar world has reignited academic interest in systemic theories of international relations. These frameworks help explain not only the distribution of power but also the strategic behavior of states in an evolving global architecture. While **neorealism** remains foundational in understanding the dynamics of multipolarity, newer paradigms such as **offensive realism**, **liberal institutionalism**, and **constructivism** offer complementary perspectives that capture the nuances of today's complex international system.

Neorealism: The Structure of the System

In his seminal work Theory of International Politics (1979), Kenneth Waltz introduced neorealism (or structural realism), which posits that the anarchic structure of the international system-defined by the absence of a central governing authority-compels states to act in self-interested, survival-oriented ways. According to Waltz, the behavior of states is shaped less by human nature and more by the constraints imposed by the international system's architecture.

Under this framework, anarchy breeds insecurity, prompting states to adopt self-help strategies and to balance against perceived threats through internal (military buildup) or external (alliances) means. Waltz contends that bipolar systems (e.g., the U.S.-USSR rivalry during the Cold War) are more stable due to fewer actors and clearer strategic calculations, which reduce the likelihood of misjudgment and conflict.

In contrast, multipolar systems involve a greater number of actors and potential alignments, which increases strategic ambiguity, raises the risks of miscalculation, and encourages shifting alliances. The fluidity of such systems can lead to both overreaction and under-balancing, making conflict more likely even if unintended.

Contemporary global politics reflects this neorealist diagnosis. The current multipolar order, lacking a single hegemon, sees states pursuing flexible, interest-based alignments rather than fixed ideological camps. For instance, India's dual engagement with both the QUAD (aligned with the U.S. and its allies) and BRICS (which includes China and Russia) illustrates strategic hedging-balancing power without full commitment. Similarly, Turkey's maneuvering between NATO membership and growing ties with Russia and regional powers reflects Waltz's ideas of buck-passing and balance-of-power behavior.

In essence, Waltz's neorealism helps explain the instability and complexity of multipolarity, where state behavior is driven not by shared norms but by systemic pressures and the imperative of strategic survival.

Offensive Realism: The Pursuit of Hegemony

John Mearsheimer's offensive realism, as articulated in The Tragedy of Great Power Politics (2001), offers a more assertive and conflict-prone interpretation of international relations than Waltz's defensive neorealism. While both scholars agree on the anarchic structure of the international system, Mearsheimer argues that states do not merely seek to survive-they strive to maximize their power relentlessly, aiming for regional hegemony and, if possible, global dominance.

According to offensive realism, great powers are inherently revisionist, not status quo actors. They are compelled by systemic incentives to expand their influence, reduce the power of rivals, and shape the rules of the international order to their advantage. This drive stems not from ideology or miscalculation, but from a rational calculation of survival in a competitive, anarchic world.

Contemporary developments vividly illustrate Mearsheimer's thesis. China's strategic behavior in the Indo-Pacific-including its militarization of the South China Sea, assertiveness over Taiwan, and expansion of naval capabilities-reflects its ambition to become the undisputed regional hegemon. Likewise, initiatives such as the Belt and Road Initiative (BRI) and the creation of parallel institutions like the Asian Infrastructure Investment Bank (AIIB) are seen through an offensive realist lens not just as tools of development, but as mechanisms for geopolitical leverage and normative dominance.

Similarly, Russia's assertive posture in Eastern Europe, particularly the annexation of Crimea, its war in Ukraine, and military interventions in Syria, point to a revisionist agenda aimed at reasserting its sphere of influence and undermining Western hegemony, especially NATO and EU expansion.

Offensive realism thus suggests that multipolarity does not promote balance or stability, but rather fuels intensified rivalry, as each power seeks to reshape the order in its favor, often at the expense of cooperative mechanisms or equilibrium.

Liberal Institutionalism: Cooperation under Anarchy

While realism emphasizes power politics and conflict, liberal institutionalism, championed by scholars like Robert Keohane, presents a more optimistic view of international relations. In his influential work After Hegemony (1984), Keohane argues that even in an anarchic international system-where no central authority exists-cooperation among states is not only possible but essential for managing interdependence and shared challenges.

According to Keohane, international institutions-such as treaties, norms, and formal organizations-can reduce the anarchic uncertainty that realism predicts by lowering transaction costs, enhancing information-sharing, and promoting trust and reciprocity. Institutions thus act as "rules of the game," enabling states to coordinate actions and overcome collective action problems even in the absence of a hegemon.

This logic is evident in the sustained relevance of bodies like the World Trade Organization (WTO), the World Health Organization (WHO), and the United Nations Framework Convention on Climate Change (UNFCCC). Despite rising geopolitical tensions and national rivalries, these institutions continue to facilitate global cooperation in trade, health, and climate governance, underscoring the liberal belief in rule-based multilateralism.

However, liberal institutionalism is not blind to the limits of existing institutions. It recognizes that to remain legitimate and effective, institutions must evolve in response to changes in global power structures. The growing demand for reform in the UN Security Council and the IMF reflects widespread concerns that these institutions still privilege post–World War II power dynamics, underrepresenting emerging actors like India, Brazil, and African states.

If such demands remain unaddressed, institutions risk losing legitimacy, prompting the rise of alternative platforms-such as BRICS and the New Development Bank-that aim to provide more inclusive and flexible governance models outside the traditional Western-led order.

Constructivism and Identity Politics

While liberal institutionalists such as Robert Keohane accept the realist premise of an anarchic international system, they diverge sharply in their conclusions. In After Hegemony (1984), Keohane argues that anarchy does not preclude cooperation. Instead, international institutions help manage interdependence by reducing uncertainty, lowering transaction costs, and promoting predictability through norms and reciprocity. Institutions like the WTO, WHO, and UNFCCC serve as platforms for ongoing dialogue, rule-setting, and dispute resolution-even among rivals-demonstrating that rational actors can cooperate without a hegemon.

However, Keohane also recognizes that institutional legitimacy depends on adaptability and fairness. The persistent calls for reform in global governance bodies like the UN Security Council and IMF reflect growing frustration among emerging powers, who view existing institutions as disproportionately shaped by Western interests. If these demands go unmet, institutional erosion or the creation of parallel governance structures, such as BRICS and the New Development Bank, becomes more likely.

In contrast, constructivist thinkers like Alexander Wendt emphasize that state behavior is not predetermined by material structures but is shaped by socially constructed identities, historical memory, and normative frameworks. Wendt's famous assertion that "anarchy is what states make of it" (1992) suggests that the international system's meaning is subject to interpretation and change through interaction and shared understandings.

For instance, China's assertive foreign policy is often rooted in its historical grievance narrative-the "century of humiliation"-and the pursuit of national rejuvenation. Russia's strategic behavior is similarly shaped by its post-Cold War trauma and distrust of NATO, rather than purely material concerns.

Constructivism also explains why states with similar capabilities behave differently. Germany and Japan, despite their economic strength, adopt restrained military roles due to deeply internalized pacifist norms born from World War II experiences. Meanwhile, India and Brazil often articulate their international aspirations not just in terms of power, but as civilizational responsibilities to represent the Global South, invoking post-colonial solidarity and moral leadership.

Together, liberal institutionalism and constructivism highlight how ideas, norms, and institutions play crucial roles in shaping global order-not merely power dynamics. Where realism sees conflict and competition, these perspectives offer tools for understanding cooperation, identity formation, and normative evolution in world politics.

Postcolonial and Global South Perspectives

In recent years, scholars from the Global South have mounted a compelling critique of the dominant Eurocentric traditions in international relations (IR). Postcolonial IR theory emphasizes that global politics cannot be fully understood without grappling with the enduring legacies of colonialism, imperial domination, and structural inequality. It argues that mainstream theories-such as realism and liberalism-too often universalize Western experiences, while ignoring the historical injustices and developmental asymmetries that continue to shape the agency of formerly colonized nations (Acharya & Buzan, 2019).

This perspective has found growing resonance in the political push for reform across global institutions. Demands for a more equitable UN Security Council, fairer voting rights in the IMF, and greater voice for developing countries in trade and climate negotiations reflect a deeper call to decolonize global governance. Likewise, the rise of regionalism in Africa, Asia, and Latin America-and the emergence of alternative platforms like BRICS, the African Union, and CELAC-signal efforts to reshape international order on more inclusive, pluralistic foundations.

One of the most influential contributions to this discourse is Amitav Acharya's "multiplex world" thesis. He argues that today's global order is no longer structured around a single hegemonic center, whether Washington or a rising Beijing, but consists of multiple overlapping orders-including regional groupings, civilizational identities, and normative communities-that coexist and compete (Acharya, 2017). This vision shifts the focus from hierarchical polarity to horizontal pluralism, recognizing that different worldviews and governance logics now coexist in a fragmented yet interdependent international system.

Moreover, Southern epistemologies-ways of knowing rooted in indigenous, postcolonial, and non-Western traditions-are increasingly informing global debates on development, sovereignty, justice, and human security. These perspectives challenge the assumption that Western liberalism holds a monopoly on legitimate international norms, and instead promote concepts like self-determination, solidarity, and ecological justice.

In essence, postcolonial and Global South approaches recenter international relations around historical consciousness, moral responsibility, and epistemic diversity-expanding the boundaries of what counts as legitimate knowledge and power in world politics.

Case Studies in Multipolar Practice

To better understand how multipolarity manifests in practical terms, it is essential to examine key geopolitical flashpoints and diplomatic manoeuvres where multiple actors engage simultaneously-often with overlapping, competing, or complementary interests. These case studies reveal that multipolarity is not just a theoretical construct but a lived reality shaping crisis responses, alliance formations, and global norms.

A. The South China Sea Dispute: Power Projection and Legal Contestation

The South China Sea (SCS) stands as one of the most contested and symbolically charged arenas in global geopolitics, embodying the complexities of an increasingly multipolar world. China claims nearly 90% of this vital maritime region through its self-declared "nine-dash line"-a loosely defined boundary based on historical maps that lacks legal standing under international law. Despite widespread criticism and a landmark 2016 ruling by the Permanent Court of Arbitration under the United Nations Convention on the Law of the Sea (UNCLOS), which rejected its claims in favor of the Philippines (PCA, 2016), China has continued to assert its dominance by constructing artificial islands and militarizing key features.

While the United States holds no territorial claims in the SCS, it maintains a strong strategic presence. Through regular Freedom of Navigation Operations (FONOPs), Washington seeks to counter Chinese expansionism and defend the principles of international maritime law and open sea lanes. The region, therefore, is not merely a hotspot of territorial dispute but a stage for broader power projection and the contest between sovereignty-based approaches and a rule-based global order.

The dispute's multipolar character is accentuated by the active involvement of regional middle powers. Vietnam, Malaysia, the Philippines, and Indonesia assert overlapping maritime claims while carefully navigating between engagement with China and strategic partnerships with external players such as the U.S., Japan, and Australia. These countries strive to preserve their autonomy and national interests amidst growing great-power competition.

Regional diplomacy, however, remains constrained. The Association of Southeast Asian Nations (ASEAN), though central to regional dialogue, has struggled to forge a unified position due to internal divisions and varying levels of economic and political alignment with China. This lack of cohesion undermines efforts to establish a collective front on issues of maritime sovereignty and regional security.

Adding another layer to the geopolitical dynamic is the Indo-Pacific strategy, particularly articulated through the Quadrilateral Security Dialogue (QUAD), comprising the United States, India, Japan, and Australia. The QUAD emphasizes a "free, open, inclusive, and rules-based Indo-Pacific," with the South China Sea as a critical zone of focus (Medcalf, 2021). This strategic alignment underscores the growing convergence of interests among like-minded democracies seeking to uphold international law and check unilateral actions.

In sum, the South China Sea represents a volatile nexus of legal contestation, strategic rivalry, and diplomatic maneuvering. As great powers and regional actors continue to jostle for influence, the SCS exemplifies the broader recalibration of global power structures-where traditional maritime disputes now intersect with technological, legal, and ideological competition in shaping the 21st-century order.

B. The Russia-Ukraine War: Great Power Rivalries and Proxy Alignments

Russia's full-scale invasion of Ukraine in February 2022 marked a pivotal moment in global geopolitics, transforming what began as a regional conflict into a crucible of great power rivalries. The war has rapidly evolved into a multipolar battlefield, where competing interests, alignments, and strategic calculations intersect on a global scale.

The United States and the European Union have emerged as Ukraine's principal backers, providing extensive military aid, economic support, and imposing sweeping sanctions aimed at isolating Russia. These measures are complemented by diplomatic efforts to sustain international pressure on Moscow and reinforce the post-Cold War liberal international order. NATO, in response to the renewed threat on its eastern flank, has expanded its influence with the accession of Finland and Sweden-nations that had previously maintained long-standing policies of neutrality. This expansion signals a historic shift in European security architecture.

China's role in the conflict illustrates the nuances of strategic alignment in a multipolar world. While avoiding explicit support for the invasion, Beijing has positioned itself as a neutral actor calling for peace talks, all while maintaining close diplomatic and economic ties with Moscow. This careful balancing act reflects China's broader objective of challenging U.S. global leadership without directly exposing itself to Western sanctions or reputational risk.

India, too, has charted an independent course. Maintaining a stance of strategic autonomy, New Delhi has continued importing discounted Russian oil, citing national interest, even as it engages actively with Western-led platforms like the G7 on issues such as climate action and global development. This dual engagement underscores India's role as a swing power navigating competing spheres of influence.

The reaction from the Global South has been far from uniform. Many nations in Africa, Asia, and Latin America have refrained from taking clear sides, reflecting a growing disillusionment with Western double standards. Critics highlight the contrast between the urgency shown by the West in defending Ukraine and its comparatively muted response to long-standing crises in Yemen, Sudan, Syria, or Palestine (Acharya, 2023). This divergence underscores the fragmentation of global consensus and the emergence of a more contested moral and strategic order.

In essence, the Russia-Ukraine war is not just a test of European security-it is a mirror reflecting the reconfiguration of global power, alliance structures, and the shifting fault lines of international legitimacy.

C. Vaccine Diplomacy and India's G20 Presidency

The COVID-19 pandemic starkly revealed how global health emergencies intertwine with geopolitics, especially in a multipolar world. As vaccine nationalism gripped much of the West-with the United States and European Union prioritizing their own populations-emerging powers like China and India stepped into the void, using vaccine diplomacy as a strategic tool to expand global influence across Asia, Africa, and Latin America.

India's Vaccine Maitri initiative became a defining example of principled leadership in a time of global crisis. By supplying over 200 million vaccine doses to more than 90 countries, India reaffirmed its identity as the "pharmacy of the world" and demonstrated the hallmarks of a responsible and responsive global power (Ghosh, 2021). This act of solidarity helped India cement its credibility among developing nations and laid the diplomatic foundation for a more assertive global role.

India's growing stature was further amplified during its G20 presidency in 2023. Far from being a ceremonial chairmanship, India used the platform to signal its arrival as a power to reckon with-capable of setting the global agenda and building cross-continental coalitions. Its presidency prioritized the concerns of the Global South, focusing on inclusive development, climate resilience, digital public infrastructure, and reform of multilateral institutions to reflect contemporary power realities.

A key milestone was India's successful push for the African Union's permanent membership in the G20-an achievement that underscored New Delhi's commitment to rebalancing global governance. Simultaneously, India engaged major Western powers while amplifying voices from countries like Bangladesh, Egypt, and Nigeria, positioning itself as a diplomatic bridge in a fragmented global order.

Yet India's rise is not confined to diplomacy and development alone. Its decisive military posture has also reinforced its strategic autonomy. The successful execution of Operation Sindoor, a precision strike in retaliation to cross-border terrorism, sent an unambiguous signal about India's military capability and political will. It demonstrated that India is not only a humanitarian leader but also a sovereign security actor, unwilling to tolerate threats to its national integrity.

Together, India's global vaccine leadership, assertive diplomacy, and credible military deterrence illustrate the multidimensional nature of its rise. It is no longer merely adapting to a changing world-it is actively shaping it. As Powerplay argues, India today exemplifies a new kind of power: one that blends moral legitimacy with hard capabilities, and strategic autonomy with global engagement.

D. Technological Rivalries and Supply Chain Realignment

In today's multipolar world, technology has emerged as a key battleground for strategic dominance. The intensifying U.S.-China competition over semiconductors is a defining feature of this struggle. In 2022, the United States imposed sweeping export controls aimed at restricting China's access to advanced chip-making tools, effectively targeting major firms like Huawei and SMIC. These actions were reinforced by the CHIPS and Science Act, which allocates significant investment to revive domestic semiconductor production and reduce reliance on foreign supply chains. Simultaneously, the U.S. is strengthening strategic partnerships through the Chip 4 alliance with Taiwan, South Korea, and Japan to secure the global chip ecosystem (Segal, 2023).

China, in response, has accelerated its push for technological self-sufficiency under its "Made in China 2025" strategy. It is channeling state-backed investment into frontier technologies like quantum computing, 5G infrastructure, and artificial intelligence to reduce dependence on Western innovation and assert its own technological leadership.

Elsewhere, other global players are recalibrating their digital priorities. India and the European Union are advancing digital sovereignty agendas-focusing on data localization, regulation of foreign digital platforms, and support for domestic innovation. These efforts reflect growing concerns about the geopolitical implications of tech dependence and the desire to reclaim control over critical digital infrastructure.

Together, these shifts underscore how technological competition is no longer confined to economic rivalry; it now shapes strategic alliances, national security policies, and global supply chain architecture. In this evolving landscape, cooperation is increasingly fragmented, and no single country can unilaterally dominate the innovation ecosystem-highlighting the deeply multipolar nature of geotechnology today.

E. Climate Diplomacy: Shared Challenges, Fragmented Responsibility

Climate change remains a defining global challenge, but efforts to address it reveal the complexities of multipolarity. The Paris Agreement (2015) marked a landmark in collective climate ambition, yet its implementation has exposed sharp fault lines. Recent COP26 and COP28 summits underscored growing divides: developed countries continue to push for aggressive net-zero timelines and global carbon markets, while developing nations emphasize historical responsibility and demand greater financial support to adapt and transition.

Major emitters like China and India have pushed back against pressure to rapidly curb emissions, arguing that their development trajectories require energy security and equitable carbon space. At the same time, vulnerable nations-especially small island states and parts of Africa-have intensified calls for climate justice, including compensation for irreversible climate-related losses and damages.

The rise of "climate clubs," such as the EU's Carbon Border Adjustment Mechanism (CBAM), points to a trend toward fragmented climate governance. These mechanisms risk creating regional carbon regimes that may advance climate goals but also raise concerns about trade protectionism and fairness in global burden-sharing (Victor, 2022).

Despite the divides, pragmatic partnerships are emerging. Initiatives like the India-U.S. Climate and Clean Energy Agenda 2030 and Just Energy Transition Partnerships (JETP) with South Africa and Indonesia represent innovative financing models that blend public-private investments and international cooperation. These efforts signal that even in a fractured climate landscape, multipolarity can foster flexible, targeted solutions to shared environmental threats.

Opinion:

The age of multipolarity is not a return to Cold War-style bipolarity, nor is it a stable balance-of-power system. It is a dynamic and fluid terrain marked by overlapping alliances, contested norms, technological disruption, and competing visions of order. Rather than presenting perfect symmetry or predictable equilibrium, today's global system is defined by strategic complexity-where volatility and opportunity coexist, and where power is increasingly exercised through influence rather than domination.

While traditional realism may anticipate instability in the absence of a clear hegemon, this new multipolar moment defies simple categorization. It is a multiplex world, where regional actors assert agency, institutions struggle for legitimacy, and non-state forces-from tech giants to climate coalitions-reshape the rules of engagement. Power is no longer concentrated; it is distributed, negotiated, and often contested across arenas that include cyberspace, the Indo-Pacific, global health, and critical supply chains.

At the center of this unfolding order stands India-a nation that exemplifies how emerging powers are no longer merely reacting to global shifts but actively engineering them. Through decisive actions like Vaccine Maitri, its assertive G20 presidency, and military operations like Operation Sindoor to neutralize cross-border threats, India has projected not just capacity, but clarity of purpose. Its embrace of multi-alignment, strategic autonomy, and regional leadership underscores the growing importance of normative middle powers in shaping tomorrow's rules.

The challenge ahead is not simply preventing great power rivalry, but managing strategic pluralism: how to uphold cooperation on transnational issues like climate change, AI governance, and public health, even amidst sharp geopolitical divergences. This requires more than traditional diplomacy. It demands an interdisciplinary lens-one that blends historical awareness, theoretical grounding, and empirical attention to the rise of new actors, technologies, and regional narratives.

In this era, coexistence will not mean consensus, and cooperation will often be contested. But therein lies the essence of powerplay in the 21st century: the ability to navigate uncertainty, shape norms, and build influence without imposing hegemony. The future of global order will not be dictated-it will be co-authored by a more plural, interconnected, and strategically agile community of states.

India's emergence at this juncture signals a broader truth: the unipolar moment is over-not with a crash, but with a recalibration. What follows is not chaos, but a new choreography of power-complex, crowded, and deeply consequential.

CHAPTER FOUR

China's Belt and Road Initiative (BRI): Strategy or Hegemony?

Introduction: Revisiting the Silk Roads for Modern Power

In 2013, President Xi Jinping unveiled the Belt and Road Initiative (BRI) during state visits to Kazakhstan and Indonesia, introducing it as a vision for "mutual benefit and common development." At first glance, the BRI appears to be an ambitious global infrastructure and connectivity project, echoing China's historical trading legacy. But a deeper analysis reveals that BRI is as much about **geopolitical restructuring** as it is about economic opportunity. It is a cornerstone of China's broader strategic doctrine-framed within its concept of a *"Community of Shared Future for Mankind"*-aimed at reshaping global governance, reducing dependence on Western-led institutions, and asserting China's place as a normative power.

The BRI comprises two major axes: the **Silk Road Economic Belt**-connecting China with Central Asia, the Middle East, and Europe through rail and road-and the **21st Century Maritime Silk Road**, aimed at deepening maritime trade networks across the Indo-Pacific and into Africa and the Mediterranean. As of 2024, over **150 countries and 30 international organizations** have signed cooperation agreements under the BRI umbrella, with total investment commitments exceeding **$1.2 trillion**, making it the world's most expansive development initiative.

Yet, the BRI's rapid expansion has drawn sharp scrutiny. Critics question whether the initiative is a benign economic integration strategy or a veiled hegemonic tool for asserting Chinese dominance. The lines between **partnership and patronage**, between **development and debt**, are often blurred. Increasingly, BRI is seen as the **geoeconomic wing of China's grand strategy**, aiming to rewire the circuits of global trade, influence, and ideology.

Reference: Jonathan Hillman, *The Emperor's New Road* (Yale University Press, 2020), underscores how infrastructure diplomacy has become a vehicle for China's soft and hard power projection under the BRI framework.

Historical Antecedents: From Silk Roads to Strategic Revivalism

To fully grasp the strategic essence of the BRI, one must trace its intellectual and historical roots in China's dynastic traditions of diplomacy and trade. The **Silk Road**, dating back to the Han Dynasty (206 BCE – 220 CE), was not merely a trade route but an imperial artery that projected Chinese cultural and political influence westward. Caravans carried not only silk, jade, and paper but also **Confucian thought, Buddhist texts, and diplomatic envoys**, establishing a form of proto-globalization led by ancient China.

The Tang (618–907 CE) and Song (960–1279 CE) dynasties extended and institutionalized these trade routes, facilitating intellectual exchanges and tributary relations from Persia to the Indian Ocean. The Silk Road was not just a corridor of goods-it was a mechanism of **Sinocentric international order**, premised on China's perception of itself as the "Middle Kingdom."

During the Yuan Dynasty under Mongol rule (1271–1368), the road was revitalized into a vast transcontinental network that connected East Asia with Europe. Marco Polo's journeys in this era symbolize the early global curiosity about Chinese civilization and its economic models. Later, in the early 15th century, Admiral **Zheng He's "treasure fleets"**-massive naval expeditions under the Ming Dynasty-ventured into Southeast Asia, the Arabian Peninsula, and East Africa. These were not only diplomatic missions but also declarations of China's technological superiority and maritime prowess.

Modern Chinese strategic thinkers draw from these histories. The revival of Silk Road symbolism in BRI is not accidental-it seeks to **legitimize contemporary geopolitical outreach** through the narrative of a peaceful, interconnected past. In speeches and official documents, the Chinese Communist Party (CCP) presents the BRI as a "civilizational bridge," not unlike the ancient routes that enabled harmonious trade and cultural exchange.

However, historical analogies can mask strategic intent. As scholars such as Nadège Rolland argue (*China's Eurasian Century?*, NBR, 2017), the Silk Road narrative serves as a **soft-power camouflage** for a hard-power agenda. While ancient China promoted harmony through hierarchical tributary relations, BRI similarly aims to construct a **Sino-centric world order**-this time through contracts, ports, and pipelines.

Reference: State Council of the People's Republic of China, *Vision and Actions on Jointly Building Silk Road Economic Belt and 21st-Century Maritime Silk Road* (2015); Nadège Rolland (2017), *China's Eurasian Century*; and Joseph Nye's theory of "soft power," which the BRI increasingly adapts into infrastructure diplomacy.

Current Landscape: Debt Diplomacy, Infrastructure Dominance, and Maritime Expansion

The modern architecture of the Belt and Road Initiative transcends mere infrastructure. It constitutes a **layered strategic ecosystem**-encompassing railways, ports, energy grids, digital infrastructure, and financial systems. While marketed as a development partnership, BRI has increasingly drawn critique for enabling **"debt diplomacy," fostering asymmetric dependencies**, and redefining global infrastructure norms.

1. Debt Diplomacy: Strategic Leverage or Economic Partnership?

One of the most controversial aspects of the BRI is the financing model deployed. Predominantly backed by **Chinese state-owned banks**, such as the Export-Import Bank of China and China Development Bank, BRI loans are often extended at market or near-market interest rates, unlike concessional loans typically offered by Western or multilateral institutions. The lack of transparency in loan terms has led to growing concern about **sovereign debt sustainability** in several BRI countries.

The **Hambantota Port in Sri Lanka** stands as a cautionary tale. Constructed with $1.5 billion in Chinese loans, the port was leased to China Merchants Port Holdings for 99 years in 2017 after Sri Lanka defaulted on repayments. This incident prompted scholars and governments alike to view BRI through the lens of **strategic asset acquisition via financial leverage**.

A similar pattern is observable in **Zambia**, where concerns emerged in 2018 that the government might relinquish control of key assets like the Kenneth Kaunda International Airport if it failed to repay Chinese loans-though officials denied these claims, the speculation alone revealed the fragility of BRI financing.

Laos too has become heavily indebted to China, particularly after the construction of the **China-Laos Railway**, which cost $6 billion (one-third of the country's GDP). The financing structure, with a heavy loan component, is expected to burden Laos with decades of repayments, raising concerns about long-term economic autonomy.

Reference: Deborah Brautigam and Meg Rithmire, "The Chinese 'Debt Trap' Is a Myth," *The Atlantic* (2021); CSIS BRI Tracker.

2. Infrastructure Dominance: From Roads to Digital Silk Roads

China's BRI is not confined to physical infrastructure; it extends deeply into **digital and energy infrastructure**, creating what scholars now call the **"Digital Silk Road."** This includes investments in fiber-optic cables, 5G technology, satellite navigation systems, and cloud computing.

Huawei and ZTE, major Chinese telecommunications firms, have become vehicles of digital expansion under BRI, installing networks and surveillance systems across Africa and Southeast Asia. In Kenya, for instance, Huawei-built Safe City surveillance systems have been praised for reducing urban crime, yet human rights advocates raise concerns about surveillance and data control.

Moreover, China is pushing its own **Beidou satellite system** in lieu of the U.S.-based GPS, promoting it as an alternative navigation network in BRI countries-a subtle but profound form of **technological sovereignty**.

Energy infrastructure is another pillar. China has financed over **$160 billion in energy projects**, particularly coal and hydropower plants. While this boosts energy access, critics note that it **locks countries into carbon-intensive pathways**, contradicting China's green development rhetoric.

Reference: Hillman, Jonathan, *The Digital Silk Road: China's Quest to Wire the World and Win the Future*, CSIS (2020); IEA Energy Outlook for Emerging Markets (2023).

3. Maritime Expansion: Commercial Ports or Strategic Chokepoints?

The BRI's maritime strategy centre's on securing **strategic logistics hubs** and enhancing access to key sea lanes through the **21st Century Maritime Silk Road**. Chinese companies have acquired or developed major stakes in **at least 40 ports across Asia, Africa, and Europe**, many of which have dual-use potential.

- **Djibouti**: Home to China's first overseas military base, it also hosts a commercial port operated by Chinese firms, located near the Bab el-Mandeb Strait-a chokepoint for global oil shipping.
- **Piraeus Port, Greece**: Acquired by COSCO, it is now the fastest-growing container port in Europe, giving China a critical foothold in the Mediterranean.
- **Gwadar Port, Pakistan**: Located near the Strait of Hormuz, this facility connects inland western China to the Arabian Sea, bypassing the Malacca Strait and reducing China's vulnerability to U.S. naval influence.

China's maritime push has led to rising tensions, particularly in the **South China Sea**, where its militarization of artificial islands contradicts the "peaceful development" rhetoric of BRI. These developments suggest that **infrastructure and strategy are increasingly intertwined.**

Reference: *The Economist* (2023), "The Global Port Grab"; IISS Asia-Pacific Security Report.

Case Studies: Africa, Europe, and Central Asia

Africa: Ethiopia and Kenya

In Africa, BRI investments are significant and symbolic. In **Ethiopia**, the Addis Ababa–Djibouti railway-financed and constructed by China-marked the first transnational electrified railway in the region. Yet, the railway has struggled financially, earning only a fraction of its operating costs, and Ethiopia's debt burden has worsened.

In **Kenya**, the $3.2 billion Standard Gauge Railway (SGR) connecting Mombasa to Nairobi, funded by China Exim Bank, has been criticized for its high cost, opaque procurement, and limited returns. The Kenyan Auditor General's report raised alarm about the risk of Chinese lenders taking control of Mombasa Port in case of default.

Despite these issues, many African leaders view BRI as essential to economic transformation. China is now Africa's largest trading partner, and Chinese-built infrastructure often fills critical gaps ignored by Western financiers.

Reference: World Bank BRI in Africa Report (2021); African Centre for Strategic Studies.

Europe: Italy's Pivot and Pushback

Italy became the first G7 country to formally join the BRI in 2019, signing agreements worth billions in infrastructure, energy, and cultural exchange. The decision drew sharp criticism from Brussels and Washington, who feared a fracture in Western unity.

However, by 2023, Italy began **scaling back its BRI commitments**, citing limited economic returns and growing political risks. Prime Minister Giorgia Meloni's government officially announced its exit from BRI cooperation in 2024, making Italy a case study in the volatility of China-Europe relations.

The **European Union's Global Gateway Initiative** is now seen as a response to BRI-emphasizing transparency, green investment, and local stakeholder engagement.

Reference: European Commission (2023), *Global Gateway Strategy*; *Foreign Policy*, "Italy's Exit from BRI: A Cautionary Tale."

Central Asia: Kazakhstan's Balancing Act

Kazakhstan, where Xi Jinping first announced the Silk Road Economic Belt, is a critical land bridge in BRI. Through **rail networks and energy pipelines**, China has linked itself directly to Europe via Kazakhstan.

However, Kazakhstan treads a careful path. It welcomes Chinese investment but is wary of overdependence. Public protests against Chinese land acquisitions and industrial projects reflect popular suspicion. Moreover, Kazakhstan is simultaneously courting Russia, Turkey, and the EU to **balance Chinese influence**.

The government's "Nurly Zhol" national development program is being aligned with BRI selectively, emphasizing **co-financing and local content requirements**.

Reference: NBR Report (2020), "China's Strategy in Central Asia"; Kazakhstan Ministry of Foreign Affairs.

Geostrategic Effects: Corridors of Influence and Contours of Contestation

The Belt and Road Initiative has transcended its original framing as a development project to emerge as a **geostrategic lever**. Through its infrastructure corridors, digital systems, and financial entanglements, China is redrawing the **map of global influence**. While some nations embrace BRI as a catalyst for growth, others see in it the **emergence of a multipolar world order**-with China poised as a rule-setter. This shift has produced both cooperation and contestation across key regions.

Asia-Africa Economic Corridors: Nodes of Interdependence

The growing physical and digital corridors connecting **China to Africa via Asia** mark a tectonic shift in global trade flows. The BRI aims to realign traditional supply chains toward Eurasia and Africa, reducing China's reliance on Western-controlled chokepoints like the Malacca Strait.

Projects such as the **East African Railway, Bagamoyo Port in Tanzania**, and **the Nairobi Inland Container Depot** are not just economic nodes-they are political statements. Chinese-built industrial parks in Ethiopia and Egypt are being promoted as part of a new Sino-African economic axis, complete with **joint security agreements, digital governance models**, and **currency swaps.**

These corridors also advance China's **resource security strategy**, particularly in energy, rare earth minerals, and agriculture, all crucial for long-term economic and technological self-reliance.

Reference: Brookings Institution, *China's Engagement with Africa: From Trade to Strategic Entrenchment* (2023).

Europe's Ambivalence: Between Engagement and Strategic Autonomy

Europe is increasingly split in its approach toward BRI. On one hand, **Eastern and Southern European countries**-such as Serbia, Hungary, and Greece-have embraced Chinese capital and infrastructure, often bypassing EU bureaucratic hurdles. The **China-CEEC (17+1) format** once appeared as a Chinese effort to fragment the EU's internal consensus.

However, **Germany, France, and the EU Commission** have grown more skeptical. The COVID-19 pandemic exposed vulnerabilities in European supply chains dependent on China, leading to calls for "**strategic autonomy**" in trade, technology, and infrastructure.

The EU's **Global Gateway Initiative**, launched in 2021, is a direct institutional response to BRI-promoting green, transparent, and inclusive connectivity projects. Brussels is now pushing for regulatory standards in BRI projects involving European companies or assets.

Reference: European External Action Service, *EU-China Strategic Outlook* (2023); Chatham House, "Europe's Connectivity Conundrum" (2022).

U.S. Countermeasures: Containment Through Competition

The United States views the BRI through a security lens-framing it as an instrument of **authoritarian expansion and digital coercion**. Since 2018, successive U.S. administrations have launched counter-initiatives, including:

- **Build Back Better World (B3W)**: A G7 partnership aimed at mobilizing $600 billion in infrastructure investment by 2027 to rival BRI.
- **Indo-Pacific Economic Framework (IPEF)**: Promotes transparent trade, data governance, clean energy, and resilient supply chains.
- **Blue Dot Network**: A certification mechanism for global infrastructure projects based on transparency, accountability, and sustainability.

Military strategists also note the dual-use nature of BRI ports and railways, potentially allowing China to **project naval power** in the Indian Ocean, the Red Sea, and the Mediterranean. The Pentagon's 2022 report to Congress on China emphasized the security implications of **logistics bases** in Djibouti, Pakistan, and Cambodia.

Reference: U.S. Department of State (2022), *Countering Authoritarian Influence through Strategic Infrastructure*; RAND Corporation, "The Strategic Logic of BRI.

The Indo-Pacific Response: India, Japan, and the Quad

China's expanding footprint in South Asia and the Indian Ocean has galvanized strategic coordination among regional democracies. **India**, which sees BRI's **China-Pakistan Economic Corridor (CPEC)** as a violation of its territorial sovereignty, has categorically rejected the initiative.

Instead, India has deepened maritime cooperation with the U.S., **Japan**, and **Australia** under the **Quadrilateral Security Dialogue (Quad)**. The **Quad Infrastructure Coordination Group**, formed in 2022, aims to offer **high-standard, market-driven alternatives** to BRI across Southeast Asia and the Pacific Islands.

Japan's **Partnership for Quality Infrastructure**, launched in 2015, promotes energy, digital, and transport projects that emphasize local employment and long-term viability. Tokyo has also co-financed projects with India in **Africa and the Indo-Pacific**, building strategic counterweights to BRI corridors.

Reference: Observer Research Foundation (ORF), *India's Strategic Response to BRI*; Japan Ministry of Foreign Affairs, *PQI Annual Report* (2023).

Chokepoints and Strategic Maritime Contestation

A major concern among global navies and geopolitical analysts is China's ability to control-or influence-**global maritime chokepoints** through BRI-linked ports. Key maritime passageways affected include:

- **Strait of Malacca:** China's vulnerability here explains its push for overland connectivity via Myanmar and Pakistan.
- **Bab el-Mandeb:** Control via Djibouti supports Chinese naval presence in the Red Sea and Eastern Africa.
- **Suez Canal and Mediterranean Gateways:** Control of Piraeus Port and investment in Egyptian infrastructure links China to Europe's southern flank.

In this framework, BRI becomes part of a broader **grand strategy of access denial and positional advantage**, often described by analysts as "**geoeconomic statecraft.**"

Reference: IISS Strategic Survey (2022), "Chokepoints and the China Challenge"; National Defence University Review.

Opinion: Strategy Masked as Partnership or Hegemony in Motion?

The Belt and Road Initiative stands at the intersection of aspiration and apprehension. For some countries, it remains an indispensable conduit for **infrastructure development, economic growth, and regional integration.** For others, it signals the quiet advance of a **neo-mercantilist world order**, with China at the helm, reshaping not only economic flows but also **rules, norms, and alliances.**

The BRI is undeniably transformative. It has connected previously unlinked geographies, infused capital into infrastructure-starved economies, and redefined China's role on the global stage. Yet, the nature of its influence is complex. The very features that make BRI attractive-speed of execution, scale of funding, and flexible implementation-are also what raise concerns about **debt dependency**, **sovereign compromise**, and **geopolitical entanglement.**

What sets the BRI apart from historical empires or Western-led development paradigms is its subtlety. China does not impose military bases or ideological regimes. Instead, it builds **ports, railways, fiber networks, and financial pipelines**-tangible assets with long-term strategic consequences. The challenge lies not merely in China's intent, but in the **infrastructural logic of power** that the BRI creates. Roads do not just connect-they direct. Ports do not just open-they anchor.

As the world transitions into a **multipolar era**, the BRI becomes a prism through which new alignments are shaped. Whether it evolves into a framework of equitable cooperation or a scaffolding for hegemonic influence will depend on several factors: **the transparency of China's ambitions, the agency of partner nations, and the emergence of credible alternatives.**

In this fluid terrain, nations must make choices not just about infrastructure-but about their **strategic autonomy, long-term economic sustainability, and place in the international order.** For researchers, policymakers, and citizens alike, understanding the BRI is no longer optional-it is essential.

CHAPTER FIVE

Russia-Ukraine War: Reshaping the European Security Order

Introduction: An End to the Post-Cold War Illusions

The Russian invasion of Ukraine in February 2022 marked a **watershed moment** in modern international relations, ending the relative stability that had characterized the European security order since the end of the Cold War. For decades, despite tensions, European policymakers operated under the belief that globalization, interdependence, and diplomacy could contain or moderate Russian ambitions. The war shattered these assumptions, reintroducing **large-scale interstate warfare** to the European continent, reviving **great-power competition**, and forcing a wholesale reassessment of security, energy, and defence policies.

To understand the seismic implications of the 2022 invasion, one must first grasp the **legacy issues** that framed it: the expansion of NATO eastward into former Soviet spheres, the breach of trust surrounding Russia's annexation of Crimea in 2014, and the steady erosion of post-Cold War arms control agreements like the **INF Treaty** and **Open Skies Treaty**. The war is not merely a localized territorial dispute; it reflects a **fundamental clash** between competing visions of Europe: one based on **liberal, rules-based international order**, and another rooted in **revanchist, imperial aspirations.**

The conflict has triggered cascading effects across multiple domains-**military modernization**, **energy security**, **cyber and hybrid warfare**, and **geoeconomic realignment**-drawing comparisons with past eras of systemic upheaval, such as the post-World War II division of Europe. Whether the continent emerges stronger and more unified, or fragmented and militarized, remains an open question. What is clear is that the **European security order has been irrevocably reshaped**, and the consequences will reverberate globally for decades to come.

Reference: RAND Corporation, *The Return of Great-Power Competition* (2022); Chatham House, *Russia's War Against Ukraine: Strategic Implications for Europe* (2023).

Historical Context: NATO Expansion and Crimea's Annexation

The Evolution of NATO and Russia's Security Anxiety

The end of the Cold War ushered in an era of optimism. The 1990 Paris Charter proclaimed a "Europe whole and free," and discussions centered around integrating Russia into a cooperative European security framework. However, this vision soon diverged. NATO, originally founded to counter Soviet aggression, expanded into former Warsaw Pact countries through successive rounds:

- **1999**: Poland, Hungary, and the Czech Republic joined.
- **2004**: Baltic states (Estonia, Latvia, Lithuania) and others like Romania and Bulgaria entered.
- **2009–2020**: Further additions included Albania, Croatia, Montenegro, and North Macedonia.

For the West, NATO enlargement was a triumph of democratic transformation. For Russia, it was perceived as a **strategic encirclement** and a **betrayal** of verbal assurances allegedly given to Soviet leaders in 1990-91, although no formal treaty codified such promises.

Russian leaders from **Boris Yeltsin to Vladimir Putin** voiced repeated concerns. The 2007 **Munich Security Conference Speech** by Putin starkly articulated Russian grievances, criticizing U.S. "unipolarity" and warning against NATO's eastward drift.

Reference: Chatham House, *Russia's Strategic Narratives and NATO Expansion* (2021); Gorbachev Foundation Archives on 1990-91 negotiations.

Crimea 2014: The Turning Point

The seeds of the 2022 invasion were sown in **2014**, when Russia annexed **Crimea** following Ukraine's **Euromaidan Revolution**, which ousted the pro-Russian president Viktor Yanukovych. Viewing Ukraine's drift toward the European Union and NATO as an existential threat, Russia rapidly deployed troops, held a controversial referendum in Crimea, and formally absorbed the peninsula.

Simultaneously, **pro-Russian separatist movements** erupted in the Donetsk and Luhansk regions of eastern Ukraine, triggering a conflict that smouldered for eight years. Despite the signing of the **Minsk Agreements** (2014, 2015) aimed at de-escalation, sporadic violence continued, resulting in **over 14,000 deaths** before the full-scale invasion in 2022.

The annexation of Crimea was a clear violation of the **Budapest Memorandum (1994)**, in which Russia, along with the U.S. and the U.K., had committed to respecting Ukraine's sovereignty in exchange for Ukraine giving up its Soviet-era nuclear arsenal. The erosion of this agreement gravely damaged trust in **security assurances** and set a dangerous precedent for future nuclear non-proliferation diplomacy.

From Moscow's perspective, Crimea was not merely about strategic access to the Black Sea-it was about reversing what Putin and Russian elites saw as the **humiliation** of the post-Soviet era and reasserting Russia's great-power status.

Reference: United Nations General Assembly Resolution 68/262 (2014) condemning Crimea's annexation; Carnegie Moscow Center, *The Logic Behind Crimea's Seizure* (2015).

Prelude to 2022: Frozen Conflict and Escalating Tensions

The period between 2015 and 2021 represented a deceptively quiet phase in the Ukraine-Russia conflict-often termed a "frozen conflict"-but beneath the surface, geopolitical pressures were steadily building. Following the 2014 annexation of Crimea and the outbreak of war in the Donbas region, Russia entrenched its position using a hybrid warfare strategy. Moscow officially denied direct involvement in eastern Ukraine, but it covertly supplied separatist forces with arms, logistical support, intelligence, and even personnel. This strategy gave Russia significant influence over the conflict's trajectory while shielding it from full-scale retaliation or sanctions beyond those already in place.

On the Ukrainian side, the response was two-pronged: military resilience and diplomatic alignment with the West. Ukraine strengthened its armed forces with the help of Western military training programs, while also receiving financial assistance and limited defensive weapons from the United States, NATO, and EU partners. Yet despite these efforts, Ukraine failed to retake control of the separatist-held territories of Donetsk and Luhansk, and the frontlines hardened into static battlefields. Over 14,000 lives were lost during this period, underscoring the conflict's enduring toll.

Diplomacy continued but stagnated. Efforts such as the Minsk Agreements (2014 and 2015) and the Normandy Format talks involving France, Germany, Ukraine, and Russia aimed to de-escalate tensions and lay the groundwork for a political resolution. However, both sides accused each other of non-compliance, and the agreements remained largely unimplemented. Ceasefires came and went, often breaking down within days or weeks due to renewed shelling or troop movements.

Meanwhile, Russia took decisive steps to solidify its hold over Crimea. The peninsula was rapidly militarized, becoming a strategic outpost in the Black Sea equipped with advanced S-400 missile systems, naval forces, and electronic warfare installations. Infrastructure projects like the Kerch Strait Bridge symbolized Russia's intent to integrate Crimea economically and politically into its federation. Beyond Crimea, Moscow also worked to inflame separatist sentiment in other vulnerable Ukrainian regions, including parts of Kharkiv, Odesa, and the wider Donbas area.

By late 2021, the simmering tensions reached a boiling point. Russia began amassing an unprecedented number of troops-eventually exceeding 150,000-along Ukraine's eastern borders and in Belarus. Satellite imagery showed heavy equipment, field hospitals, and logistical chains being positioned for potential large-scale operations. Western intelligence agencies raised alarms, warning that Russia's actions went far beyond typical exercises. The Kremlin, however, insisted it had no intention of invading, accusing NATO and the West of provocation and encirclement.

Simultaneously, disinformation campaigns, cyberattacks on Ukrainian infrastructure, and inflammatory rhetoric surged, indicating the multidimensional nature of Russia's strategy. The build-up wasn't merely a show of force—it was preparation for a full-spectrum escalation. Despite last-ditch diplomatic efforts in Geneva, Brussels, and via backchannel talks, the standoff hardened.

The frozen conflict had become a pressure cooker. As 2022 dawned, it became evident that Europe was on the brink of its most serious military crisis since the Cold War. Western intelligence increasingly warned that the frozen conflict was transitioning toward a high-intensity confrontation, setting the stage for Russia's full-scale invasion in February 2022.

Reference: RAND Corporation, *Russia's Hybrid Warfare Campaigns* (2021); UN OHCHR, *Human Rights Situation in Ukraine Reports* (2014–2022)

The 2022 Invasion: Military, Diplomatic, and Economic Fallout

Military Dimensions: Blitzkrieg Failure and the Evolution of the War

When Russia launched its so-called "special military operation" on February 24, 2022, it envisioned a rapid, decisive campaign that would topple the Ukrainian government within days. The operation was designed as a blitzkrieg-a fast, overwhelming assault intended to paralyze Ukrainian command structures, capture Kyiv, and install a Moscow-friendly regime with minimal resistance. Russian troops poured in from three primary directions: from the north via Belarus toward Kyiv, from the east through the Donbas region, and from the south via Crimea, aiming to encircle and divide Ukrainian defenses.

Russian military planners misjudged several critical factors. First, they underestimated both the will and the capability of Ukrainian forces. Years of NATO-assisted training since 2014 had modernized Ukraine's army, making it more mobile, coordinated, and battle-hardened. Second, Moscow's assumptions of a welcoming Ukrainian populace and a disoriented leadership proved disastrously wrong. Instead, Ukrainians rallied in defense of their sovereignty, and President Volodymyr Zelenskyy's decision to stay in Kyiv became a powerful symbol of national resistance.

Additionally, the Russian offensive suffered from major logistical failures and poor battlefield coordination. Long supply lines stalled, armoured columns were ambushed in dense urban and forested environments, and communication breakdowns plagued Russian command. The lack of air superiority also prevented Moscow from establishing uncontested operational dominance-a critical failure in modern warfare.

Key Military Engagements and Turning Points:

Battle of Kyiv (Feb–April 2022):
Russia's attempt to seize the Ukrainian capital from the north through a rapid mechanized thrust was decisively thwarted. The infamous 64-kilometer-long Russian convoy north of Kyiv became emblematic of strategic overreach and logistical paralysis. Ukrainian forces, armed with U.S.-supplied Javelin anti-tank missiles, Turkish Bayraktar drones, and Western intelligence support, mounted an effective asymmetric defense, targeting fuel convoys, command vehicles, and high-value assets. By early April, Russian forces were forced to retreat entirely from Kyiv Oblast, abandoning their original objective of regime change.

Siege of Mariupol (March–May 2022):
While the northern front collapsed, Russia found partial success in the south. The port city of Mariupol became a focal point of brutal urban warfare. Encircled and bombarded relentlessly, the city endured one of the war's most devastating assaults. The Azovstal steel plant became the last bastion of Ukrainian resistance, with fighters from the Azov Regiment and civilians sheltering underground for weeks. Though Russia ultimately captured Mariupol, over 90% of the city was destroyed, and the siege drew global outrage for targeting civilian infrastructure and causing widespread humanitarian suffering.

Kharkiv and Kherson Counteroffensives (Sept–Nov 2022):
By mid-2022, Ukraine shifted to the offensive, capitalizing on Russian

exhaustion and supply deficiencies. In September, a surprise Ukrainian counteroffensive in the Kharkiv region recaptured thousands of square kilometers in just days-demonstrating superior mobility, intelligence-led operations, and battlefield morale. In the south, Ukraine's months-long pressure campaign on Kherson forced Russia to retreat from the city in November, marking a significant strategic and symbolic victory. The withdrawal from Kherson-the only regional capital Russia had captured-highlighted the vulnerability of Russian positions west of the Dnipro River.

These developments made clear that Russia's initial war objectives had failed. Rather than achieving a quick and decisive campaign, Moscow became mired in a protracted, grinding conflict. The Russian military then pivoted to a strategy of attrition, leveraging its advantage in artillery and missile stockpiles to target Ukrainian cities, energy grids, railways, and water systems. Civilian infrastructure became a key target, particularly in winter, in a calculated attempt to demoralize the population and pressure the Ukrainian government into concessions.

This phase of the war also witnessed increased reliance on Iranian-supplied drones, such as the Shahed-136, for targeted strikes on energy facilities, further globalizing the conflict and expanding its technological and diplomatic scope.

Opinion:

The failure of Russia's blitzkrieg revealed critical flaws in its military doctrine, exposed the limits of its expeditionary capabilities, and underscored the resilience and adaptability of Ukrainian defense forces. The war transitioned from a planned short-term incursion into a drawn-out, high-cost war of attrition-one that redefined modern warfare through the interplay of asymmetric resistance, real-time intelligence-sharing, and hybrid tactics across kinetic and digital domains.

Reference: RAND Corporation, *The Russian Military's Lessons from Ukraine* (2023); IISS, *The Military Balance* (2023).

Economic Fallout: Sanctions, Decoupling, and Energy Warfare

The Russian invasion of Ukraine in February 2022 triggered one of the most far-reaching and coordinated sets of economic sanctions in modern history. Led by the United States, European Union, United Kingdom, Canada, Japan, and several other allies, the Western response aimed to cripple Russia's financial architecture, isolate its economy, and constrain its war-making capacity. Unlike previous sanctions, which were often limited to specific individuals or sectors, this wave targeted the systemic foundations of Russia's global economic integration.

Financial Sanctions and Institutional Decoupling-

SWIFT Expulsion:

One of the most significant early measures was the removal of major Russian banks-including Sberbank, VTB, and Gazprombank-from the SWIFT international payment network. This effectively severed their ability to conduct cross-border transactions in dollars and euros, paralyzing trade finance, disrupting supply chains, and isolating Russia's financial institutions from the global economy.

Central Bank Asset Freeze:

In a move without precedent against a G20 country, Western governments froze approximately $300 billion of Russia's foreign exchange reserves held abroad. This action undermined Moscow's financial cushion and blocked its ability to stabilize the ruble through currency interventions. The measure also eroded investor confidence, leading to fears about the sanctity of sovereign reserves in geopolitically volatile scenarios.

Sanctions on Oligarchs and Elites:

A parallel strategy focused on the Russian elite, aiming to fracture the domestic power base around President Vladimir Putin. Dozens of oligarchs with known Kremlin ties faced asset seizures-luxury properties in London, yachts moored in European ports, and stakes in Western businesses were frozen or confiscated. While symbolic in part, these actions sent a signal that personal wealth and global mobility were no longer guaranteed for Russia's ultra-rich.

Technology and Industrial Embargoes:

Perhaps the most strategically impactful measures were export controls on dual-use technologies. Western countries banned the export of advanced semiconductors, aircraft components, microchips, sensors, and software-disabling Russia's capacity to manufacture high-end military hardware, modern vehicles, and even civilian electronics. This technological decoupling created long-term structural damage to Russia's defense sector and industrial modernization plans.

Russia's Economic Countermeasures and Energy Retaliation

In response, Russia weaponized its dominant role in global energy markets, particularly its leverage over European gas and oil supplies. This marked the emergence of energy as a strategic retaliatory tool-one that exposed the vulnerabilities of even advanced economies to supply-side shocks.

Gas Supply Curtailments to Europe:

Beginning mid-2022, Russia systematically reduced natural gas exports to Europe via key pipelines, including Nord Stream 1. Countries such as Germany, Austria, and Italy, heavily reliant on Russian energy, experienced a surge in prices, industrial disruptions, and fears of winter shortages. The crisis prompted emergency EU responses, including rationing plans, accelerated LNG imports, and joint procurement initiatives. The European energy market was effectively restructured overnight, with long-standing dependence on Russian gas abruptly replaced by diversification efforts.

Oil Trade Diversion to the East:

To offset revenue losses from Western embargoes and price caps, Russia redirected significant volumes of crude oil exports to India, China, and other non-aligned countries-often at discounted rates. This pivot partially cushioned the financial blow but also reduced Russia's profit margins. Meanwhile, the G7-led oil price cap initiative aimed to keep Russian oil flowing to global markets while restricting its earnings-a delicate balancing act between economic pressure and energy stability.

Nord Stream Pipeline Sabotage (September 2022):

In a dramatic development, underwater explosions severely damaged the Nord Stream 1 pipeline and disabled the never-activated Nord Stream 2. The blasts-occurring in international waters in the Baltic Sea-were widely seen as a turning point in infrastructure warfare. Though the perpetrators remain officially unidentified, the incident underscored the geopolitical risk surrounding critical infrastructure and heightened concerns about hybrid warfare targeting energy grids, undersea cables, and pipelines.

Broader Economic and Geostrategic Implications

Global Inflation and Commodity Shock:

The war and its economic repercussions triggered a spike in global energy, food, and fertilizer prices. Wheat exports from both Russia and Ukraine-two of the world's largest producers-were disrupted, contributing to food insecurity in the Global South. Inflationary pressures intensified worldwide, complicating monetary policy and social stability from Europe to Africa to Southeast Asia.

Russia's Pivot to Autarky and Parallel Systems:

Facing long-term exclusion from Western systems, Moscow accelerated its move toward economic self-reliance and alignment with non-Western powers. Russia expanded use of the Chinese yuan and Indian rupee in bilateral trade, promoted its own Mir payment system as an alternative to Visa and Mastercard, and explored de-dollarization with BRICS countries. While these measures offer partial relief, they cannot fully substitute the scale and efficiency of the Western-dominated financial system.

Deindustrialization Risks and Brain Drain:

As Western companies exited the Russian market-over 1,000 firms by some estimates-the economy experienced a rapid decline in foreign investment, technology transfers, and skilled labor. Many multinational production facilities were nationalized or sold at distressed prices. Simultaneously, a wave of skilled workers, tech professionals, and young entrepreneurs fled the country, deepening the long-term economic damage.

Opinion:

The economic front of the Russia-Ukraine war evolved into a full-spectrum contest of sanctions, decoupling, and resource leverage. While sanctions have severely impaired Russia's economy and strategic industries, Moscow's energy retaliation caused acute pain in Europe and demonstrated the interdependence of global markets. The net result has been a structural rupture in the post-Cold War economic order-pushing the world toward greater economic fragmentation, realignment of trade flows, and politicization of global finance.

Reference: Chatham House, *Russia's Economic Isolation: Effectiveness and Limits* (2023); UNCTAD, *World Economic Impact of the War in Ukraine* (2022).

Diplomatic Fallout: Global Fractures and Realignments

The Russia-Ukraine war did not just redraw military frontlines-it redrew diplomatic ones, revealing the widening fractures in the global order and underscoring the erosion of consensus on core principles of international conduct. While Western democracies responded with striking unity, much of the rest of the world adopted a more cautious or ambivalent stance, exposing deep rifts in how different regions interpret legitimacy, sovereignty, and global responsibility.

United Nations and the Limits of Consensus

The United Nations became an early arena for diplomatic contestation. In March 2022, the UN General Assembly adopted Resolution ES-11/1, condemning Russia's invasion and reaffirming Ukraine's territorial integrity. The resolution passed with 141 votes in favor-signifying widespread formal disapproval of Moscow's actions. Yet, notable absences from this moral majority highlighted the fractured nature of global opinion.

Key Abstentions:

China, India, South Africa, Iran, and several African and Southeast Asian countries abstained. These abstentions did not necessarily imply support for Russia but reflected discomfort with what many perceived as Western double standards, NATO's eastward expansion, or fear of economic retaliation from either side.

Security Council Paralysis:

As expected, the UN Security Council-where Russia holds a permanent seat-remained gridlocked. Veto powers were used to block stronger action, reinforcing criticism that the UN's institutional structure is outdated and ill-equipped to manage 21st-century crises.

China's Calculated Ambiguity

China's diplomatic posture became a case study in strategic hedging. Beijing affirmed respect for Ukraine's sovereignty while simultaneously refusing to condemn Moscow's actions, abstaining from UN votes, and amplifying narratives that shifted blame onto NATO and the West. It positioned itself as a potential mediator, unveiling a 12-point peace plan in early 2023 that emphasized ceasefires, negotiations, and sovereignty but omitted explicit criticism of Russia's aggression.

Critics viewed the plan as pro-Russian in tone and content, noting its call for lifting Western sanctions and avoiding "bloc confrontation"-a thinly veiled reference to U.S. alliances.

Despite its public neutrality, China deepened energy and trade ties with Russia, significantly increasing its imports of Russian oil and gas at discounted prices, while also coordinating joint military drills in the Pacific.

This posture allowed Beijing to project neutrality to the Global South, retain strategic leverage over Russia, and avoid alienating the West, all while quietly benefiting from the geopolitical vacuum.

The Global South's Dissonant Response

In contrast to the West's view of the war as a clear-cut battle between democracy and authoritarianism, many countries in the Global South interpreted the conflict through historical and pragmatic lenses.

Historical Grievances:

African, Latin American, and some Asian nations cited Western interventions in Iraq, Libya, and Afghanistan, arguing that principles of sovereignty were selectively applied. The lack of accountability for those invasions undermined Western efforts to frame the Ukraine war as a moral struggle.

Economic Pragmatism:

Many developing countries remained reluctant to antagonize Russia, given their dependency on Russian energy, arms, grain, and fertilizer. They prioritized national interests-food security, affordable energy, and geopolitical balance-over alignment with a Western-led sanctions regime.

Calls for Reform:

The mixed responses from the Global South highlighted calls for a reformed multilateral order where emerging powers like India, Brazil, and South Africa have a stronger voice-particularly within institutions like the UN Security Council and the IMF.

Western Diplomacy: Unity and Acceleration

While fractures emerged globally, the war catalyzed a remarkable diplomatic consolidation within the West, particularly across NATO and the European Union.

NATO Article 4 Consultations:

In the early days of the invasion, NATO invoked Article 4-which allows member states to consult on threats to their territorial integrity or political independence. This marked a coordinated return to collective deterrence and rapid intelligence-sharing.

Strategic Recalibration:

NATO's 2022 Strategic Concept, adopted at the Madrid Summit, declared Russia the "most significant and direct threat" to Euro-Atlantic security and identified China as a long-term systemic challenger-signifying a doctrinal shift from post-9/11 counterterrorism to traditional great power rivalry.

EU's Military and Financial Mobilization:

For the first time in its history, the EU activated the European Peace Facility to provide billions of euros in military aid, lethal weaponry, and humanitarian assistance to a non-member state-Ukraine. This move redefined the EU's identity, marking a shift from soft-power diplomacy toward hard-power engagement.

Emerging Realignments and Strategic Hedging

The diplomatic landscape post-2022 has been defined by fluid realignments and hedging strategies:

India maintained a deliberate neutrality, refusing to condemn Russia at the UN while expanding trade in discounted oil and fertilizer. Simultaneously, it hosted Western leaders during its G20 presidency and strengthened its QUAD commitments with the U.S., Japan, and Australia-underscoring its multi-alignment doctrine.

Turkey leveraged its position as a NATO member with ties to Russia and Ukraine to broker the Black Sea Grain Initiative, allowing for resumed Ukrainian grain exports under UN supervision. Ankara's balancing act enhanced its geopolitical relevance while frustrating both Brussels and Moscow.

Middle Eastern States like the UAE and Saudi Arabia pursued strategic autonomy-engaging with Moscow in OPEC+ coordination, even as they maintained security ties with the West. Their posture signaled a broader post-American recalibration of foreign policy among Gulf states.

Opinion:

The diplomatic fallout of the Russia-Ukraine war has fractured global alignments, reinforced the West's strategic cohesion, and amplified the geopolitical assertiveness of middle powers. It has highlighted the limits of Western influence in the Global South, revived great-power competition, and reshaped the contours of global diplomacy. While Europe and North America moved in lockstep, the rest of the world carved more ambiguous, interest-driven paths—reshaping a world where influence is now as contested diplomatically as it is militarily.

Reference: UNGA Resolution ES-11/1 (2022); Brookings Institution, *China's Strategy in the Ukraine War* (2022); Chatham House, *The Global South's Response to Ukraine* (2023).

Geopolitical Outcomes: NATO Realignment, Energy Reconfigurations, EU Assertiveness, Expansion, Deterrence, and Strategic Depth

The full-scale Russian invasion of Ukraine in February 2022 acted as a seismic shock to the post-Cold War security architecture of Europe. It upended decades of strategic assumptions, reactivated dormant security mechanisms, and revitalized alliances once thought obsolete. NATO, which French President Emmanuel Macron had famously described as "brain dead" in 2019, emerged from the crisis with renewed purpose, cohesion, and momentum. The invasion served not only as a threat but as a catalyst-reshaping European defence strategy, altering energy geopolitics, and transforming the European Union's role in global security.

NATO Expansion: Redrawing the Strategic Map of Northern Europe

Finland and Sweden Break with Neutrality

In a historic reversal of decades-long non-alignment policies, Finland and Sweden submitted formal applications to join NATO in May 2022-triggered by Russia's aggressive actions and existential threat perceptions. Their accession marked one of the most consequential expansions of NATO since the end of the Cold War.

Finland became NATO's 31st member in April 2023, extending the alliance's direct border with Russia by over 1,300 kilometers-transforming NATO's strategic posture in the High North and placing additional pressure on Russia's Western Military District.

Sweden overcame political resistance from Turkey and Hungary, joining in 2024 after making concessions on counterterrorism cooperation and arms export policies.

This dual accession has dramatically shifted the Baltic Sea into a NATO-controlled basin, enabling more secure supply chains, air defence coordination, and maritime operations, while also reinforcing deterrence in the Arctic and North Atlantic theatres.

Forward Deployments and Eastern Flank Fortification

In response to Russian aggression, NATO accelerated the deployment of multinational battlegroups in Central and Eastern Europe. New forces were positioned in Romania, Slovakia, Hungary, and Bulgaria, augmenting existing units in Poland and the Baltics.

These deployments are part of NATO's broader Enhanced Forward Presence strategy, designed not merely for deterrence but for immediate reaction capability. The presence of U.S., British, French, and other allied troops sends a clear signal that any attack on member states will invoke

Article 5 collective defense commitments.

The establishment of permanent infrastructure-command centers, logistics hubs, and joint training facilities-represents a shift from "tripwire" deterrence to pre-integrated, interoperable combat readiness.

Defence Spending Surge: Rearmament and Strategic Convergence

The invasion shattered long-held illusions in Western Europe about the durability of peace and the adequacy of post-Cold War military capabilities.

Germany's Historic Pivot:

Berlin, long criticized for underinvestment in defense, unveiled a €100 billion special defense fund and committed to meeting NATO's 2% GDP spending target. This marked a break from its post-WWII aversion to militarization and introduced debates on long-term force modernization and industrial capacity.

Poland's Military Renaissance:

Poland committed to raising its defense spending to over 4% of GDP-among the highest in NATO. It expanded procurement of tanks, artillery, fighter jets, and missile defense systems, aspiring to become the linchpin of NATO's eastern flank.

Nordic and Baltic Buildups:

Denmark, Norway, and the Baltic states increased investments in air defense, cybersecurity, and mobility infrastructure, emphasizing resilience against hybrid threats and potential Russian provocations.

Collectively, these efforts signal the end of Europe's post-Cold War military drawdown and the beginning of a continental rearmament era-driven not by expeditionary warfare but by territorial defense and strategic deterrence.

Strategic Concept 2022: Reframing Threats and Priorities

At the Madrid Summit in June 2022, NATO adopted its first New Strategic Concept since 2010—a document that codified the alliance's doctrinal evolution.

Key highlights include:

Russia was identified as the "most significant and direct threat" to Euro-Atlantic security, replacing the previous phrasing that described it as a "partner."

China was named for the first time as a "systemic challenge", citing its coercive diplomacy, technological influence, and strategic partnership with Russia.

The document emphasized the need for 360-degree security, recognizing threats from the south (North Africa and the Sahel) as well as the east.

It also reaffirmed commitments to cyber defense, resilience to hybrid attacks, and climate-security linkages, expanding NATO's purview beyond traditional kinetic threats.

This strategic reorientation is not just reactive-it reflects a long-term adaptation to a more volatile, multipolar world order.

EU Assertiveness: From Soft Power to Strategic Actor

While NATO focused on military deterrence, the European Union stepped into a more assertive geopolitical role, particularly in economic, humanitarian, and defense funding dimensions.

European Peace Facility (EPF):

For the first time, the EU financed the delivery of lethal weapons to a conflict zone-marking a departure from its traditionally pacifist posture. Over €10 billion was allocated in military aid to Ukraine, covering ammunition, air defense, and combat vehicles.

Strategic Compass (2022):

The EU's new defense white paper called for the creation of a Rapid Deployment Capacity of 5,000 troops, improved joint procurement, and increased strategic autonomy in security matters.

Energy and Economic Decoupling:

The EU rapidly diversified away from Russian gas-once constituting over 40% of its energy mix-by securing LNG contracts with the U.S., Qatar, and Norway, accelerating the development of renewable infrastructure, and implementing joint gas procurement mechanisms.

Together, these moves signified a geopolitical awakening of the EU, blending economic clout with emerging hard-power tools.

Opinion:

The Russian invasion of Ukraine catalyzed a tectonic realignment in European and transatlantic security. NATO's geographical expansion, doctrinal recalibration, and military forward positioning signaled a return to high-stakes deterrence reminiscent of the Cold War-but adapted to hybrid and multidomain threats. Simultaneously, the EU evolved into a more agile and assertive actor in both defense and energy geopolitics.

What emerged is a more cohesive, strategically awake Western bloc-though still grappling with long-term sustainability, defense industrial gaps, and questions of burden-sharing. At its core, this geopolitical transformation is about reclaiming strategic depth, deterrence credibility, and institutional resilience in an era of contested norms and open-ended rivalry.

Reference: NATO Strategic Concept 2022; RAND Corporation, *NATO After Ukraine: Deterrence Recalibrated* (2023).

Energy Reconfigurations: Europe's Great Decoupling

The war in Ukraine forced Europe into one of the most dramatic and rapid energy realignments in its modern history. Prior to the invasion, Russia was Europe's single largest energy supplier-providing roughly 40% of its natural gas and 30% of its oil imports. This dependency had long been seen as a strategic vulnerability, but inertia and cost-efficiency kept ties intact. The outbreak of war and Russia's weaponization of energy exports jolted European policymakers into action, prompting an ambitious and multi-pronged decoupling effort.

Key Developments and Strategic Shifts:

LNG Infrastructure Boom:

To substitute Russian pipeline gas, European nations massively expanded liquefied natural gas (LNG) imports. Germany, historically resistant to LNG, opened its first floating LNG terminal in Wilhelmshaven in under a year-a pace unmatched in prior infrastructure development. Similar projects advanced in the Netherlands, Italy, and the Baltic states.

Diversification through Energy Diplomacy:

The EU secured new supply agreements with Norway, the U.S., Algeria, Azerbaijan, and Qatar, significantly reducing Russia's market share in European gas imports. Norway overtook Russia as Europe's top gas supplier by early 2023, while U.S. LNG exports to Europe reached record highs.

Renewable Energy Acceleration:

The crisis catalyzed Europe's green transition. Under the REPowerEU plan, the EU fast-tracked investments in solar, wind, hydrogen, and energy efficiency measures, targeting 45% renewable energy consumption by 2030. Germany and Spain led solar and wind expansions, while France emphasized nuclear revival.

Managing Energy Price Shocks:

The winter of 2022–23 brought historic price spikes in gas and electricity, but fears of blackouts and industrial collapse did not materialize. A combination of energy savings, public subsidies, full gas storage, and unseasonably mild weather helped Europe withstand the shock.

Opinion:

This decoupling marks a geopolitical and structural turning point. It not only reduced Russia's leverage over Europe, significantly cutting into Moscow's energy revenues, but also redirected the EU's energy model toward resilience, sustainability, and strategic autonomy. The long-term outcome is a greener, more diversified energy architecture-less vulnerable to coercion and more aligned with climate goals.

Reference: European Commission, *Repower EU: Plan for Energy Independence* (2022); International Energy Agency, *Energy Security in Europe 2023.*

EU Assertiveness: From Economic Bloc to Strategic Actor

The war in Ukraine marked a historic inflection point in the European Union's geopolitical identity. Long seen primarily as an economic and regulatory superpower, the EU began shedding its reluctance toward hard security matters and emerged as a more strategically assertive actor-capable of responding with speed, unity, and substance to a major war on its borders.

Key Strategic Shifts:

European Peace Facility (EPF):

In a break from precedent, the EU used the EPF to finance lethal military aid to Ukraine, including ammunition, air defense systems, and armored vehicles. This move blurred the line between economic diplomacy and defense support, signaling a bold new role in crisis response.

Strategic Compass (2022):

The EU adopted its first-ever comprehensive security doctrine. Key objectives included:

Establishing a 5,000-troop rapid deployment force for crises.

Enhancing cybersecurity and hybrid defense capacities.

Launching joint defense procurement programs to reduce fragmentation and strengthen Europe's defense industry.

Defense Spending Coordination:

The European Defence Agency (EDA) gained a stronger mandate to coordinate defense investments among member states-aiming to reduce wasteful duplication and improve interoperability across armed forces.

Sanctions Leadership:

The EU imposed 13 consecutive sanctions packages against Russia, targeting banking, energy exports, dual-use technologies, disinformation networks, and hundreds of individuals. This marked a new level of sanctions diplomacy, demonstrating cohesion across 27 member states under crisis conditions.

Opinion:

This assertiveness does not compete with NATO but rather complements it, filling critical gaps in economic coercion, hybrid warfare, cybersecurity, and post-war reconstruction planning. The EU is now not just a market regulator but a geo-strategic pillar in the evolving European security architecture-blending hard power tools with economic influence and diplomatic reach.

Reference: European External Action Service, *Strategic Compass for Security and Defence* (2022); Chatham House, *Europe's Geopolitical Awakening* (2023).

Conclusion: The Collapse of the Post-Cold War Order and the Birth of a New Europe

The Russian invasion of Ukraine in 2022 did not merely ignite another regional war-it shattered the underlying assumptions of the **post-Cold War European security architecture**. The belief that economic interdependence, multilateral diplomacy, and soft power could prevent great-power conflict has been gravely undermined. Instead, the war revealed that **force remains a central currency of international politics**, and that unresolved grievances, if ignored, can escalate into existential crises.

The immediate geopolitical outcomes have been profound. NATO has been **revitalized**, with new members, heightened military spending, and a sharpened strategic focus. Europe has embarked on an **unprecedented energy transformation**, severing ties with Russian hydrocarbons and accelerating the green transition. The **European Union has evolved** from an economic bloc into an increasingly capable geopolitical actor, willing to leverage economic, diplomatic, and military tools in defence of its values and interests.

Meanwhile, Russia faces a long-term strategic setback. Isolated economically and diplomatically in the West, it turns increasingly to China, Iran, and parts of the Global South for support-accelerating a **fractured, multipolar world order**. Yet, this pivot has its limits; dependency on China risks subordinating Russian autonomy to a rising Asian hegemon.

The war has also reshaped global alignments. The Global South's ambivalence toward Western-led sanctions and narratives indicates that **the battle for influence is far from settled**. Future security frameworks will need to account not just for hard-power balances, but for competing ideological visions about sovereignty, intervention, and global governance.

In a broader sense, the Russia-Ukraine war represents **the end of the post-Cold War illusion** that the international system was moving irreversibly toward liberalism and peace. In its place, a **messier, more dangerous, but also more realistic world** has emerged-one where deterrence, resilience, and strategic autonomy are again paramount.

The challenge ahead for Europe, and for the broader international community, will be to **build a durable security order** that acknowledges power realities without abandoning the pursuit of stability, human rights, and international law. Whether the lessons of Ukraine will lead to a more resilient and united Europe-or to a fragmented, militarized, and unstable one-remains the defining question of our time.

Reference: Chatham House, *A New European Security Order?* (2023); UN Security Council Reports on Ukraine Crisis (2022–2024).

Case Study 1

Nord Stream Sabotage - The New Age of Infrastructure Warfare

In September 2022, powerful explosions damaged the Nord Stream pipelines in the Baltic Sea, halting gas supplies from Russia to Europe. The sabotage occurred in international waters and is widely believed to be a state-level operation, though official investigations by Germany, Sweden, and Denmark are still ongoing.

This marked a turning point in modern conflict, highlighting how critical energy infrastructure can be weaponized even outside of traditional war zones.

Key Implications:

- Energy Security: Europe quickly reduced its dependence on Russian gas, building new LNG terminals in Germany, Poland, and the Netherlands.
- Infrastructure Protection: NATO set up a Critical Undersea Infrastructure Coordination Cell to monitor and protect undersea assets.
- Information Warfare: The sabotage triggered conflicting narratives in Western and Russian media, turning infrastructure damage into a tool of disinformation and influence operations.

Reference: European Commission, *Safeguarding Critical Infrastructure Report* (2023); IISS, *New Frontiers in Hybrid Warfare* (2023).

Case Study 2

Turkey's Balancing Act

Turkey, a NATO member with significant ties to Russia, exemplified the delicate diplomatic balancing amid the Ukraine war:

- Facilitated the **Black Sea Grain Initiative**, allowing Ukrainian grain exports through Russian-controlled waters under UN auspices.
- Refused to join Western sanctions, maintaining robust trade with Russia, yet sold **Bayraktar drones** to Ukraine, which became iconic in early Ukrainian defences.
- Blocked, then allowed, Sweden and Finland's NATO accession bids, extracting concessions on counterterrorism cooperation.

Turkey's nuanced diplomacy enhanced its **geopolitical leverage** but also strained ties within NATO, revealing cracks in alliance unanimity.

Reference: International Crisis Group, *Turkey's Strategic Calculus in the Ukraine War* (2023); UN Black Sea Grain Initiative Agreements (2022).

Case Study 3

Poland and the New Frontline States

Countries like **Poland, the Baltic States (Estonia, Latvia, Lithuania)**, and **Romania** emerged as critical frontline actors in the new security environment.

- Poland became Ukraine's logistical and diplomatic hub-facilitating the transfer of military aid, welcoming over **3 million refugees**, and advocating for maximum pressure on Russia.
- Defence Modernization: Poland announced one of the largest defence buildups in Europe, planning to spend **4% of its GDP on defence** and ordering hundreds of tanks, fighter jets, and air defence systems from the U.S. and South Korea.
- Strategic Posture: Warsaw's leadership reshaped intra-European security debates, pushing back against earlier Franco-German models of engagement with Russia.

Poland's rise highlights a broader **eastward shift** in European security leadership-a dynamic likely to persist even after the Ukraine conflict stabilizes.

Reference: Polish Ministry of Defence, *National Defence Strategy 2023*; Carnegie Europe, *The New European Frontlines* (2023).

CHAPTER SIX

India-Pakistan Relations After the Pahalgam Attack: Escalation, Diplomacy, and Global Consequences

Introduction:

A Shocking Attack

On 22 April 2025, a devastating terror attack struck Pahalgam, a popular town in Jammu and Kashmir known for its scenic beauty and pilgrimage routes. The assault claimed the lives of several Indian security personnel and civilians, shaking the entire nation. Investigations and intelligence reports quickly pointed to Pakistan-based militant groups, bringing long-standing tensions between India and Pakistan back into the spotlight.

This tragic event was not an isolated incident - it was part of a long and painful history of cross-border terrorism and unresolved disputes over the Kashmir region. The attack once again reminded both nations and the world of how fragile peace in South Asia can be, especially between two nuclear-armed neighbours with a troubled past.

The Historical Context

To understand why such incidents keep happening, one must look at the roots of the Kashmir conflict. The issue dates back to 1947, when British India was divided into two independent nations - India and Pakistan. At that time, the princely state of Jammu and Kashmir, ruled by a Hindu Maharaja but with a Muslim-majority population, had the choice to join either country. The Maharaja chose to accede to India, leading Pakistan to launch military aggression in 1947-48 to seize the territory.

This decision ignited the first Indo-Pak war, and since then, the two nations have fought multiple wars over Kashmir - in 1947–48, 1965, and the Kargil conflict of 1999. Beyond open wars, the region has endured decades of insurgency and militancy, particularly since 1989, when Pakistan began to support and train militant groups operating across the border. India has repeatedly accused Pakistan of backing organisations such as Jaish-e-Mohammed (JeM) and Lashkar-e-Taiba (LeT), which have been responsible for many major terror attacks.

A Pattern of Terror Strikes

Over the years, several significant attacks have left deep scars on India's national psyche. The 2001 Indian Parliament attack targeted the very heart of Indian democracy. The 2008 Mumbai attacks left over 160 people dead and brought global attention to Pakistan's role in harbouring terrorists. The 2016 Uri attack on an Indian Army camp near the Line of Control was another turning point, prompting India to carry out surgical strikes across the border.

The Pahalgam attack of 2025 thus appeared as part of this grim pattern - one that combines local insurgency with cross-border planning. It revived memories of earlier tragedies and reignited anger and grief among citizens who have long demanded stronger action against terrorism.

The Pahalgam incident brought these historical grievances and fault lines back into sharp focus. Within hours, Indian political and military leaders condemned the attack in the strongest terms, vowing a "decisive response." The public mood across India was one of outrage, leading to widespread calls for retribution and national unity. Pakistan denied any state involvement and urged de-escalation, but its credibility was undermined by the continued presence of groups like Jaish-e-Mohammed and Lashkar-e-Taiba operating from its soil. The episode echoed earlier inflection points like the Pulwama-Balakot exchange in 2019, suggesting the onset of a dangerous and familiar escalation cycle in South Asia.

Bilateral Breakdown: Diplomatic, Military, and Economic Reactions

In the wake of the Pahalgam attack, India undertook a comprehensive recalibration of its engagement with Pakistan across diplomatic, military, and economic domains. Diplomatically, India withdrew its High Commissioner from Islamabad and expelled Pakistan's envoy from New

Delhi, effectively freezing formal bilateral dialogue. The Ministry of External Affairs (MEA) issued a series of strong statements linking Pakistan's territory to cross-border terrorism and reiterated India's demand for verifiable action against terror groups sheltered in Pakistan. Cultural exchanges, bilateral sporting events, and Track II diplomacy initiatives were indefinitely suspended.

In the hours following the Pahalgam terror strike, India's political and military leadership reacted with firmness and clarity. The Prime Minister, along with senior ministers and defence officials, condemned the attack in the strongest possible terms, assuring the nation that a "decisive response" would follow. This was not only a military warning but also a signal of India's intent to use every available lever of national power to respond to terrorism.

One of the first major steps announced was the suspension of the Indus Waters Treaty of 1960 with immediate effect. The treaty, brokered by the World Bank, had long governed the sharing of river waters between India and Pakistan-allocating the three eastern rivers (Ravi, Beas, Sutlej) to India and the three western rivers (Indus, Jhelum, Chenab) to Pakistan. Despite wars and hostilities, India had continued to honour this agreement for over six decades, making it a rare example of cooperation between the two rivals. The suspension, therefore, carried strong symbolic and strategic weight-it showed that India was now willing to reconsider even long-standing commitments if Pakistan failed to curb cross-border terrorism.

On the military front, India heightened its operational readiness along the Line of Control (LoC) and the International Border (IB). Deployment of additional infantry battalions, heightened surveillance using UAVs and satellite imagery, and activation of quick reaction teams in key sectors signalled a calibrated but resolute posture. The Indian Air Force was reportedly put on high alert, while the Indian Navy was directed to increase patrols in the Arabian Sea to deter potential maritime threats. Strategic discussions within the Cabinet Committee on Security explored kinetic options, including the possibility of cross-border precision strikes akin to the Balakot airstrike of 2019.

Economically, India intensified pressure through both symbolic and substantive measures. The Most Favoured Nation (MFN) status accorded to Pakistan was revoked, and customs duties on imports from Pakistan were hiked significantly. Joint infrastructure initiatives like the Kartarpur Corridor were placed under review. India also lobbied within the Financial

Action Task Force (FATF) to retain Pakistan on the grey list, citing lack of credible action on terror financing. Cross-border bus and train services such as the Samjhauta Express and Delhi–Lahore bus were suspended.

Across the country, the public mood was one of outrage and unity. From the bustling streets of Delhi to the quiet towns of the hinterland, people expressed their anger and grief through candlelight marches, tributes to fallen soldiers, and social media campaigns calling for justice. The nation stood together in solidarity, sending a clear message: India would neither forget nor forgive such an act of violence.

In response, Pakistan closed its airspace to Indian flights for several days and mobilized reserve forces in key garrison towns near the border. Anti-India protests broke out in major Pakistani cities, fuelled by a media narrative portraying India's stance as aggressive and unjustified. Diplomatic overtures by Pakistan to allies like China, Turkey, and the Organization of Islamic Cooperation (OIC) aimed to rally international support and shift global opinion against India's retaliatory posture.

On the diplomatic front, India intensified efforts to isolate Pakistan internationally. Through sustained lobbying at global forums such as the United Nations, the Financial Action Task Force (FATF), and the G20, India emphasized Pakistan's continued support for terror financing and its failure to dismantle extremist networks. As a result, Pakistan faced mounting global scrutiny and risked deeper economic consequences if it remained non-compliant with anti-terror commitments.

Additionally at the strategic level, India's decision to suspend people-to-people links-such as the Samjhauta Express and the Delhi–Lahore bus service-carried deep symbolic meaning. These initiatives had once stood as rare bridges of hope between the two nations. Their suspension reflected the collapse of trust and India's firm resolve that normal relations could not coexist with terrorism.

Together, these actions formed a comprehensive doctrine of deterrence. Instead of reacting only to individual incidents, India began building a framework that imposed sustained pressure across all fronts-economic, diplomatic, cultural, and strategic. This holistic response marked the emergence of a new phase in India's counter-terrorism policy, where the country's strength was demonstrated not just through its armed forces, but through its economic resilience, diplomatic influence, and national unity.

Limited vs. Full-Scale Conflict Scenarios: Strategic and Humanitarian Risks

In analysing potential military trajectories following the Pahalgam attack, defence strategists largely outlined two possible pathways: limited conflict or full-scale war. A limited military engagement-similar to India's 2016 surgical strikes or the 2019 Balakot airstrike-was widely considered the more probable scenario. These operations were calibrated to inflict punitive damage on terror infrastructure without crossing nuclear red lines. Such responses typically included precision air raids, covert operations by special forces, or artillery strikes confined to strategic sectors near the Line of Control (LoC).

However, even limited actions carried an inherent risk of miscalculation. Pakistan's military doctrine-particularly its emphasis on the early use of tactical nuclear weapons under its "full spectrum deterrence" strategy-complicated India's operational calculus. The danger was that any Indian retaliatory move, however targeted, might have been perceived by Pakistan as existential, thereby triggering an escalatory spiral.

A full-scale conventional war would have involved the deployment of ground forces, air dominance strategies, naval blockades, and potentially long-range missile strikes. Such a scenario was expected to result in mass displacement, significant military and civilian casualties, and financial market destabilization in both countries. Urban centres such as Delhi, Lahore, Karachi, and Mumbai would likely have become high-value targets, raising fears of large-scale destruction.

The humanitarian consequences would have been dire: refugee flows across internal and international borders, the collapse of basic services, disruption of food and medical supply chains, and psychological trauma on a mass scale. International humanitarian organizations, including the Red Cross and UNHCR, had historically warned that a South Asian war involving nuclear states could trigger the worst refugee crisis since World War II.

Further complicating the scenario was the potential for a two-front situation, should China have chosen to exploit regional instability by pressuring India along its northern borders. The Galwan Valley clash of 2020 served as a stark reminder of how quickly a localized confrontation could escalate into a multi-front strategic crisis. In such a volatile environment, the lack of reliable de-escalation mechanisms or institutionalized military-to-military hotlines between India and Pakistan made the situation even more precarious.

Operation Sindoor: India's Precision Strike Doctrine and the Strategic Shift It Heralds

In response to the Pahalgam terror attack of April 22, 2025, which claimed the lives of 26 innocent men, India launched a decisive and symbolic military operation known as Operation Sindoor, carried out between May 6 and May 10, 2025. For the families who lost their loved ones-especially the young widows forced to wipe away their sindoor-the operation was more than a counter-strike; it was a message that their pain had not gone unnoticed.

Operation Sindoor marked a turning point in India's national security and cultural consciousness. It was not only about eliminating terror camps across the border but also about redefining what national strength means. For the first time, a military response was blended with cultural symbolism, showing that India's power lies not just in its armed forces but also in its values, emotions, and unity. By naming the operation after a sacred symbol of womanhood, India sent a clear message to the world-that its strength comes not only from its soldiers, but also from the spirit of its people, especially the women whose resilience turns tragedy into national pride.

The Symbolism Behind "Sindoor" -

The name "Sindoor" was deliberately chosen to evoke India's civilizational ethos, linking national grief to a powerful cultural signifier. The operation's name-Sindoor, a sacred symbol of dignity and strength for married Hindu women-transformed grief into resolve. It signaled the emergence of "narrative warfare": India's cultural identity fused with its military resolve to create a potent strategic message. Sindoor became a metaphor for national willpower and strategic clarity. The operation thus transformed sorrow into resolve-weaponizing emotion into doctrine.

As Indian officials consistently underscored, Operation Sindoor was far more than a conventional military response-it marked a strategic and psychological turning point. It declared, with clarity and conviction, that India would no longer endure terrorism in silence. Sindoor evolved into more than an operation; it became a strategic philosophy-a fusion of cultural identity, national pride, and calibrated military power. It redefined the contours of response, where symbolism met strength, and doctrine emerged from dignity.

India's Message to the World Was Unambiguous:

It would no longer suffer terror in silence.

It would no longer rely on global mediation.

It would retaliate with proportionality, purpose, and pride.

As one official summarized, "The red of Sindoor is no longer just a mark of tradition-it became a metaphor for India's modern resolve."

A Historic Departure from Past Conflicts

Operation Sindoor represented a decisive break from past Indian military engagements with Pakistan. For the first time:

India refused any prisoner swaps or land-for-peace overtures.

Backchannel diplomacy was absent.

India dictated the terms-from escalation to cessation-without blinking.

Military historian Tom Cooper remarked: "This was the first time India didn't just respond-it commanded the narrative, signaled dominance, and set new rules of engagement."

Doctrinal Shift: The Birth of a Strategic Philosophy

Sindoor codified a new Indian doctrine rooted in three pillars:

Defensive Realism: Assertively protecting sovereignty while showing calibrated restraint.

Narrative Warfare: Leveraging civilizational symbolism-like "Sindoor"-to shape legitimacy and public morale.

Active Deterrence: Establishing a new norm of immediate and precise retaliation to any cross-border terror attack.

This wasn't merely strategy-it was a declaration of strategic maturity.

Hybrid Warfare: Weaponizing Water and Narrative

Alongside the airstrikes, India suspended cooperation under the **Indus Waters Treaty**, invoking its rights without breaching international law. This signaled a shift toward integrated hybrid warfare-blending military force, hydro-diplomacy, and global narrative control.

As John Spencer of West Point noted, "India practiced weaponized water diplomacy without breaking the law-this was hybrid warfare in its most modern, ethical form."

Precision Execution and Fifth-Generation Warfare

India launched 24 coordinated airstrikes in just 23 minutes, deploying Rafale jets equipped with SCALP and Hammer missiles. The mission neutralized over 70 high-value terror targets across Bahawalpur, Muridke, Muzaffarabad, and other zones in Pakistan and Pakistan-occupied Kashmir (PoK).

Tom Cooper observed: "This wasn't just an air raid-it was the dismantling of a terror infrastructure with surgical precision. India executed a fifth-generation playbook-on par with the U.S. or Israel."

India deliberately avoided Pakistani military installations, signaling restraint and compliance with international norms-but drawing an uncompromising red line against terror sanctuaries.

Analysts outlined two broad trajectories - a limited, targeted military operation or a full-scale war. Guided by experience, the government opted for a measured yet firm approach, combining military precision with political prudence.

Under Prime Minister Narendra Modi's leadership, India chose the path of decisive restraint-a response strong enough to punish, yet calculated enough to prevent uncontrolled escalation. This approach reflected a matured national security doctrine: hit hard, hit precisely, and withdraw on your own terms.

Operation Sindoor became the embodiment of this doctrine. Much like the 2016 surgical strikes and the 2019 Balakot air operation, it was designed to deliver a swift, accurate, and high-impact blow to terror infrastructure without crossing the thresholds that could lead to an all-out war. Over several days between May 6 and May 10, 2025, India executed a series of precision air raids, special forces incursions, and coordinated artillery strikes on identified terror launch pads and training facilities along and beyond the Line of Control (LoC). Each target was chosen based on real-time intelligence and satellite data, ensuring minimal collateral damage and maximum operational success.

These operations showcased India's technological edge and strategic discipline-combining drones, radar mapping, cyber surveillance, and high-accuracy missile systems. The strikes crippled multiple terror camps and destroyed key logistics hubs that had been used to channel arms and recruits across the border. Most importantly, the operations remained contained and controlled, avoiding civilian zones and limiting escalation opportunities for Pakistan's military.

Despite its bluster, Pakistan quickly realised the gravity of India's response. Within days of sustained Indian offensives, Islamabad sent back-channel messages through diplomatic intermediaries, pleading for a ceasefire. Facing mounting international isolation and internal panic, Pakistan's leadership sought urgent de-escalation. India, having achieved its strategic and symbolic objectives, agreed to a cessation of hostilities-but strictly on its own terms.

Operation Sindoor thus marked a turning point in India's defence posture. It demonstrated that India could neutralise threats with surgical precision, control escalation dynamics, and force adversaries to the negotiating table without entering a prolonged war. For many observers, this balance between strength and restraint reflected the Modi government's evolved strategic vision-one that blends military confidence with political maturity.

By stopping short of a full-scale confrontation, India not only safeguarded regional stability but also redefined the concept of deterrence in South Asia. Operation Sindoor sent a clear message to the world: India's pursuit of peace is not out of weakness, but out of strategic self-assurance-a nation capable of acting with force, leading with discipline, and ending conflicts on its own command.

Pakistan's Retaliatory Collapse and Ceasefire Plea

Despite launching drone strikes and limited cross-border shelling, Pakistan failed to generate a credible military response. On May 10, 2025, its Director General of Military Operations (DGMO) officially requested a ceasefire, marking a rare moment in South Asian history where:

India refused third-party mediation.

Pakistan offered terms, not India.

New Delhi secured strategic dominance through unilateral action.

Diplomatic Backing and Global Messaging: Backchannel Diplomacy and Global Mediation Efforts-

Backchannel diplomacy, often facilitated by neutral intermediaries such as the United Arab Emirates, Norway, and Switzerland, was swiftly activated to contain escalation and maintain communication between India and Pakistan after the Pahalgam attack. Under the strategic direction of Prime Minister Narendra Modi and the astute diplomatic handling of External Affairs Minister Dr. S. Jaishankar, India engaged in these channels with clarity and confidence. The focus was on upholding India's firm stance against terrorism while keeping dialogue options open through trusted partners.

Although these backchannels managed to preserve minimal lines of communication between intelligence and military officials on both sides, they did not yield any major breakthroughs. This was largely due to the domestic political climates in both nations-India gearing up for state elections and Pakistan facing internal instability-which left little room for compromise or flexibility. Nonetheless, India's conduct during this phase reflected maturity and restraint, hallmarks of Prime Minister Modi's calm yet commanding leadership style, which ensured that diplomacy complemented deterrence rather than undermined it.

Global Strategic Dialogues and India's Balanced Posture-

Strategic dialogues initiated by countries such as the United States and France were welcomed as gestures of concern but had limited practical impact. Both India and Pakistan today operate with far greater strategic autonomy than in the past, reducing the scope for external mediation. Under Modi's vision of "multi-alignment"-an approach that allows India to engage constructively with diverse global powers-New Delhi continued to balance its role within the Quad alliance (with the U.S., Japan, and Australia) while preserving independent relationships with Russia, Europe, and the Global South.

Meanwhile, Pakistan leaned more heavily toward China and Russia, further polarising the regional landscape. Yet, throughout this complex diplomatic web, Prime Minister Modi's mature statesmanship and Dr. Jaishankar's skilful foreign policy execution ensured that India's global standing only grew stronger. India emerged not as a reactive state, but as a responsible regional power, navigating crisis through strength, dialogue, and dignity-reinforcing its reputation as the voice of balance and reason in the Global South.

(Major powers rallied behind India:

The United States upheld India's right to self-defence.

Russia condemned the Pahalgam attack as a "barbaric provocation."

France, Israel, the UK, and Australia issued strong endorsements of India's measured retaliation.

China, notably, offered only a non-committal statement of "regret", reflecting unease with India's rising strategic autonomy.)

Strategic Communication: Women and Kashmir at the Helm

In a carefully choreographed press briefing, Foreign Secretary Vikram Misri-a native of Jammu and Kashmir-stood flanked by Wing Commander

Vyomika Singh and Colonel Sofiya Qureshi. The imagery conveyed:

National unity across region and gender.

A symbolic rebuke to terrorists who targeted women by killing their husband brazenly in front of them in Pahalgam.

India's assertion of womanhood as strength, not vulnerability.

Sindoor as a Strategic Doctrine-

Operation Sindoor was more than retaliation-it was a doctrine in motion. It embodied a new strategic philosophy for a new India: one that fuses military precision with cultural symbolism, domestic unity with international clarity, and decisive action with normative restraint.

The name "Sindoor" was chosen with deep thought and emotion-it is not just a word, but a powerful symbol in Indian culture. In Hindu tradition, sindoor is the red vermilion powder that a married woman applies in the parting of her hair, signifying love, commitment, and the sacred bond of marriage. It represents her husband's life and the continuity of their shared journey. When a woman becomes a widow, she wipes away her sindoor, marking an end to that sacred bond-a gesture filled with pain and loss.

By naming the military retaliation Operation Sindoor, India gave this cultural symbol a new meaning. It transformed sindoor from a sign of personal love and devotion into a national metaphor of strength, dignity, and resilience. The name honoured the widowed women of the Pahalgam attack, whose husbands-26 civilians-were brutally killed in the terror strike. Their grief became a reflection of the nation's own sorrow. Yet, through the operation, India sought to turn that pain into power, conveying that every drop of sindoor lost would be avenged with courage and unity. In essence, "Sindoor" came to represent both sacrifice and resolve-the sacred red turning from the colour of loss into the colour of India's determination

As analysts worldwide concluded, India had turned the page-not just on the Pahalgam attack, but on its own strategic history.

Global Implications: Nuclear Anxiety, Economic Fallout, and Geopolitical Realignment

The Pahalgam attack reverberated far beyond the Indian subcontinent, drawing sharp international attention due to the potential for escalation between two nuclear-armed adversaries. Global powers, international organizations, and markets responded with a mix of concern, caution, and contingency planning. The spectre of nuclear conflict reintroduced Cold

War-style anxieties into 21st-century geopolitics, where deterrence is complicated by tactical nuclear doctrines, asymmetrical warfare, and nationalist political climates.

The United Nations Secretary-General and several Security Council members issued immediate calls for restraint, urging both sides to pursue diplomatic channels. The United States, a key strategic partner of India and a security aid provider to Pakistan, found itself walking a tightrope. While reiterating India's right to self-defence, Washington also pressured Islamabad to crack down on terror networks. France and the UK expressed solidarity with India while simultaneously emphasizing the need to avoid destabilization in a region that affects global trade and security. China, a close ally of Pakistan and an economic competitor of India, issued a carefully worded statement urging de-escalation while subtly reinforcing its support for Pakistan's sovereignty and strategic interests.

Global financial markets reacted with unease. The Indian rupee and Pakistani rupee both depreciated sharply in the immediate aftermath, while regional stock indices slumped on fears of war. Crude oil prices spiked due to fears of a broader regional conflagration, given the proximity of conflict zones to key maritime chokepoints like the Strait of Hormuz. Foreign institutional investors (FIIs) pulled back from South Asian markets, and multilateral institutions flagged the risk of negative credit ratings for both countries if hostilities escalated.

From a geopolitical perspective, the attack accelerated India's pivot towards more robust security alignments. New Delhi intensified defence cooperation with the United States, Japan, Australia, and France-particularly under the Quad framework-seeking greater intelligence sharing, joint drills, and defence technology transfers. Simultaneously, India renewed its efforts in multilateral platforms like the Financial Action Task Force (FATF) to isolate Pakistan diplomatically over terror financing concerns.

Pakistan, on the other hand, responded by doubling down on its strategic alliances with China, Turkey, and increasingly Russia and Iran. Islamabad leveraged forums such as the Organization of Islamic Cooperation (OIC) to rally support on Kashmir and portray itself as a victim of Indian aggression. These divergent alignments highlighted a hardening of regional blocs and an emerging bipolarity in South Asia's security architecture.

Furthermore, global non-proliferation advocates expressed grave concerns about the long-term implications of repeated brinkmanship between India and Pakistan. Think tanks and strategic experts underscored the urgency of re-establishing crisis communication channels and institutional mechanisms to avoid accidental escalations. As U.S. influence in South Asia becomes more complex and China's regional role expands, the potential for misinterpretation and delayed de-escalation grows.

In sum, the fallout from the Pahalgam attack extended far beyond immediate military responses, touching global markets, diplomatic balances, and nuclear stability frameworks. It exposed the enduring fragility of regional peace in South Asia and underscored how localized violence can ripple through the interconnected fabric of the global order.

International Mediation and Diplomatic Deadlock-

In the aftermath of the Pahalgam attack, international actors scrambled to contain a spiralling crisis between two of Asia's most volatile nuclear states. The United Nations, major global powers, and multilateral forums attempted mediation in varying forms. However, deep-rooted historical mistrust, conflicting national narratives, and rigid diplomatic posturing quickly revealed the limitations of international diplomacy in the India–Pakistan context.

The United Nations Secretary-General offered to facilitate dialogue, invoking the UN Charter's principles of conflict prevention and peaceful resolution. However, India, adhering to its consistent position since the Shimla Agreement of 1972, categorically rejected third-party mediation, asserting that all issues with Pakistan, including terrorism and Kashmir, must be resolved bilaterally. This position was echoed in official statements from the Ministry of External Affairs (MEA), which underscored that internationalization of the Kashmir dispute would only embolden non-state actors and destabilize regional peace.

Pakistan, conversely, made a concerted push for international intervention. Prime Minister and Foreign Minister engaged in a diplomatic outreach campaign targeting the United Nations, the Organization of Islamic Cooperation (OIC), the European Union, and influential capitals like Washington, Ankara, and Beijing. Pakistani officials argued that the security situation in Kashmir posed a threat to global peace and warranted UN-led or third-party mediation. Islamabad also raised the issue at the OIC, where it received rhetorical support but limited concrete backing.

Backchannel diplomacy, often facilitated by neutral actors like the United Arab Emirates, Norway, and Switzerland, was activated to prevent escalation. However, while these channels succeeded in maintaining minimal communication between intelligence and military officials, they failed to produce any major breakthroughs. The domestic political environment in both countries, marked by electoral cycles and heightened nationalism, further constrained the space for compromise.

Strategic dialogues initiated by the United States and France, although appreciated, faced limits due to the increasing strategic autonomy exercised by both India and Pakistan. With India aligned more closely with the Quad and pursuing multi-alignment, and Pakistan deepening ties with China, the room for mutually acceptable mediation narrowed.

This diplomatic paralysis highlighted the enduring fragility of South Asia's security architecture. Despite repeated crises-from Kargil to Balakot-no institutionalized de-escalation mechanism or crisis hotline exists between the two countries that could serve as a stabilizing force during such emergencies. The reliance on ad hoc backchannels, informal interlocutors, and reactive diplomacy remains a key vulnerability in the region's conflict management framework.

The Way Forward: India's Vision for Regional Stability

Looking ahead, the path to lasting peace in South Asia must involve more than reactive diplomacy. Both nations-and the wider international community-must recognise the need for institutionalised crisis management frameworks that prevent small incidents from spiralling into major conflicts. These mechanisms can include military hotlines, intelligence-sharing platforms, civil society engagement, and economic interdependence strategies that create shared stakes in peace. At the same time, India believes that such efforts must remain regionally led and bilaterally driven, not externally imposed.

Prime Minister Modi's leadership offers a blueprint for this vision-anchored in diplomacy, deterrence moderation, and the rebuilding of mutual trust. His consistent emphasis on dialogue, development, and dignity illustrates that India's rise as a global power is not just measured in military or economic terms, but in its ability to lead with moral authority.

India's Steadfast Leadership Amid the Fragility of Regional Peace-

The Pahalgam terror attack and its aftermath revealed once again the fragile nature of peace in South Asia, where a single act of violence can send shockwaves across borders and institutions. Yet, amid this volatility, India has emerged as the principal pillar of stability and responsibility. Under Prime Minister Narendra Modi's decisive and composed leadership, India demonstrated a rare blend of strategic firmness and diplomatic restraint-acting with strength but avoiding unnecessary escalation. Rather than succumbing to reactive impulses, India's response through Operation Sindoor reflected maturity, precision, and clarity of purpose, underscoring that peace and power can coexist when guided by disciplined leadership.

India's Role in a Multipolar World

As global power centres become increasingly fragmented and preoccupied-from the Russia-Ukraine war to the U.S.-China rivalry-India stands out as a stabilising force and a moral anchor in a multipolar world. While other powers often view South Asia through lenses of competition or containment, India's approach under Modi has been defined by engagement without dependency and assertion without aggression. With a growing voice in the G20, BRICS, and the Quad, and as a leading figure of the Global South, India continues to project an image of measured power and responsible statecraft. Prime Minister Modi's charismatic diplomacy and global credibility have positioned India as not just a regional actor, but a shaping power influencing peace, dialogue, and economic stability across continents.

India's Strategic Maturity and Bilateral Approach

While South Asia lacks formal institutions like ASEAN or the OSCE for conflict resolution, India has consistently filled this vacuum through its own diplomatic maturity and bilateral engagement. Rejecting the notion of "diplomatic paralysis," New Delhi has shown that it does not require third-party mediation to pursue peace. India's belief that the India–Pakistan equation is a bilateral matter reflects confidence in its institutional and diplomatic capability. Under Modi's vision of "multi-alignment," India has deepened ties with multiple global powers while maintaining its strategic autonomy, ensuring that its foreign policy remains guided by national interests rather than external influence.

Strength with Restraint: The Modi Doctrine in Practice

In an era where populist politics often drives aggression, India's conduct under Prime Minister Modi has showcased a model of strength balanced with restraint. From Balakot to Pahalgam, India's responses have been swift, calibrated, and principle-driven-designed to uphold deterrence while preventing war. This discipline reflects Modi's evolved doctrine of statecraft, where national pride operates hand in hand with global responsibility. His foreign policy team, led by External Affairs Minister Dr. S. Jaishankar, has reinforced this balance-strengthening India's partnerships while ensuring that dialogue remains open where it matters most. The world increasingly views India as a responsible power, capable of transforming grief into resolve and crises into opportunities for peace.

India: A Beacon of Stability in an Uncertain World

Ultimately, the Pahalgam episode serves as a reminder that the absence of war is not the presence of peace. Yet, with India at the centre of South Asia's strategic landscape, the region retains hope for a stable and prosperous future. In a world marked by shifting alliances and competing crises, India's steady hand-guided by Modi's mature and visionary leadership-remains the most dependable force for balance and peace. Through a blend of courage, composure, and conviction, India today stands as a beacon of stability-a nation that not only defends its borders but also shapes the moral and diplomatic contours of peace in a turbulent multipolar world.

Opinion:

Triggered by the brutal Pahalgam terror attack on April 22, 2025-which killed 26 civilians, mostly married men and left many women widowed-Operation Sindoor marked a decisive shift in India's counter-terror doctrine. Operation Sindoor marked a turning point in India's national security and cultural consciousness. It was not only about eliminating terror camps across the border but also about redefining what national strength means. For the first time, a military response was blended with cultural symbolism, showing that India's power lies not just in its armed forces but also in its values, emotions, and unity. By naming the operation after a sacred symbol of womanhood, India sent a clear message to the world-that its strength comes not only from its soldiers, but also from the spirit of its people, especially the women whose resilience turns tragedy into national pride.

Between May 6-10, India executed deep-penetration airstrikes, annihilating major terror camps and disabling critical Pakistani military infrastructure. The operation demonstrated India's mastery of fifth-generation warfare, deploying advanced indigenous technologies such as BRAHMOS, Rudram, NAVIC, and Akashteer. With calibrated restraint, India maintained escalation control, sending a clear message: terror would now be met with doctrine-backed retaliation.

Pakistan's retaliatory attempts-ranging from drone strikes to missile launches-were neutralized with unmatched efficiency, underscoring India's superior cyber, air, and information warfare capabilities. The operation culminated with Pakistan's plea for a ceasefire, which India accepted on its own terms-without third-party mediation.

More than a tactical victory, Operation Sindoor reaffirmed India's emergence as a mature global military power. It signaled that India no longer absorbs provocation passively, but responds with precision, proportionality, and psychological strength. With its indigenous defense capability, doctrinal clarity, and diplomatic finesse, India has redefined modern warfare and solidified its position as a rising pillar of global stability and strategic autonomy.

CHAPTER SEVEN

Energy Geopolitics and Resource Competition: Old Battles, New Frontiers

As the struggle for energy and critical minerals intensifies, another powerful front in the geopolitical contest is taking shape-one that wields economic interdependence as a strategic weapon. In today's deeply interconnected world, the battlefield has expanded beyond pipelines and ports to include tariffs, sanctions, financial systems, and trade regimes. This is the arena of geo-economics, where markets are militarized, and economic policies become instruments of global influence. As states compete for control over supply chains, manufacturing hubs, and investment flows, they are rewriting the rules of globalization to serve strategic ends. The following chapter delves into this rising dimension of power politics, where economics is no longer just about prosperity-but about persuasion, pressure, and pre-emptive control.

1. Introduction: Energy as the Engine of Geopolitics

Throughout modern history, control over energy resources has been synonymous with geopolitical power. In the 20th century, oil served as the lifeblood of industrial economies and modern militaries. Its centrality shaped the colonial partitioning of the Middle East, drove Cold War alliances, and triggered defining conflicts such as the Suez Crisis (1956) and the Gulf War (1990–91). The creation of the Organization of Petroleum Exporting Countries (OPEC) institutionalized the role of energy in international politics, introducing a new era of resource-driven leverage.

In the 21st century, however, the geopolitical map of energy is being radically redrawn. The global transition toward decarbonization and clean energy has shifted the focus from fossil fuels to critical minerals—including lithium, cobalt, nickel, graphite, and rare earth elements-which are essential for electric vehicles, batteries, wind turbines, semiconductors, and advanced defence systems. These materials are not only finite and geographically concentrated, but their refining and processing chains are often controlled by a limited set of actors, creating new strategic chokepoints.

This emerging contest has been aptly described as the "New Great Game", echoing the 19th-century rivalry between imperial Britain and Tsarist Russia. But this time, the arena spans from the Arctic tundras and African mines to the Indo-Pacific seabed's and the lithium-rich deserts of Latin America. The stakes are not just in extraction-but in technological leadership, industrial policy, ethical mining practices, and global sustainability.

References: International Energy Agency (IEA), The Role of Critical Minerals in Clean Energy Transitions (2021); Global Energy Monitor, Critical Minerals Tracker (2023).

2. The Classical Era of Energy Geopolitics: Fossil Fuels and Strategic Coercion

In the 20th century, fossil fuels-especially oil-played a pivotal role in defining strategic doctrines, alliances, and wars.

Key episodes:

- 1973 Oil Embargo: Arab producers used oil as leverage during the Yom Kippur War, triggering an energy crisis and transforming Western foreign policy.
- Iran–Iraq War (1980–88) and Gulf War (1990–91): Both were deeply linked to oil security and regional dominance.
- U.S. Energy Doctrine: From the Carter Doctrine (1979) to the shale revolution in the 2000s, securing global oil flows became a strategic priority for the United States.
- Pipeline Politics: Infrastructure such as Russia's Nord Stream pipelines and the Baku–Tbilisi–Ceyhan corridor reflect how energy transport

routes became geopolitical instruments.

The centrality of oil gave rise to energy nationalism in states like Venezuela, Iran, and Russia, which wielded energy as a tool of coercion or resilience against sanctions.

3. Transitioning to Clean Energy: Strategic Shifts and Emerging Vulnerabilities

Today's energy transformation is creating a paradox: while the shift away from fossil fuels is essential for climate mitigation, it has introduced new dependencies-particularly on countries with rich deposits of critical minerals.

Key Drivers:

- Technological Evolution: EVs and renewables are far more mineral-intensive. An electric car needs 6× more mineral input than a conventional one; a wind plant needs 9× more than a gas-fired power plant (IEA, 2021).
- Geopolitical Rationale: Post-Russia's weaponization of gas in 2022, the EU and other actors now see green energy as a security imperative.
- Supply Chain Nationalism: Legislation such as the U.S. Inflation Reduction Act and the EU's Critical Raw Materials Act are designed to reduce dependency on Chinese or unstable supply lines.

4. Critical Minerals: The New Strategic Chokepoints

Unlike oil-traded through mature global markets-critical minerals are mined, refined, and manufactured through highly concentrated and fragile supply chains.

Key Global Distributions:

- Lithium: Dominated by the "Lithium Triangle" - Argentina, Bolivia, Chile.
- Cobalt: Over 70% comes from the Democratic Republic of Congo (DRC).
- Rare Earths: China controls over 80% of global refining capacity.
- Nickel: Predominantly from Indonesia, the Philippines, and Russia.

These supply chains are non-fungible and technologically layered. Most refining is monopolized by China, giving it strategic leverage in the clean tech race.

5. Strategic Responses: Decoupling, Diversification, and Domestic Re-shoring

Global powers are responding by reshaping their resource and industrial strategies:

- United States: The CHIPS and Science Act (2022) seeks to localize semiconductor and rare earth processing.
- European Union: Through Global Gateway, the EU funds mining/refining projects in Africa and Central Asia to build alternatives to BRI routes.
- India: Public-private initiatives like the PLI for Advanced Chemistry Cells and MOUs with Argentina and Australia aim to secure lithium and rare earth access.

6. New Frontiers and Flashpoints: Africa, Latin America, and the Arctic Africa:

A key battleground, with China investing in infrastructure-for-resources deals, while the U.S. and EU seek more transparent, sustainable alternatives.

Africa is at the heart of the critical minerals race, particularly for minerals essential to **batteries, electronics, and clean energy systems.**

- **Democratic Republic of Congo (DRC)**: Produces over **70% of global cobalt** and is a major source of copper. However, mining is plagued by **human rights abuses, child labor**, and **environmental degradation**. Chinese firms control much of DRC's cobalt supply chain, leading to concerns about monopolistic practices.
- **South Africa**: A major producer of **platinum group metals (PGMs)**-vital for hydrogen fuel cells and catalytic converters. South Africa's mineral wealth is critical for both energy transition and automotive industries.
- **Namibia and Niger**: Emerging as significant **uranium suppliers**, vital for nuclear energy expansion in a low-carbon future.

Yet, Africa faces serious challenges:

- **Resource Nationalism**: Governments are increasingly demanding better terms, local beneficiation, and environmental protections.
- **Security Risks**: Instability, especially in the Sahel region and eastern Congo, threatens supply chain reliability.

Example: The **U.S.-DRC-Zambia MoU** (2022) on EV battery value chains highlights a growing move to **ethically source** and **domestically process** critical minerals rather than simply exporting raw materials.

Reference: Global Energy Monitor, *Africa's Critical Minerals and Clean Energy* (2023); World Bank, *The African Mining Vision* (2022).

Latin America:

The Lithium Triangle is rich in resources but marked by rising protests over water use, Indigenous rights, and environmental degradation. China dominates, but Western countries are recalibrating climate-linked partnerships.

Latin America's "Lithium Triangle"-**Chile, Argentina, and Bolivia**-contains **over 60% of the world's lithium reserves**, crucial for battery technologies.

- **Chile**: The second-largest lithium producer globally. Political debates over resource nationalization intensified in 2023, with new frameworks proposed to balance foreign investment and public control.
- **Argentina**: Lithium production is booming, with new mines opening in Salta and Jujuy provinces. The government has pursued a **more open investment climate** compared to Chile and Bolivia.
- **Bolivia**: Despite vast reserves, development has been hampered by political instability and technological challenges in extracting lithium from its high-altitude salt flats.

Beyond lithium, Latin America is rich in copper (Chile, Peru), silver (Mexico), and rare earth potential.

However, the region is seeing a resurgence of **resource nationalism**, where states demand **greater control over mining sectors**, reflecting broader trends of economic sovereignty post-COVID.

Example: Mexico nationalized lithium production in 2022, creating a state-owned company, *LitioMx*, while simultaneously courting partnerships with U.S. and Canadian firms under the USMCA framework.

Reference: BP Statistical Review (2023); U.S. Geological Survey, *Lithium Statistics and Information* (2022).

Arctic: Melting ice is exposing mineral reserves, making it a contested zone. The U.S., China, and Russia are expanding scientific and military presence, especially around Greenland and the Northern Sea Route. The Arctic, once a frozen and inaccessible frontier, is rapidly emerging as a **geopolitical hotspot** due to climate change. Melting ice is opening up previously unreachable reserves of **oil, natural gas, and critical minerals** like rare earths, zinc, and nickel.

Key developments:

- **Russia's Arctic Strategy**: Russia controls roughly **half of Arctic coastline** and has aggressively invested in Arctic infrastructure-building icebreakers, military bases, and energy projects like the **Yamal LNG plant.** Russia's 2020 Arctic Strategy explicitly prioritizes critical mineral extraction.
- **U.S. and Allies**: The U.S. Geological Survey estimates that the Arctic holds **13% of undiscovered oil** and **30% of undiscovered gas resources** globally. The U.S., Canada, and Nordic countries are ramping up Arctic security strategies, balancing resource extraction with environmental protection.
- **China's "Near-Arctic State" Policy**: China, despite its geographical distance, declared itself a "near-Arctic state" and is investing in Arctic mining projects in Greenland and Canada.

Beyond hydrocarbons, the Arctic is rich in **rare earths**-essential for electronics and defence technologies. Greenland alone is estimated to hold **25% of the world's rare earth reserves.** Chinese-backed companies have sought to dominate Greenlandic mining, prompting pushback from Denmark and the U.S.

Reference: Arctic Council Reports (2022); U.S. Geological Survey, *Circum-Arctic Resource Appraisal* (2021).

Indo-Pacific: Australia, Indonesia, and Deep-Sea Mining

The Indo-Pacific is a **strategic fulcrum** for critical minerals, with vast reserves in Australia, Indonesia, and the deep seabed.

- **Australia**:
    - The world's **largest lithium producer** (53% of global supply).
    - Major reserves of cobalt, rare earths, and nickel.
    - Canberra has signed critical minerals partnerships with the U.S., India, Japan, and South Korea to secure non-Chinese supply chains.
- **Indonesia**:
    - The world's **largest nickel producer**.
    - Jakarta has banned raw nickel exports to boost domestic refining and battery industries, a model of resource nationalism gaining momentum elsewhere.
- **Deep-Sea Mining**:
    - The Clarion-Clipperton Zone (CCZ) in the Pacific Ocean holds enormous reserves of polymetallic nodules rich in nickel, cobalt, and manganese.
    - Companies like The Metals Company (TMC) are pushing forward, but environmental groups warn of irreversible ecosystem damage.

The **Indo-Pacific mineral supply chain** is increasingly a **theater of competition** between China and U.S.-aligned states seeking to **diversify supplies and ensure ethical sourcing.**

Reference: Australian Government, *Critical Minerals Strategy* (2022); International Seabed Authority Reports (2023).

7. Energy Infrastructure as a Geopolitical Weapon
Infrastructure is now both an economic artery and a vulnerability:

- Nord Stream Sabotage (2022): Demonstrated how underwater pipelines are susceptible to hybrid warfare.

- China's Port Strategy: Control of facilities in Djibouti, Piraeus (Greece), and Gwadar (Pakistan) raises concerns about dual-use military logistics under BRI.
- Cyber Threats: Attacks like the Colonial Pipeline hack (2021) show how national energy grids are now primary cyberwarfare targets.

8. The Climate–Energy Nexus: Cooperation or Competition?

The global transition poses a dilemma: will it foster cooperation or fragment the system further?

Fragmentation Risks:

- Climate Clubs like the EU's CBAM (Carbon Border Adjustment Mechanism) could penalize developing nations.
- Green arms race over access to minerals and manufacturing technologies could widen the Global North–South divide.

Signs of Pragmatic Cooperation:

- India–U.S. Climate and Clean Energy Agenda 2030.
- Just Energy Transition Partnerships (JETPs) with South Africa and Indonesia.
- African Union's critical minerals platform, promoting coordinated bargaining power.

9. Conclusion: From Barrel Diplomacy to Battery Politics

The classic era of energy geopolitics-dominated by oil wars, pipeline diplomacy, and petro-hegemony-is evolving. The new competition centre's on "mineral diplomacy," technological autonomy, and supply chain resilience. But the strategic implications remain just as profound.

Energy security is no longer about the control of refineries and rigs. It now hinges on access to rare earth elements, industrial innovation, ethical mining, and climate governance. Whether this transition fosters inclusive global cooperation or reproduces extractive geopolitical hierarchies under new labels will define the balance of power in the 21st century.

While critical minerals and green transitions are redefining energy geopolitics, they are inextricably linked to technological sovereignty. As the next chapter explores, the pursuit of technological advantage, control over trade routes, and strategic economic dependencies represents a parallel front in the evolving struggle for global power-one where geo-economics takes center stage.

CHAPTER EIGHT

Geo-Economics and Trade Wars

As the global transition to clean energy and mineral diplomacy reshapes the foundations of geopolitical rivalry, another powerful axis of competition has come to the fore: economic statecraft. In an interconnected world where markets can be militarized and trade weaponized, nations increasingly rely on tools like sanctions, tariffs, and supply chains to assert influence. This evolving domain-where power is exercised not through force but through finance, trade frameworks, and regulatory leverage-marks the rise of geo-economics as a central pillar of modern geopolitics.

Simultaneously, climate change is redefining the contours of global risk and responsibility, intersecting with the deeper currents of economic power and strategic interdependence. As environmental vulnerabilities shape both national policies and international alliances, economic instruments are being recalibrated to serve geopolitical ends. In an era where traditional military confrontations are often replaced by economic coercion, the strategic deployment of trade agreements, sanctions, and technological restrictions reveals a world where the boundaries between markets and geopolitics are increasingly blurred.

This weaponization of interdependence-evident in tariff wars, investment screening, and efforts at technological decoupling-demands closer scrutiny. Understanding this shift requires unpacking the logic behind economic confrontation, the resurgence of protectionism, and the reconfiguration of globalization in a fractured yet tightly interwoven world.

Contemporary Dynamics: Trade, Military Alliances, and Regional Tensions

U.S.-India Strategic Convergence: From Hesitation to Partnership

Over the past two decades, U.S.-India relations have evolved from **mutual suspicion** to **strategic partnership**. Shared concerns about China's assertiveness, combined with India's economic liberalization and military modernization, created fertile ground for expanded ties.

Key developments:

- **Defence Cooperation:**
  - Signing of foundational agreements:
    - **Logistics Exchange Memorandum of Agreement (LEMOA)** (2016): Mutual logistics support.
    - **Communications Compatibility and Security Agreement (COMCASA)** (2018): Enhanced secure communication interoperability.
    - **Basic Exchange and Cooperation Agreement (BECA)** (2020): Sharing of geospatial intelligence.
  - Rising arms trade: U.S. arms sales to India grew dramatically, making the U.S. India's second-largest defence supplier after Russia.
  - Joint military exercises: **Malabar Naval Exercises, Yudh Abhyas, Tiger Triumph** enhance interoperability.
- **Economic Engagement:**
  - Bilateral trade crossed **$190 billion** in 2022, making the U.S. India's largest trading partner.
  - Launch of the **U.S.-India Initiative on Critical and Emerging Technologies (iCET)** in 2023 to promote collaboration in AI, quantum computing, semiconductors, and defence tech.

Despite occasional trade disputes (e.g., tariffs under the Trump administration), the trajectory of U.S.-India relations reflects **deepening strategic alignment**.

Reference: CFR, *The U.S.-India Partnership in a Changing Global Order* (2023); Carnegie India, *iCET: Deepening the U.S.-India Tech Partnership* (2023).

India-China Tensions: The Galwan Valley Clash and Beyond

While India and China share over **3,400 kilometres** of disputed border, tensions escalated dangerously in recent years.

- **Galwan Valley Clash (June 2020):**
    - First deadly encounter between Indian and Chinese troops since 1975.
    - At least **20 Indian soldiers** and an undisclosed number of Chinese troops killed in brutal hand-to-hand combat.
- **Aftermath:**
    - Massive military deployments along the Line of Actual Control (LAC).
    - Infrastructure build-up by both sides (roads, airfields, bridges).
    - Diplomatic disengagement efforts through Corps Commander-level talks, but **trust deficit remains deep**.

Beyond borders:

- China's growing naval presence in the Indian Ocean, including port investments in Sri Lanka (Hambantota) and Pakistan (Gwadar), heightens Indian concerns about **strategic encirclement** (**"String of Pearls"** theory).
- India has **banned over 200 Chinese apps**, restricted Chinese investments, and scrutinized tech imports as part of a broader **economic de-risking strategy**.

Reference: ORF, *Galwan Clash and the Future of India-China Relations* (2021); Brookings, *The India-China Conundrum: Border, Trade, and Trust* (2022).

U.S.-China Strategic Competition: A Global Rivalry with Regional Impacts

The U.S.-China relationship has shifted from **strategic engagement** to **strategic competition** across military, economic, technological, and ideological dimensions.

Key flashpoints:

- **Taiwan Strait**: Escalating tensions after U.S. visits to Taiwan and Chinese military exercises.
- **South China Sea**: Freedom of navigation operations (FONOPs) by U.S. Navy challenge China's expansive territorial claims.
- **Tech Decoupling**:
    - Export controls on advanced semiconductors to China.
    - Restrictions on U.S. investments in Chinese AI, quantum computing, and defence-related tech sectors.

For India, this **U.S.-China rivalry opens strategic space** but also introduces complexities:

- Aligning too closely with the U.S. risks retaliation from China.
- Remaining too detached risks missing opportunities for technology access and security partnerships.

India's approach remains pragmatic: **partnering selectively** with both sides where interests align.

Reference: Brookings Institution, *The U.S.-China Strategic Rivalry and its Implications for India* (2023); CFR, *U.S.-China Technology Decoupling: Risks and Opportunities* (2022).

India's Strategic Balancing: Between Economic Pragmatism and Security Realism

Despite border tensions, China remains a significant economic partner for India:

- China is India's **second-largest trading partner**, though the trade deficit heavily favours China (~$100 billion in 2022).

- Indian pharmaceutical, IT, and manufacturing sectors depend on Chinese inputs (APIs, electronics components).

India's balancing act:

- **Strategic Caution**: India remains outside U.S.-led security alliances (e.g., AUKUS) and refuses to adopt formal alliances, preserving strategic autonomy.
- **Economic De-Risking**: Focused on diversifying supply chains via:
    - **Production-Linked Incentive (PLI)** schemes to boost domestic manufacturing.
    - Joining the **Indo-Pacific Economic Framework for Prosperity (IPEF)** to develop resilient supply chains.

In essence, India is pursuing a strategy of "**alignment without alliance**"-strengthening partnerships with the U.S. and other democracies while keeping open channels with China and Russia.

Reference: Carnegie India, *India's Multi-Alignment Strategy in the Indo-Pacific* (2022); ORF, *De-Risking India's China Exposure* (2023).

U.S.-India-China dynamic-Strategic Outlook:
The QUAD: From Dialogue to Security Architecture, De-Risking from China, and India's Balancing Act

The **Quadrilateral Security Dialogue (QUAD)**-comprising the United States, India, Japan, and Australia-has evolved from a **tentative consultative mechanism** into a **critical platform for Indo-Pacific security cooperation.**

- **Origins**:
    - Initiated in 2007 after the Indian Ocean tsunami relief efforts.
    - Dormant for nearly a decade due to geopolitical sensitivities (particularly India's hesitations).

- **Revival**:

  - Reactivated in 2017 amidst growing concerns over China's assertiveness.
  - Elevated to **Leaders' Summits** in 2021 and 2022, signalling deeper commitment.

Focus areas:

- Maritime security and **freedom of navigation**.
- Critical and emerging technologies (5G, AI, cybersecurity).
- Vaccine diplomacy during COVID-19.
- Infrastructure development as alternatives to China's BRI.

Despite rhetoric downplaying military aims ("not an Asian NATO"), the QUAD is increasingly seen as a **soft security coalition** aimed at **balancing Chinese influence**.

India's role:

- Critical as a "resident power" in the Indian Ocean.
- Offers strategic depth and geographical centrality to QUAD operations.

Reference: Brookings, *The Future of the QUAD in the Indo-Pacific* (2023); ORF, *India's Maritime Imperatives and the QUAD* (2022).

De-Risking from China: Economic Strategy without Decoupling

While the United States pursues a partial **decoupling** from China (especially in tech sectors), India has adopted a more measured **de-risking** approach.

Key Indian strategies:

- **Diversifying Imports**: Boosting partnerships with Southeast Asia (Vietnam, Indonesia), Japan, Australia, and the EU to reduce dependence on Chinese goods.
- **PLI Schemes**: Incentivizing domestic production in sectors like electronics, semiconductors, solar manufacturing, and electric vehicles.
- **Screening Investments**: Tightening scrutiny over foreign direct investments (FDI) from bordering countries (implicitly targeting Chinese inflows) in sensitive sectors.

- **Infrastructure Resilience**: Collaborating with partners to develop critical supply chain infrastructure (e.g., semiconductor fabrication, battery manufacturing).

However, complete decoupling remains impractical given:

- India's reliance on Chinese intermediate goods.
- The complex web of global supply chains where China remains a dominant player.

Thus, India's economic approach is best described as "**selective disengagement**"-minimizing vulnerabilities while retaining pragmatic engagement where necessary.

Reference: Carnegie India, *Strategic De-Risking: India's Response to China's Economic Challenge* (2023); CFR, *Economic Resilience and Supply Chain Diversification in Asia* (2022).

India's Balancing Act: Multi-Alignment in a Fractured World

India's foreign policy remains rooted in the principle of **strategic autonomy**, updated for the multipolar realities of the 21st century.

Key dimensions of India's balancing act:

- **QUAD and Beyond**:
  - Deepening ties with QUAD members while avoiding formal alliances.
  - Participating in new Mini lateral groupings like the **I2U2** (India-Israel-UAE-USA) focused on food security, technology, and infrastructure.
- **Global South Leadership**:
  - Projecting itself as a voice for the Global South at platforms like the G20 and BRICS, advocating for more inclusive global governance.
- **Engagement with Russia**:

- ◦ Maintaining strong defence ties with Russia (critical for India's military hardware) despite Western pressure post-Ukraine invasion.
- ◦ Pursuing discounted Russian oil imports as part of energy diversification.

India's vision aligns with what External Affairs Minister **S. Jaishankar** has termed "**multi-alignment**"-engaging simultaneously with multiple power centre's to maximize strategic options.

Challenges:

- Navigating U.S. expectations for greater alignment against China.
- Managing Chinese sensitivities without appearing weak domestically.
- Sustaining credible deterrence at disputed borders while advancing economic growth imperatives.

Reference: ORF, *India's Strategic Autonomy: Principles and Practice in the Indo-Pacific Era* (2022); Carnegie Endowment, *India at the Crossroads of Great Power Competition* (2023).

Taken together, the forces explored across these diverse yet interconnected dimensions-ranging from shifting power hierarchies and regional flashpoints to resource rivalries, technological frontiers, environmental crises, and economic statecraft-reveal a global order in flux. Geopolitics in the 21st century is no longer confined to traditional notions of hard power or territorial expansion; it is increasingly shaped by hybrid threats, systemic vulnerabilities, and the entanglement of domestic and international imperatives. As states navigate this complex terrain, their strategies reflect both the enduring logic of realpolitik and the evolving demands of an interdependent world. With this holistic understanding, we are now positioned to synthesize the key insights and reflect on the broader implications for global stability, cooperation, and conflict in the years ahead.

Conclusion: The Unfinished Triangle

The evolving strategic triangle between the United States, India, and China represents one of the defining configurations of 21st-century geopolitics. It is a triangle marked not by rigid alliances or clear rivalries but by **fluid competition, selective cooperation, and cautious containment**.

India occupies a uniquely pivotal position. It shares democratic values and strategic objectives with the United States, particularly in preserving a free and open Indo-Pacific. Yet it simultaneously values **strategic autonomy**, engages economically with China, and maintains ties with other major powers like Russia. India's balancing act reflects both its historical ethos of non-alignment and its pragmatic recognition of **multipolar complexity**.

For the United States, strengthening ties with India is critical to its Indo-Pacific strategy, but it must do so with sensitivity to India's independent posture. For China, managing the India relationship is equally vital to avoid encirclement and mitigate the formation of anti-China coalitions.

Thus, India is not merely a passive actor in great-power politics-it is an active shaper of the emerging global order.

Whether this strategic triangle evolves into **competitive confrontation**, **cooperative equilibrium**, or a **dynamic but fragile balancing system** will depend on how the three powers navigate issues of **trust, competition, and strategic convergence** over the coming decades.

The triangle remains unfinished-and its final shape will profoundly influence the architecture of the Indo-Pacific and the world beyond.

Opinion:

As states recalibrate alliances, impose sanctions, and restructure trade flows to secure strategic advantage, another force-more pervasive and irreversible-is reshaping the foundations of global power: the planet itself. Climate change is no longer a distant environmental concern-it has become a central axis of geopolitical strategy, influencing everything from resource access and migration patterns to national security priorities. The vulnerabilities exposed by global warming intersect with existing inequalities and fault lines, creating new arenas of competition, cooperation, and crisis. In this next chapter, we explore how rising seas, melting glaciers, and shifting climate zones are not just ecological phenomena, but deeply political forces-redefining sovereignty, redrawing borders, and demanding a new kind of international response.

Reference: Carnegie India, *India's Role in a Rebalancing Indo-Pacific* (2023); Brookings, *Navigating the Strategic Triangle: U.S., India, and China*

(2022).

CHAPTER NINE

Climate Change and Environmental Geopolitics

While the contest for technological supremacy and cyber dominance reflects the cutting edge of modern geopolitics, an equally profound—yet existential—dimension is emerging from the planet itself. Climate change is no longer a peripheral issue confined to environmental summits; it has rapidly become a central axis of global political strategy.

Rising temperatures, sea-level encroachments, water scarcity, and extreme weather events are not only redrawing coastlines and displacing populations—they are also reshaping national security priorities and foreign policy agendas. Environmental vulnerabilities, particularly in fragile and resource-stressed regions, often intensify existing geopolitical tensions. As nations confront both the physical consequences and diplomatic imperatives of a warming planet, the politics of sustainability, adaptation, and ecological responsibility have emerged as new arenas of competition, cooperation, and coercion.

To grasp the full spectrum of 21st-century geopolitics, it is imperative to examine how environmental transformations are redefining global power structures and recalibrating the strategic calculus of states.

Introduction:

From Peripheral Threat to Central Strategic Variable: Climate change has transcended its traditional classification as an environmental concern and emerged as a core issue in geopolitical strategy. As global warming accelerates, extreme weather events, resource scarcity, rising sea levels, and forced migration are reshaping state behavior, altering diplomatic alignments, and influencing defence policy. What was once a distant ecological challenge is now directly impacting national security, economic resilience, and regional stability.

Climate Security and National Sovereignty

Nations are increasingly framing climate threats through the lens of sovereignty and territorial integrity. Rising sea levels threaten the very existence of small island states like the Maldives and Tuvalu, while desertification and water scarcity in regions like the Sahel and South Asia are exacerbating tensions over land and river access. Climate-induced crop failures and erratic monsoons have already triggered localized instability in parts of India, Pakistan, and Bangladesh, complicating traditional border security and humanitarian coordination mechanisms.

In militarized contexts, climate change is increasingly acting as a "threat multiplier." In South Asia, transboundary rivers like the Indus and Brahmaputra are emerging flashpoints. Glacial retreat and shifting rainfall patterns are intensifying water stress, raising the risk of diplomatic standoffs between India, Pakistan, and China.

Following the Pahalgam terror attack, India placed the Indus Waters Treaty under review—a significant shift from decades of adherence, signaling how climate-linked agreements can become tools of strategic pressure. Meanwhile, China's upstream projects on the Brahmaputra and limited data sharing have heightened downstream concerns in India and Bangladesh.

These dynamics reflect how climate change amplifies existing rivalries, turning environmental issues into core national security challenges.

Resource Competition and Environmental Nationalism

Access to clean water, arable land, and mineral resources critical for the green transition is fostering new forms of environmental nationalism. As countries race to secure lithium, cobalt, and rare earth metals for batteries and renewable energy infrastructure, competition over ecological zones—from the Arctic to deep-sea reserves—has intensified. The geopolitics of the energy transition is increasingly being shaped not only by technological innovation but also by geographical control of eco-strategic zones.

Africa and Latin America, rich in biodiversity and mineral wealth, are witnessing renewed strategic interest from global powers seeking to green their economies. However, this external interest often sidelines local communities and exacerbates environmental degradation, raising concerns about a neo-extractive global order under the guise of climate cooperation.

Climate Diplomacy and Global Governance

It Challenges Multilateral efforts like the Paris Agreement and subsequent COP summits have institutionalized climate diplomacy, but with uneven results. While there is growing consensus on the need for urgent action, divergences between developed and developing countries persist over funding, technology transfer, and emission targets. The concept of "common but differentiated responsibilities" remains contested, with the Global South demanding reparative justice and climate finance to adapt and mitigate climate risks.

The rise of "climate clubs"—like the European Union's Carbon Border Adjustment Mechanism (CBAM)—has introduced carbon tariffs as tools of trade leverage, blurring the lines between environmental regulation and protectionist economic policy. This risks deepening global inequality, especially for countries unable to rapidly decarbonize due to developmental constraints.

Climate Refugees and Human Security

One of the most tangible impacts of climate change is on human displacement. The World Bank estimates that over 200 million people could be displaced by climate change by 2050, particularly in hotspots like Sub-Saharan Africa, South Asia, and Latin America. These climate refugees, lacking legal recognition under the 1951 Refugee Convention, exist in a legal grey zone and pose complex challenges for national immigration policies, urban planning, and international humanitarian law.

In South Asia, the Sundarbans delta—a shared ecosystem between India and Bangladesh—is shrinking due to sea-level rise and soil salinization. This has already triggered internal migration and could eventually spark bilateral tensions over cross-border humanitarian access and resource allocation.

Environmental Geopolitics in a Multipolar World

The intersection of climate change and geopolitics is particularly stark in a multipolar international system. Unlike during the Cold War, where bipolar superpower rivalry offered some predictability, today's fragmented power structure creates governance vacuums. Countries often prioritize short-term national interests over long-term ecological sustainability.

China's Belt and Road Initiative, for instance, has been criticized for financing coal plants in developing countries even as it leads in solar panel production. Similarly, climate leadership by the EU and the U.S. is frequently undermined by domestic political backlashes and inconsistent implementation.

Opinion: Toward Cooperative Environmental Sovereignty

As this chapter has explored, climate change is no longer a slow-moving backdrop to global affairs—it is an accelerating force reshaping the geopolitical stage itself. From the retreating glaciers of the Himalayas to the sinking deltas of the Global South, environmental disruptions are reframing the very notions of borders, sovereignty, and security.

Nations are increasingly forced to reconcile the imperatives of ecological sustainability with the instincts of strategic competition. Water disputes, climate-induced displacement, and eco-strategic resource grabs have emerged as flashpoints of instability, while carbon tariffs, green technology races, and climate clubs signal the growing weaponization of environmental policy. Yet, amid these tensions, climate change also offers an opportunity for reimagining global governance—not as a zero-sum contest, but as a platform for shared responsibility and resilience.

Whether states choose to compete over collapsing ecosystems or collaborate toward inclusive sustainability will shape the architecture of peace, power, and prosperity in the decades to come. As the planet warms, the question facing humanity is no longer just how to adapt, but whether we can transform the logic of geopolitics itself to meet the greatest collective challenge of our time.

CHAPTER TEN

U.S.-India-China Strategic Triangle: Cooperation, Competition, and Containment

Introduction: Emergence of the Strategic Triangle

The early 21st century has witnessed the consolidation of a **strategic triangle** between the United States, India, and China - a dynamic marked by **cooperation, competition, and containment**. As the global balance of power shifts from the Atlantic to the Indo-Pacific, these three actors increasingly shape regional and global order, influencing not only trade and security frameworks but also technological standards, supply chain architectures, and diplomatic alliances.

Historically, India's policy of **non-alignment** allowed it to avoid entanglement in Cold War bipolarity. However, the evolving security environment, economic interdependencies, and China's assertive foreign policy have compelled India to **reassess its strategic posture**. Simultaneously, the U.S.-China relationship, once defined by engagement and cautious optimism, has deteriorated into **strategic rivalry** marked by military brinkmanship, economic decoupling, and ideological contestation.

India's unique position-geographically proximate to China, economically linked to both superpowers, and increasingly aligned with U.S.-led initiatives-renders it the critical "**swing state**" in this emerging triangular dynamic. How India manages its relationships with the U.S. and China will significantly determine the future of the Indo-Pacific order.

Reference: Carnegie India, *The Strategic Choices Before India* (2023); Brookings Institution, *The Emerging U.S.-India-China Triangle* (2022).

Historical Background: From Non-Alignment to Indo-Pacific Strategy

India's Non-Aligned Roots and the Rise of Strategic Power

During the Cold War, India emerged as a founding pillar of the Non-Aligned Movement (NAM)-an initiative aimed at maintaining independence from the two dominant power blocs led by the United States and the Soviet Union. Alongside nations like Egypt, Indonesia, and Yugoslavia, India sought to forge a third path in global politics, grounded in strategic autonomy, peaceful coexistence, and anti-colonial solidarity.

Guided by Prime Minister Jawaharlal Nehru's vision, non-alignment was not passive neutrality but an assertive foreign policy doctrine rooted in sovereignty, disarmament, and the moral leadership of the developing world. Nehru envisioned a world where newly independent nations would not serve as proxies in superpower rivalries but as architects of a more just and multipolar global order.

Though India occasionally tilted toward the Soviet Union-especially with the 1971 Indo-Soviet Treaty of Peace, Friendship, and Cooperation-it steadfastly resisted alignment with military blocs like NATO or the Warsaw Pact. Instead, India championed South–South cooperation, global disarmament, and developmental equity through platforms like the United Nations.

This foundational ethos of non-alignment and strategic autonomy has evolved-but not vanished. Under Prime Minister Narendra Modi, India has recalibrated its global posture while staying true to its core principles. Today, India asserts itself not just as a voice of the Global South, but as a decisive global power-one that balances ties with major players like the U.S., Russia, and the EU, while fiercely protecting its strategic independence.

From leading multilateral coalitions like the International Solar Alliance to chairing the G20 with a Global South–centric agenda, India's foreign policy reflects a matured non-aligned legacy-one that adapts to powerplay in a multipolar world without compromising its sovereignty or moral authority.

India is no longer merely navigating global currents-it is helping shape them.

Reference: ORF, *Non-Alignment in Indian Foreign Policy: Relevance and Evolution* (2021).

The 1991 Liberalization and Shift in Strategic Thinking

India's economic liberalization in 1991 was a watershed moment that reshaped not just its economy but also its global strategic outlook. As India opened its markets to foreign investment and global trade, the collapse of the Soviet Union-its long-time partner-forced a fundamental recalibration of foreign policy priorities.

By the late 1990s, India began to pivot toward a more outward-looking and pragmatic approach. Relations with the United States improved significantly, particularly after India's 1998 nuclear tests, which, despite initial sanctions, paved the way for deeper strategic engagement-culminating in the landmark U.S.-India Civil Nuclear Agreement (2005).

At the same time, China's rapid economic rise and growing assertiveness, especially in territorial disputes like the South China Sea, raised concerns in New Delhi. In response, India adopted a policy of multi-alignment-building strong relationships with multiple global powers without entering into exclusive alliances.

This evolving strategy laid the groundwork for India's active role in Indo-Pacific initiatives, reflecting its aim to uphold regional balance, safeguard maritime interests, and assert itself as a key player in a multipolar world order.

Reference: Carnegie India, *India's Foreign Policy Transformation Post-1991* (2022).

Rise of the Indo-Pacific Concept

The emergence of the Indo-Pacific as a strategic framework has significantly shaped India's external outlook. Linking the Indian and Pacific Oceans, the concept was first advanced by Japan's Prime Minister Shinzo

Abe and later embraced by the United States and other regional powers. It emphasizes key principles such as freedom of navigation, a rules-based international order, ASEAN centrality, and infrastructure connectivity as strategic alternatives to China's Belt and Road Initiative (BRI).

For India, the Indo-Pacific aligns closely with its evolving strategic priorities. It is seen as:

A natural extension of its **Act East Policy**, deepening engagement with East and Southeast Asia.

A platform to counterbalance China's influence, particularly through initiatives that promote transparency and sovereignty.

An opportunity to strengthen ties with like-minded democracies, including the U.S., Japan, Australia, and other QUAD members.

India's commitment to this vision was formalized through the launch of the Indo-Pacific Oceans Initiative (IPOI) in 2019, which outlines its approach to a free, open, inclusive, and cooperative regional order focused on maritime security, connectivity, and sustainable development.

Reference: Brookings, *The Indo-Pacific Construct and India's Foreign Policy* (2022); CFR, *The Indo-Pacific Strategy and the Rise of India* (2023).

China's Rise and the Strategic Rebalancing

China's meteoric economic and military rise, culminating in initiatives like the **Belt and Road Initiative (BRI)** and its growing naval presence in the Indian Ocean, posed new challenges for India.

- Border disputes, particularly along the **Line of Actual Control (LAC)**, simmered for decades, occasionally erupting into skirmishes.
- China's deepening ties with Pakistan, including through the **China-Pakistan Economic Corridor (CPEC)**—which passes through contested Kashmir-further aggravated tensions.
- At the multilateral level, China's assertiveness within organizations like BRICS and the Shanghai Cooperation Organization (SCO) created both opportunities and frictions for India.

Consequently, India began **incrementally strengthening strategic ties** with the United States, Japan, Australia, and European partners-while maintaining cautious engagement with China in forums like the BRICS, SCO, and RIC (Russia-India-China dialogue).

Reference: Carnegie Endowment for International Peace, *India and China: Strategic Rivalry and Engagement* (2022).

CHAPTER ELEVEN

Artificial Intelligence and the Future of Geopolitical Power

Introduction: The Strategic Stakes of the AI Race

In the 21st century, artificial intelligence (AI) has emerged as a transformative force not only in economic development but also in the very architecture of international power. As with nuclear technology in the Cold War era, AI now occupies the core of strategic calculations among major powers. Its applications-from autonomous weapons to surveillance regimes and economic modelling-suggest that whoever dominates AI may hold disproportionate sway in global affairs. This chapter explores AI as a new domain of geopolitical competition, drawing on theoretical frameworks, real-world policy initiatives, and emerging alliances around technological sovereignty.

Historical Context: From Technological Superiority to Algorithmic Dominance

Throughout history, technological revolutions have consistently reshaped global power dynamics. The Industrial Revolution equipped Britain with unmatched economic and military capacity, fueling its imperial expansion. In the 20th century, nuclear technology defined the bipolar world order, with the U.S. and the Soviet Union asserting dominance through deterrence and arms races. The post-Cold War digital era introduced transformative innovations in global connectivity and communication-but artificial intelligence (AI) represents a paradigm shift of a different order.

Unlike past technologies, AI introduces autonomous learning systems that can not only process data but also predict, decide, and manipulate outcomes at scale-blurring the lines between automation and cognition. The rise of AI is fundamentally altering not just economic productivity but also warfare, governance, surveillance, and strategic influence.

The roots of the current AI race trace back to the early 2010s, when breakthroughs in deep learning, neural networks, and big data analytics began to unlock new possibilities. Recognizing AI's transformative potential, China launched its "Next Generation AI Development Plan" in 2017, with a bold ambition to become the global leader in AI by 2030. The strategy combines state investment, private-sector mobilization, and data-driven infrastructure to gain technological superiority.

The United States, initially led by its private tech giants, responded with the "American AI Initiative" in 2019, signaling a more coordinated national approach to innovation, research funding, and AI talent development. Meanwhile, the European Union and countries like India have focused on crafting AI strategies that prioritize ethical frameworks, data sovereignty, and strategic autonomy-reflecting concerns about privacy, algorithmic bias, and monopolistic platforms.

Together, these developments mark a transition from mere technological superiority to algorithmic dominance, where code, data, and cognitive automation become tools of national power, economic leverage, and geopolitical competition.

Strategic Domains of AI Geopolitics

1. Military Applications and Autonomous Warfare

Artificial intelligence is rapidly transforming the nature of warfare, shifting the balance from manpower-centric strategies to algorithm-driven combat systems. Autonomous drones, AI-enabled surveillance, robotic infantry, and decision-support tools are now integral to battlefield operations, enhancing speed, precision, and coordination in ways traditional systems cannot match.

The United States' Joint All-Domain Command and Control (JADC2) initiative exemplifies this shift-aiming to create a seamless network that integrates land, air, sea, cyber, and space assets through real-time AI-powered data analysis. Similarly, China's concept of "intelligentized warfare" seeks to embed AI across its military doctrine, emphasizing predictive warfare, swarm drone technology, and automated logistics.

Russia, too, is integrating AI into missile defense and combat simulation systems, using machine learning to enhance threat detection and response capabilities.

Yet, this rapid militarization of AI introduces complex ethical, legal, and strategic dilemmas. One major concern is the rise of "black box" systems-AI tools whose decision-making processes are opaque even to their developers. In high-stakes conflict scenarios, such lack of interpretability could lead to unintended escalation or catastrophic miscalculations.

Moreover, the absence of internationally accepted norms or treaties governing lethal autonomous weapons (LAWs) leaves a troubling regulatory gap. Without clear frameworks to define accountability, compliance, or red lines, AI-enabled warfare risks outpacing diplomacy, creating a future where machines may make life-and-death decisions with minimal human oversight.

In essence, while AI offers military advantages, it also underscores the urgent need for global cooperation on norms, transparency, and responsible use to prevent destabilization in an already volatile security environment.

2. AI and Economic Competitiveness

Artificial intelligence is emerging as a key driver of global economic transformation, with estimates projecting it could contribute up to $15.7 trillion to the global economy by 2030 (PwC, 2018). Nations that lead in AI development and deployment are poised to reshape labor markets, manufacturing systems, and innovation ecosystems, gaining significant strategic and economic advantages.

China has surged ahead in AI application, dominating global rankings in AI patents, particularly in areas like facial recognition, fintech, and logistics automation. It has also scaled deployment rapidly through state-driven integration into governance and infrastructure. By contrast, the United States remains the global frontrunner in foundational AI research, high-end semiconductor design, and the strength of its tech ecosystem-anchored by firms like Google, Nvidia, and OpenAI.

This technological race also fuels strategic dependencies, especially around semiconductors, the backbone of AI systems. Taiwan's TSMC, the world's most advanced chipmaker, has become a geopolitical chokepoint, given its centrality to global AI supply chains and the ongoing U.S.-China tech rivalry.

To mitigate these vulnerabilities, governments are taking action. The U.S. CHIPS and Science Act (2022) allocates billions to revive domestic chip manufacturing and reduce reliance on foreign sources. Similarly, the EU's Digital Compass aims to achieve digital sovereignty by investing in local innovation, supply chain security, and AI infrastructure.

In this emerging AI economy, technological leadership translates directly into geopolitical influence, making economic competitiveness a core component of national power in the multipolar world.

3. AI in Surveillance and Statecraft

Artificial intelligence has become a powerful tool of governance, particularly in the realm of surveillance and political control. AI-powered systems are now widely used by states to monitor populations, track behavior, and preempt dissent-blurring the lines between national security and social control.

Nowhere is this more evident than in China, where the state's Social Credit System combines facial recognition, real-time data analytics, and predictive policing to assess individual behavior and enforce compliance. These systems serve as pillars of digital authoritarianism, enabling the state to manage public sentiment, curb opposition, and centralize political control under the guise of stability and efficiency.

In contrast, liberal democracies face a different dilemma: how to harness AI's benefits in governance and security without undermining civil liberties. The European Union's AI Act represents a proactive response-seeking to regulate or ban high-risk surveillance technologies, including biometric mass surveillance and emotion recognition, especially in public spaces. This regulatory approach reflects a broader normative divide between techno-authoritarian and democratic models of AI governance.

As AI reshapes statecraft, the choices countries make-whether toward control or accountability-will profoundly influence not just domestic governance, but also the global discourse on digital rights, privacy, and freedom.

4. Norm Setting and Global Governance

Geopolitical competition over artificial intelligence increasingly revolves not only around hardware production and algorithmic capability but also around the power to shape the normative frameworks and global standards that govern its use. In this emerging digital order, norm setting has become a strategic battleground, where states compete to embed their values, regulatory philosophies, and technological ecosystems into global governance structures.

Multilateral and technical bodies such as the International Telecommunication Union (ITU), International Organization for Standardization (ISO), and Institute of Electrical and Electronics Engineers (IEEE) have become key arenas of soft power projection. China has been particularly assertive in leveraging its influence within these forums to promote standards aligned with its model of state-led digital governance. For instance, Chinese proposals for "smart cities" and "facial recognition infrastructure" have made their way into international standard-setting agendas-often bundled with equipment exports to the Global South, thereby creating both technical lock-in and normative alignment.

By contrast, the United States and its allies have emphasized frameworks rooted in liberal democratic principles, including privacy, transparency, accountability, and human rights. This divergence reflects deeper ideological contestation: while the Chinese model promotes surveillance-enabled governance under the rubric of efficiency and order, Western frameworks advocate for AI systems that are fair, explainable, and aligned with human dignity.

Important multilateral initiatives have attempted to bridge this divide. The **OECD's AI Principles (2019)**-endorsed by over 40 countries-laid out foundational commitments to inclusive growth, human-centered values, transparency, robustness, and accountability in AI deployment. Similarly, UNESCO's **Recommendation on the Ethics of Artificial Intelligence (2021)** represents the first global normative instrument on AI, adopted by all 193 member states. It calls for banning social scoring and biometric mass surveillance systems, emphasizing inclusivity and sustainability.

Yet these initiatives face two principal challenges. First, **implementation remains fragmented**, with stark differences in national regulatory capacities and political will. Second, **great power rivalry continues to obstruct the formation of binding global treaties**. Unlike in the nuclear or climate regimes, there is no consensus on enforcement mechanisms, jurisdictional reach, or institutional authority over AI ethics and safety.

Furthermore, the private sector-particularly Big Tech firms-plays a pivotal role in shaping global norms. Companies like Google, Microsoft, Alibaba, and Huawei are not merely subjects of regulation but also norm entrepreneurs, often outpacing governments in technological innovation and lobbying efforts. This complicates governance efforts, especially in jurisdictions where public-private boundaries are blurred or where state and corporate interests are tightly interwoven.

As AI becomes more autonomous and embedded in critical sectors-from defence and healthcare to education and criminal justice-the urgency for a coherent and inclusive global governance framework intensifies. Without such frameworks, the world risks a future of **regulatory fragmentation**, **technological bifurcation**, and **normative disarray**-where ethical standards vary not by values, but by the prevailing political power behind the code.

Reference Highlights:

- OECD. (2019). *OECD Principles on Artificial Intelligence*
- UNESCO. (2021). *Recommendation on the Ethics of Artificial Intelligence*
- Segal, A. (2022). *The AI Governance Gap: Competing Visions, Missing Rules*. Council on Foreign Relations
- Kania, E. (2019). *AI Weapons and Global Norms: Chinese Approaches to Governance*. CNAS
- United Nations Office of the High Commissioner for Human Rights (2021). *The Right to Privacy in the Digital Age*

5. AI in Military Strategy and Autonomous Warfare

Artificial Intelligence is rapidly transforming the nature of modern warfare, from decision-making and logistics to intelligence collection, targeting, and autonomous combat. In the geopolitical realm, AI is no longer a passive enabler of defence systems but an active force multiplier-reshaping strategic doctrines, deterrence frameworks, and the ethical calculus of war itself.

AI as a Force Multiplier

Artificial Intelligence (AI) is rapidly emerging as a force multiplier in military strategy-an asset that significantly enhances a nation's combat capabilities without proportionally increasing its military footprint. Leading powers such as the United States, China, and Russia have identified AI as a game-changing technology capable of transforming the battlefield across all domains: land, air, sea, cyber, and space.

Key applications include autonomous drones for real-time reconnaissance and precision strikes, predictive analytics to anticipate enemy movements, algorithmic target identification that enables faster and more accurate threat assessment, and AI-enabled surveillance systems for persistent monitoring of operational theatres. These technologies are no longer experimental-they are becoming central to defense planning and modernization.

In the United States, maintaining strategic overmatch-the ability to decisively outperform any adversary-is a top priority. The Joint Artificial Intelligence Center (JAIC) was established to integrate AI across military operations, while programs like Project Maven apply machine learning to process vast amounts of battlefield imagery for intelligence analysis. The Third Offset Strategy, developed by the Department of Defense, envisions AI as a key tool to counterbalance emerging threats through innovation in autonomous systems, logistics, and command-and-control mechanisms.

China, meanwhile, has embedded AI into its military doctrine through "Intelligentized Warfare"-a concept that emphasizes information dominance and the integration of AI across sensors, weapons platforms, and decision-making systems. Under its civil-military fusion strategy, breakthroughs in the private tech sector are funneled into military applications, including drone swarms, cyber warfare tools, and AI-assisted command systems.

Russia is also investing heavily in automated combat platforms, robotic artillery, and AI for electronic warfare-focusing on offsetting technological gaps with high-impact innovations.

Together, these efforts illustrate how AI is not just an add-on to military power but a transformational capability-reshaping doctrines, reducing human latency in decision-making, and altering the very nature of deterrence and conflict in the 21st century.

Autonomous Weapons Systems (AWS) and Strategic Risk

Among the most controversial advancements in modern warfare is the emergence of Lethal Autonomous Weapons Systems (LAWS)-weapons that can identify, select, and engage targets without direct human control. Unlike remotely operated drones or automated defense systems, LAWS operate independently once activated, making battlefield decisions using algorithms, sensors, and machine learning models.

This development raises profound ethical and legal concerns, particularly with regard to international humanitarian law (IHL). Two core principles of IHL are at risk:

Distinction-the obligation to differentiate between combatants and civilians, and

Proportionality-ensuring that the military advantage of an attack is not outweighed by excessive civilian harm.

LAWS challenge both, as algorithmic decision-making lacks human judgment, empathy, and accountability.

Critics argue that removing humans from the decision-making loop increases the risk of:

Unintended escalation during conflicts due to rapid, opaque responses,

Accidental engagements resulting from misidentification, and

Algorithmic bias, where flawed or poorly trained systems disproportionately target certain populations or environments, potentially resulting in unlawful or discriminatory harm.

At the global level, the United Nations Convention on Certain Conventional Weapons (CCW) has served as the main forum for international debate on regulating or banning LAWS. Despite over a decade of discussions, attempts to reach a binding consensus-such as a global moratorium or treaty prohibiting fully autonomous lethal systems-have stalled, largely due to opposition from technologically advanced military powers like the U.S., Russia, and China, who see such systems as critical to future strategic superiority.

In essence, the rise of LAWS underscores a growing strategic and moral vacuum, where the pace of technological development is outstripping the creation of global norms and governance mechanisms-posing serious risks to human rights, battlefield accountability, and long-term global stability.

Case Study: The Nagorno-Karabakh Conflict (2020)

The 2020 Nagorno-Karabakh conflict between Azerbaijan and Armenia served as a stark demonstration of how AI-enabled warfare is reshaping modern conflicts, even outside the realm of major power rivalries. Azerbaijan leveraged a combination of Turkish-made Bayraktar TB2 drones and Israeli loitering munitions (also known as "kamikaze drones"), many of which were guided or enhanced by AI-supported targeting systems.

These technologies enabled real-time surveillance, precision strikes, and automated threat identification, allowing Azerbaijan to neutralize Armenian air defenses, artillery units, and armored vehicles with high efficiency. Crucially, this marked one of the first conflicts where algorithm-driven targeting played a decisive role in battlefield dominance.

The conflict also revealed a paradigm shift: smaller states can now alter regional military balances through access to relatively affordable, semi-autonomous systems-without the need for direct superpower involvement or large-scale ground forces. It underscored the growing accessibility and impact of algorithmic warfare, where AI enhances speed, accuracy, and lethality, often reducing human oversight in critical targeting decisions.

The Nagorno-Karabakh case thus foreshadowed the future of warfare-where precision, automation, and real-time intelligence, rather than sheer numbers or conventional firepower, can determine the outcome of conflicts.

Strategic Stability and the "Flash War" Dilemma

Artificial Intelligence introduces new complexities into the delicate balance of strategic stability, particularly in the context of nuclear deterrence and crisis escalation. AI systems enable machine-speed decision-making, automated threat detection, and cyber-enhanced early warning systems-tools designed to improve response times. However, this speed can become a liability in high-stakes scenarios where misinterpretation or malfunction could rapidly escalate tensions.

Scholars have raised concerns about the possibility of a "flash war"-a scenario in which AI-driven systems misread adversarial actions or intentions, triggering retaliatory responses before human decision-makers have the chance to intervene. In such a situation, diplomacy and de-escalation mechanisms may be outpaced by the very technologies meant to enhance security.

The opacity of black-box algorithms-systems whose internal logic is not fully understandable even to their creators—adds another layer of risk. In nuclear command and control environments, reliance on such AI tools could erode trust between rival states, especially if one side perceives its opponent to have superior or faster AI capabilities. This perception could incentivize pre-emptive actions or automated retaliation, echoing the uncertainty and fear-driven behaviors of the early nuclear arms race.

Ultimately, the integration of AI into strategic command systems demands robust norms, transparency, and human oversight to prevent unintended escalation and to maintain crisis stability in an increasingly automated security environment.

Ethical and Legal Gaps

The rapid militarization of artificial intelligence has outpaced the development of ethical frameworks and legal standards governing its use in armed conflict. Fundamental questions remain unresolved: Who bears responsibility when an AI system commits a violation of international humanitarian law? Is it the programmer, the commanding officer, the manufacturer, or is liability diluted across the system-perhaps even untraceable due to the opacity of algorithms?

This accountability vacuum poses serious challenges, particularly when AI systems operate with limited or no human oversight. The principle of combatant status-which defines who is legally entitled to engage in warfare-is also complicated by autonomous systems, which themselves cannot be held morally or legally accountable.

In response, a growing number of NGOs and international coalitions, such as Stop Killer Robots, are advocating for a pre-emptive global ban on fully autonomous weapons. Their concern is that without clear legal safeguards, such technologies could lead to unaccountable warfare, lowered thresholds for the use of force, and increased risks of civilian harm.

However, proponents of military AI argue that autonomous systems could reduce collateral damage, citing their ability to process data faster, make precise calculations, and avoid fatigue-induced errors common in human soldiers. This position, while compelling in theory, raises concerns about algorithmic bias, lack of contextual judgment, and the ethical limits of machine decision-making-all of which demand rigorous scrutiny, transparency, and international consensus.

As AI continues to reshape warfare, bridging the ethical and legal gaps is not just necessary-it is urgent.

Reference Highlights:

- Scharre, P. (2018). *Army of None: Autonomous Weapons and the Future of War.* W. W. Norton & Company.
- United Nations CCW Meetings on Lethal Autonomous Weapons (2014–2023).
- Kania, E. B. (2020). *Battlefield Singularity: China's Military Revolution in Artificial Intelligence.* CNAS.
- Boulanin, V. & Verbruggen, M. (2017). *Mapping the Development of Autonomy in Weapon Systems.* SIPRI.
- Horowitz, M. C. (2022). *AI and the Future of Deterrence: Risks and Opportunities.* Brookings Institution.

6. AI Inequality and the Global South

As the global race for artificial intelligence accelerates, a widening gap has emerged between technological leaders and the rest of the world-a phenomenon increasingly referred to as AI inequality. While the United States, China, and the European Union dominate AI research, infrastructure, patents, and regulatory frameworks, many countries across the Global South remain on the margins-either as consumers of imported technology or as passive recipients of AI-driven governance models designed elsewhere.

This disparity has geopolitical consequences, as technological dependency can translate into strategic vulnerability, limiting the Global South's ability to shape AI norms, protect data sovereignty, or assert digital autonomy. From a developmental perspective, the lack of access to AI tools and digital infrastructure deepens existing divides in education, healthcare, finance, and public services-sectors where AI could otherwise have transformative impact.

Moreover, the normative influence of dominant AI powers means that ethical standards, regulatory principles, and governance models are increasingly being exported from the Global North, often without adequate input from developing nations. This risks creating a digital hierarchy, where global AI frameworks reflect the interests of a few while neglecting the values, needs, and rights of many.

Addressing AI inequality requires inclusive global dialogue, targeted investment in digital capacity-building, and mechanisms to ensure that the benefits of AI are equitably shared-not just concentrated among technological superpowers.

Digital Dependency and Infrastructure Gaps

A core contributor to global AI inequality is the uneven distribution of digital infrastructure. The essential backbone of AI innovation-such as cloud computing hubs, advanced data centers, AI research institutions, and high-performance computing systems-is heavily concentrated in the Global North, particularly in the United States, Europe, and parts of East Asia.

In contrast, many nations across Africa, Latin America, and parts of South and Southeast Asia face significant barriers. These include limited broadband access, low data storage capacity, a shortage of skilled AI professionals, and underinvestment in tech infrastructure. Without this foundational ecosystem, developing and scaling indigenous AI solutions becomes exceedingly difficult.

This asymmetry fosters a form of technological dependency-or digital neocolonialism-where countries in the Global South must rely on foreign-designed AI systems, often developed by multinational corporations based in the West or China. These tools are frequently trained on non-representative datasets, which can result in algorithmic bias, high error rates, and cultural misalignment when deployed in local contexts.

For example, facial recognition technologies used in African or South Asian cities have shown elevated inaccuracies due to their training on datasets that lack demographic and ethnic diversity. These issues raise serious concerns around fairness, accountability, and sovereignty, particularly when legal oversight is dictated by external jurisdictions.

Closing these infrastructure gaps is essential not only for inclusive technological development but also for ensuring that AI reflects diverse realities, respects local norms, and empowers communities rather than reinforcing global hierarchies.

Let me know if you'd like to include specific country case studies

Case Study: Surveillance Technologies in Africa

China's export of **AI-driven surveillance infrastructure**-particularly under the Digital Silk Road component of the Belt and Road Initiative-has raised alarms about the entrenchment of authoritarian technology norms. In countries such as Zimbabwe, Uganda, and Ethiopia, Huawei-supplied facial recognition and monitoring systems have been deployed with little transparency or local oversight.

While such systems offer improved law enforcement tools, they also risk enabling digital authoritarianism, particularly in states with weak democratic institutions. The African Union's 2018 data breach scandal-allegedly tied to Chinese-built infrastructure-underscores the vulnerability of sovereignty in AI-enabled governance.

Lack of Representation in Global AI Governance

Despite being deeply affected by the global spread of artificial intelligence, the Global South remains largely underrepresented in key international forums that shape AI norms, standards, and governance. Platforms such as the OECD, G7, and European Union are at the forefront of setting ethical guidelines, technical benchmarks, and regulatory frameworks for AI-but participation from countries in Africa, Latin America, and parts of Asia is minimal or symbolic.

This results in a global governance imbalance, where most developing nations act as rule-takers, rather than rule-makers. The marginalization in decision-making processes reinforces technological dependency, limits policy sovereignty, and reduces the ability of these nations to advocate for equitable standards that reflect their social, cultural, and economic realities.

However, emerging coalitions and regional initiatives are beginning to challenge this dynamic. The African Union's Digital Transformation Strategy (2020-2030) includes specific commitments to data governance, AI regulation, and digital capacity-building, aiming to align technological development with African values and priorities.

Similarly, India's G20 presidency in 2023 marked a pivotal moment. By advocating for inclusive digital public infrastructure, open-source AI solutions, and global cooperation for development-focused innovation, India positioned itself as a voice for the Global South in shaping a more balanced and inclusive digital future.

These efforts reflect a growing awareness that fair and representative AI governance is essential-not just for justice, but for long-term global stability and trust in emerging technologies.

Toward Inclusive AI Diplomacy

Bridging the growing AI divide demands more than just technical solutions-it requires a fundamental reorientation of global digital diplomacy. As artificial intelligence becomes central to economic development, security, and governance, multilateral institutions, technology companies, and donor governments must work collaboratively to ensure that the Global South is not left behind.

A truly inclusive approach to AI must prioritize:

Equitable access to AI research infrastructure, including cloud computing, data centers, and open-source platforms.

Diverse and representative datasets, especially in underrepresented languages and cultural contexts, to build inclusive and fair AI models.

Global funding mechanisms to support AI education, innovation, and entrepreneurship in developing countries.

South-South cooperation to co-develop ethical AI frameworks grounded in shared values, regional priorities, and context-specific needs.

Encouraging signs of progress are emerging. UNESCO's AI Needs Assessment for Least Developed Countries (LDCs) seeks to identify gaps in digital readiness and offer tailored support. The International Telecommunication Union's AI for Good Global Summit provides a platform for dialogue and collaboration between governments, researchers, and civil society, focusing on AI's potential to advance the UN Sustainable Development Goals (SDGs).

Though still in early stages, these initiatives mark important steps toward a future where AI diplomacy is more inclusive, participatory, and globally representative-ensuring that technological progress benefits all, not just a few.

Reference Highlights:

- United Nations Economic Commission for Africa (UNECA). (2021). *Policy Framework for Africa's AI Readiness.*

- UNESCO. (2021). *AI and Inclusion: Challenges and Opportunities in the Global South.*
- Digital Watch Observatory. (2023). *Mapping the Digital Divide and AI Capability Gaps.*
- Ghosh, R. (2022). *Digital Colonialism and the Global South.* Global Policy Journal.
- African Union Commission. (2020). *Digital Transformation Strategy for Africa (2020–2030).*

CHAPTER TWELVE

Space Geopolitics – The New Strategic Frontier

1. Introduction: From Celestial Curiosity to Strategic Calculus

Since the launch of Sputnik by the Soviet Union in 1957-the first human-made satellite to orbit Earth-outer space has undergone a profound transformation. What began as a domain of scientific curiosity and symbolic competition during the Cold War has evolved into a highly strategic and contested arena. In the early years, space achievements were largely political gestures-marked by iconic milestones like moon landings and orbital missions-designed to showcase technological supremacy.

In the 21st century, however, the space race is no longer just about exploration. It is increasingly defined by the deployment of dual-use technologies-systems that serve both civilian and military purposes. These include reconnaissance satellites, positioning and navigation systems (like GPS and BeiDou), and early-warning sensors that are essential for missile defense and global surveillance. The emergence of militarized orbits, private-sector launch vehicles, and the race to control low-Earth and geostationary orbital slots reflect the growing intersection of space and security.

Today, outer space is a critical infrastructure layer in the global power matrix. It underpins everything from civilian telecommunications and weather forecasting to military command-and-control and intelligence gathering. Recognizing this, leading powers such as the United States, China, and regional alliances like NATO have officially designated space as a warfighting domain-placing it on par with land, sea, air, and cyber.

This strategic recalibration means that space is no longer an isolated or neutral realm. It is a high-altitude extension of Earth's geopolitical rivalries, where technological leadership, commercial dominance, and security doctrines converge-making outer space a pivotal theatre of global influence in the 21st century.

2. *The Militarization and Weaponization of Space*

2.1 Strategic Infrastructure in Orbit

Space is no longer a passive backdrop to terrestrial conflict-it has become a vital domain of military operations, with nations increasingly reliant on space-based infrastructure to support and enhance their defense capabilities. At the core of this transformation are satellite constellations that provide critical functions such as precision-guided targeting, encrypted military communications, missile early-warning systems, and real-time battlefield surveillance.

The United States leads this evolution, operating over 160 dedicated military satellites, integrated into platforms such as the Space-Based Infrared System (SBIRS), which provides global missile launch detection and strategic warning. Meanwhile, China and Russia are rapidly scaling their own ISR (Intelligence, Surveillance, and Reconnaissance) networks. China's Yaogan series includes remote sensing and radar satellites capable of tracking maritime and ground movements, while Russia's Lotos-S and Kosmos fleets serve electronic intelligence and early-warning roles.

A growing concern is the proliferation of dual-use satellites-technologies that appear civilian (e.g., for weather or communications) but are equipped with capabilities suited for military applications. These systems blur the line between civilian and military space assets, making arms control efforts more complex and increasing the risk of misinterpretation during times of tension or crisis.

Furthermore, the integration of these assets into national command-and-control architectures underscores their strategic value. Disruption of space-based systems-whether through cyber attacks, jamming, or kinetic anti-satellite (ASAT) weapons-can paralyze military operations, creating incentives for preemptive action and destabilizing deterrence.

In sum, the militarization of orbit is redefining space as a strategic high ground-critical not only to warfare but to national security planning and global power projection.

2.2 Anti-Satellite Weapons and Strategic Escalation

A pivotal moment in the militarization of space occurred with the advent and testing of anti-satellite (ASAT) weapons-systems designed to disable or destroy satellites in orbit. These weapons can be kinetic (physically destroying the satellite) or non-kinetic (using jamming, cyberattacks, or directed energy).

In 2007, China demonstrated the first high-profile kinetic ASAT capability by destroying one of its own defunct weather satellites with a ground-launched missile. The test created over 3,000 pieces of trackable orbital debris, raising global alarm over space safety and long-term sustainability. India joined the group of ASAT-capable nations in 2019 with "Mission Shakti", successfully targeting a satellite in low-Earth orbit (LEO). Russia followed with its own test in 2021, similarly generating large amounts of debris.

Such demonstrations have strategic and environmental consequences. They heighten the risk of triggering a Kessler Syndrome-a scenario where cascading collisions between space debris render orbital paths unusable for satellites, threatening both military and civilian space operations. These tests also underscore the emerging role of space deterrence in national defense postures, where threatening or disabling a rival's satellite infrastructure is seen as a viable tactic in future conflicts.

In response to this shifting threat landscape, the United States has significantly expanded its space command structure. The re-establishment of U.S. Space Command (SPACECOM) and the creation of the U.S. Space Force in 2019 signal the formal recognition of outer space as a warfighting domain, on par with land, sea, air, and cyber.

As more nations develop and test ASAT capabilities, the lack of binding international norms or arms control agreements for space warfare poses an escalating risk to global security, orbital sustainability, and crisis stability.

3. The Rise of Commercial Space Actors

3.1 Privatization and the New Space Economy

The landscape of space exploration and utilization has undergone a dramatic shift with the privatization of space activities. Once dominated solely by government space agencies like NASA, Roscosmos, and ISRO, the space domain is now shaped by a growing constellation of private-sector players. Companies such as SpaceX, Blue Origin, OneWeb, and Starlink have revolutionized the sector by reducing costs, accelerating innovation, and creating a competitive commercial space economy.

At the forefront of this transformation is SpaceX, whose reusable Falcon 9 launch system has significantly lowered the cost per launch, making satellite deployment more accessible than ever before. Its satellite-based broadband arm, Starlink, currently operates over 5,000 satellites in low-Earth orbit (LEO), delivering high-speed internet across more than 70 countries. Notably, Starlink's role in conflict zones-such as Ukraine-has underscored the growing strategic utility of commercial space assets. Ukrainian military units have relied on Starlink terminals for secure, real-time battlefield communications, highlighting how commercial infrastructure can directly influence military outcomes.

This evolution introduces a new dimension to geopolitics: the dual-use nature of private space infrastructure. Systems designed for civilian applications-like communication or navigation—can be rapidly repurposed for military or strategic use. As a result, private companies now wield forms of geopolitical leverage traditionally reserved for nation-states, raising questions around accountability, regulation, and sovereignty in space.

The rise of the New Space Economy-characterized by satellite constellations, private launch capabilities, and data-driven space services-has expanded access and innovation. However, it also necessitates new governance frameworks to address the blurring boundaries between commercial ambition and national security imperatives.

3.2 Lunar and Planetary Resource Politics

As technological capabilities advance, the next phase of space competition is shifting beyond Earth's orbit to focus on the extraction of extraterrestrial resources-particularly from the Moon, asteroids, and eventually Mars. This emerging domain of space resource politics is redefining global space diplomacy, legal norms, and strategic ambitions.

A key initiative shaping this future is the Artemis Accords, led by the United States and signed by over 30 countries. The Accords promote peaceful exploration, transparency, and the principle that nations have the right to extract and utilize resources from celestial bodies, including lunar regolith (moon dust and soil) and asteroid materials, for scientific and commercial purposes. These agreements are linked to NASA's Artemis Program, which aims to return humans to the Moon and establish a long-term presence.

In contrast, China and Russia, excluded from the Artemis framework due to geopolitical tensions and legislative barriers (such as the U.S. Wolf Amendment), have announced plans to jointly develop the International Lunar Research Station (ILRS). This rival initiative signals a bifurcation in lunar governance frameworks, reflecting broader competition between rival blocs in space exploration and access to off-world resources.

However, these ambitions are increasingly testing the limits of the 1967 Outer Space Treaty (OST)-the foundational legal instrument governing outer space. The OST prohibits any nation from claiming sovereignty over celestial bodies and classifies space as the province of all humankind. Yet, the legal grey zones surrounding resource extraction-where ownership of harvested materials is permitted but territorial claims are not-remain contested and unresolved.

These evolving tensions raise critical questions: Who governs space resources? How are rights to mine or inhabit celestial bodies defined and enforced? And can existing frameworks adapt to a future involving off-world mining, commercial space habitats, and potentially, planetary colonization?

The way the international community addresses-or exploits-these legal ambiguities will shape the contours of planetary governance and determine whether space remains a cooperative frontier or becomes a domain of unregulated competition.

4. *Space Governance: Fragmentation and Future Regimes*

The current framework for space governance is increasingly outpaced by the realities of modern space activity. Foundational treaties such as the Outer Space Treaty (1967)-which prohibits national sovereignty over celestial bodies and promotes space as a global commons-and the Moon Agreement (1979)-which seeks to regulate lunar resource use-form the legal backbone of space law. However, these instruments are proving insufficient in an era marked by privatization, commercial exploitation, and militarization of space.

Emerging challenges include:

Lack of enforceable debris mitigation protocols: With thousands of satellites and rising space junk, there are no binding mechanisms to ensure orbital sustainability or hold actors accountable for collisions or pollution.

Legal ambiguity around resource extraction: Treaties ban ownership of celestial bodies, yet allow for the extraction and use of space resources, creating a regulatory grey zone ripe for competing interpretations.

Inadequate regulation of satellite mega-constellations: Large-scale commercial constellations (e.g., Starlink) raise concerns about space traffic management, radio-frequency interference, and monopolization of orbital slots.

Escalation of anti-satellite (ASAT) capabilities: With no binding arms control mechanisms for space weapons, the threat of militarized space conflict continues to grow, increasing the risk of miscalculation and debris-generating confrontations.

While various initiatives are attempting to address these gaps-such as the UNOOSA Long-Term Sustainability Guidelines, the Artemis Accords, and the EU's proposed Space Code of Conduct-they remain non-binding and fragmented, lacking universal adoption and enforcement mechanisms.

This growing patchwork of rules and voluntary norms creates a high risk of norm fragmentation, where competing legal and political frameworks emerge based on geopolitical alignments. The trend mirrors what is already happening in cyberspace and artificial intelligence, where rival powers promote divergent models of sovereignty, security, and international cooperation.

In the absence of a comprehensive, enforceable global space governance regime, space risks becoming a contested and unstable domain-marked by legal ambiguity, commercial rivalry, and strategic confrontation.

5. Conclusion: The Orbital Chessboard and the Future of Sovereignty

Space is no longer a distant, symbolic frontier-it is a living, contested domain that undergirds terrestrial power. The lines between exploration, exploitation, and escalation are increasingly blurred, as great powers and private actors stake claims to orbital and celestial assets.

In the coming decades, space geopolitics will shape not just national security but also the **technological architecture of global governance**, the **ideology of sovereignty**, and the **economic foundations of future growth**. Without robust multilateral agreements, shared norms, and transparency in civil-military coordination, the strategic high ground of space may become both the arena and the accelerator of geopolitical instability.

Key References:

- United Nations Office for Outer Space Affairs (UNOOSA). (2022). *Long-Term Sustainability of Outer Space Activities*
- U.S. Department of Defence. (2020). *Defence Space Strategy Summary*
- Johnson-Freese, J. (2016). *Space Warfare in the 21st Century: Arming the Heavens*. Routledge
- Weeden, B., & Samson, V. (2023). *Global Counterspace Capabilities Report*. Secure World Foundation
- NASA. (2023). *Artemis Accords and Lunar Governance*
- Outer Space Treaty (1967); Moon Agreement (1979)

Case Study A: Starlink in the Ukraine War

The 2022 Russian invasion of Ukraine underscored the growing strategic importance of commercial space infrastructure, particularly low-Earth orbit (LEO) satellite constellations. In the early days of the conflict, SpaceX rapidly deployed Starlink satellite internet terminals to Ukraine, ensuring uninterrupted broadband connectivity amid widespread disruption of terrestrial networks.

While initially framed as humanitarian support for civilian communications, Starlink soon became a dual-use technology-serving both civilian and military functions. Ukrainian forces used Starlink to coordinate real-time drone surveillance and strikes, maintain encrypted battlefield communications, and improve situational awareness through live intelligence feeds. These capabilities significantly enhanced Ukraine's command-and-control (C2) operations and operational resilience under wartime conditions.

However, the blurred lines between civilian and military usage raised governance and accountability concerns. In 2023, media reports revealed that SpaceX had unilaterally restricted Starlink access in certain frontline areas, citing the desire to avoid escalation and direct involvement in combat operations. This incident highlighted the unprecedented influence private corporations now hold in geopolitical conflicts, where decisions made in corporate boardrooms can shape the course of warfare.

The Starlink case illustrates the complexity of dual-use governance in the new space economy. It raises critical questions about regulatory oversight, terms of use in conflict zones, and the limits of private-sector autonomy in domains once tightly controlled by nation-states. As commercial actors increasingly provide essential infrastructure for national security, the need for clear frameworks governing responsibility, neutrality, and access control in wartime becomes more urgent.

Case Study B: China's Orbital Logistics and the Tiangong Space Station

China's space program has undergone a profound transformation-shifting from technological catch-up to strategic leadership in key domains of orbital and deep-space operations. The successful deployment of the Tiangong Space Station ("Heavenly Palace")-a modular space station independently constructed and operated by China-marks a significant milestone in its ambition to become a dominant player in low-Earth orbit (LEO) and beyond.

Tiangong serves not only as a platform for scientific research and long-duration human spaceflight, but also as a symbol of technological sovereignty in an era where China is excluded from international collaborations like the International Space Station (ISS). This self-reliant infrastructure is complemented by China's rapidly advancing planetary exploration program, including the Chang'e lunar missions and the Tianwen-1 Mars mission-both signaling its long-term commitment to leading in cislunar space and interplanetary exploration.

China's Beidou Navigation Satellite System (BDS), a global alternative to the U.S.-operated Global Positioning System (GPS), further enhances its orbital logistics network. Beidou provides precise geolocation, timing, and navigation services, with applications ranging from military targeting to international trade and disaster response-positioning China as a provider of critical space services for the Global South.

Crucially, China's ambitions extend beyond technical capability to geopolitical reach. Its investments in launch and ground infrastructure across Africa and South America reflect a strategy of space diplomacy under the Belt and Road Initiative (BRI). Examples include deep-space tracking stations in Argentina and Namibia, which enable real-time communication with lunar and Martian missions while deepening bilateral cooperation with host nations.

Through these initiatives, China is embedding space infrastructure into a broader geopolitical vision-linking orbital logistics, regional influence, and technological independence. This integrated approach positions China as a counterweight to Western space leadership and reshapes the architecture of global space governance and access.

CHAPTER THIRTEEN

Digital Sovereignty and the Politics of Data

1. Introduction:

In the 21st century, data has become a cornerstone of geopolitical power, often compared to oil in the industrial era for its role in shaping economies, security systems, and global influence. From fueling artificial intelligence (AI) algorithms to enabling real-time surveillance, guiding targeted advertising, and powering smart infrastructure, data is now central to how states govern, compete, and project influence.

As digital technologies permeate every facet of modern life, control over data flows, storage infrastructure, cloud systems, and digital platforms is becoming a new arena of strategic competition. This has elevated debates around jurisdiction, ethical use, cross-border access, and data localization to the top of national policy agendas.

At the heart of this contest lies the concept of digital sovereignty-defined as the ability of a state or region to govern its digital infrastructure, protect its citizens' data, and assert regulatory authority over its information ecosystems. Unlike the earlier vision of a globally open and interoperable internet, today's digital landscape is increasingly fragmented. Nations are embracing data nationalism, motivated by concerns over cybersecurity threats, technological dependency on foreign platforms, and divergent cultural or legal norms regarding privacy, speech, and surveillance.

From Europe's General Data Protection Regulation (GDPR) and cloud sovereignty efforts, to China's Data Security Law and India's push for data localization, digital sovereignty is reshaping the global governance of the internet. It reflects a broader shift from treating data as a neutral commodity to recognizing it as a strategic asset intertwined with questions of power, autonomy, and governance.

2. Fragmenting the Internet:

The vision of a globally open, borderless internet is steadily giving way to a fragmented digital landscape, shaped by divergent regulatory models and competing geopolitical agendas. This trend-commonly referred to as the "Splinternet"-reflects the growing division of the internet into distinct digital blocs, each governed by its own legal frameworks, technological standards, and political ideologies.

The United States traditionally champions a market-driven, innovation-first approach to the internet, emphasizing minimal government interference and strong support for the private tech sector. However, this stance is evolving amid rising concerns over data privacy, platform accountability, foreign interference, and the unchecked power of Big Tech. Emerging legislation around antitrust, content moderation, and national security is slowly reshaping the American digital governance model.

The European Union promotes a rights-based digital order, rooted in the protection of user privacy, transparency, and competition. Through landmark regulations such as the General Data Protection Regulation (GDPR), the Digital Services Act (DSA), and the Digital Markets Act (DMA), the EU seeks to regulate platform behavior, curb monopolistic practices, and ensure responsible data handling. Brussels also aims to export its regulatory standards globally through normative power, influencing digital policies beyond its borders-a phenomenon known as the "Brussels Effect."

China represents the most comprehensive model of state-centric digital control. Its "cyber sovereignty" doctrine prioritizes data localization, real-name registration, censorship, and state control of internet infrastructure. Under laws such as the Data Security Law and Cybersecurity Law, China maintains strict oversight of both domestic and foreign tech platforms, advancing a model of digital authoritarianism that it promotes through partnerships within the Digital Silk Road.

Russia, Iran, and North Korea advocate for digital autarky, seeking to build sovereign internet infrastructures that can operate independently of the global web. These efforts include firewalls, localized domain name systems (DNS), and the development of national intranets to isolate content and limit external influence-often justified in terms of information security and cultural sovereignty.

This growing fragmentation is transforming the internet from a universal information commons into competing techno-political spheres, each reflecting the strategic priorities and values of its architects. As these digital blocs deepen, cross-border cooperation, interoperability, and shared norms are increasingly under strain-ushering in a new era of digital geopolitics.

3. The Sovereignty-Openness Paradox

In the digital age, states face a growing paradox: the pursuit of digital sovereignty-the ability to control data, infrastructure, and digital ecosystems within national borders-often comes at the expense of global openness, interoperability, and technological efficiency.

Governments justify increased control in the name of privacy protection, cybersecurity, economic security, and national sovereignty. One prominent mechanism is data localization-legal requirements mandating that data generated within a country be stored, processed, or mirrored locally. Countries such as India, Russia, and Brazil have introduced or proposed such measures, aiming to shield sensitive information from foreign surveillance and assert jurisdiction over digital platforms.

However, these policies have economic and technological trade-offs. Data localization can disrupt cloud-based services, complicate cross-border data flows, and hinder global value chains that depend on seamless digital connectivity. For businesses, it increases compliance costs, complicates data governance strategies, and may deter foreign investment due to regulatory uncertainty.

The push for sovereign control is also shaped by geopolitical events. The Snowden revelations in 2013 exposed the extent of foreign surveillance by U.S. intelligence agencies, prompting many nations to rethink their reliance on foreign-owned digital infrastructure. More recently, technology sanctions-such as U.S. restrictions on Chinese firms like Huawei-have further intensified concerns around technological dependency and vulnerability to foreign control.

As a result, strategic autonomy now extends beyond data to encompass the entire digital stack-from semiconductors and cloud servers to AI algorithms, software protocols, and coding standards. Countries are investing in domestic chip manufacturing, open-source alternatives, and national digital platforms to reduce exposure to external shocks and political leverage.

This tension between sovereign control and global openness defines the next phase of digital governance. Finding a balance that respects national interests without undermining the global internet's collaborative and innovative character remains a core challenge for policymakers worldwide.

4. Case Studies in Divergent Models

The global debate over data governance and digital sovereignty is reflected in two contrasting regulatory models-the European Union's rights-based framework and China's state-centric approach. Each represents a distinct vision for how data should be managed, regulated, and shared within and beyond borders.

The European Union's General Data Protection Regulation (GDPR) has become the global gold standard for privacy regulation. Enforced since 2018, GDPR is notable for its extraterritorial scope-meaning it applies to any organization, regardless of location, that processes data related to EU residents. It enshrines key principles such as data minimization, user consent, the right to be forgotten, and accountability of data controllers. GDPR's influence extends far beyond Europe, shaping laws like California's Consumer Privacy Act (CCPA) and Japan's Act on the Protection of Personal Information (APPI). However, GDPR also faces criticism for complex compliance requirements, heavy enforcement burdens on smaller businesses, and its potential to act as a barrier to digital market access, especially for non-European startups.

China's cyber-legal regime, by contrast, is built around state control, security, and data sovereignty. Through a series of laws-including the Cybersecurity Law (2017), Data Security Law (2021), and Personal Information Protection Law (PIPL, 2021)-China mandates data localization, security reviews for cross-border data transfers, and broad surveillance powers for regulators. These laws prioritize national security and social stability over individual privacy, aligning with China's broader governance philosophy. Furthermore, through initiatives like the Digital Silk Road-a component of the Belt and Road Initiative-China is actively exporting its digital governance model to developing countries in Asia, Africa, and Latin America. This includes offering infrastructure, training, and legal frameworks that promote a state-led approach to internet governance.

These case studies underscore the normative divergence in global digital governance. While the EU champions individual rights and global harmonization, China promotes state sovereignty and strategic control. As more countries choose between-or blend-these models, the future of the global digital order will be shaped by how these competing frameworks are adopted, adapted, or resisted.

5. Weaponization of Data in Geopolitical Rivalry

In the digital age, data and digital infrastructure have become central to great power competition, turning cyberspace into a new arena for strategic rivalry, economic coercion, and geopolitical influence. Far from being a neutral economic resource, data is now wielded as a tool of national power, used to advance security interests, shape alliances, and impose regulatory dominance.

The ongoing U.S.–China technology rivalry exemplifies the weaponization of digital ecosystems. Over the past few years, the United States has imposed a series of sanctions, export controls, and investment restrictions targeting key Chinese tech firms such as Huawei (telecommunications), ZTE (network equipment), ByteDance (parent of TikTok), and SMIC (semiconductor manufacturing). These actions are justified on grounds of national security, concerns over data surveillance, and fears of technological dependency, effectively curbing China's access to advanced chips, 5G components, and software systems.

In Europe, data governance tensions have surfaced through legal rulings such as Schrems II (2020), in which the European Court of Justice invalidated the EU-U.S. Privacy Shield framework. The decision was based on concerns over U.S. surveillance practices and the lack of adequate protections for European citizens' data when transferred across the Atlantic. This ruling has strained transatlantic digital cooperation and revealed the deeper incompatibility between privacy regimes and intelligence mandates.

In response to the fragmentation of global data norms, like-minded democracies have begun forming emerging data alliances. One example is the Cross-Border Privacy Rules (CBPR) Forum, led by countries such as the U.S., Japan, Canada, and South Korea. The initiative aims to harmonize privacy standards, facilitate secure data transfers, and build trust-based digital trade architectures among members who share democratic values and rule-of-law commitments.

These developments signal a clear shift: data is no longer just a commodity-it is a strategic asset, used to coerce rivals, fortify alliances, and export national governance models. In an increasingly fragmented digital world, the ability to shape data rules and infrastructure has become a defining feature of geopolitical leverage and digital sovereignty.

6. Governance Gridlock and Multilateral Gaps

Efforts to establish global frameworks for data governance have increasingly run into institutional inertia, normative divergence, and geopolitical fragmentation. Platforms such as the United Nations High-Level Panel on Digital Cooperation, the G20 digital economy tracks, and the OECD's data governance principles have proposed guidelines and norms, but have struggled to gain universal consensus or enforceable outcomes.

At the heart of this gridlock lies a profound lack of alignment on core digital values-including data privacy, platform accountability, surveillance practices, and cross-border data flows. Competing visions of the internet-ranging from open, rights-based models (as championed by the EU) to sovereign, state-centric frameworks (as promoted by China and Russia)-have made multilateral convergence increasingly difficult.

One illustrative yet stalled initiative is the proposed "Digital Geneva Convention", put forth by Microsoft and supported by various civil society actors. Intended to establish international norms for cyber warfare and data protection in conflict, the convention has gained symbolic traction but limited political momentum. The absence of binding commitments and lack of support from major state actors have rendered it largely aspirational.

These challenges are further complicated by global power asymmetries. Most of the world's dominant tech platforms and cloud providers-such as Google, Amazon, Meta, and Microsoft-are headquartered in the Global North, which gives these countries disproportionate influence over infrastructure, standard-setting, and norm development. In contrast, many nations in the Global South serve as data-rich but infrastructure-poor regions, contributing vast amounts of user data while lacking the regulatory, technological, and institutional capacity to shape global rules or demand equitable benefits.

This imbalance reinforces a "digital dependency trap", where developing countries must adopt foreign technologies and regulatory templates, often with limited sovereignty over their data ecosystems. Without meaningful representation in global standard-setting processes, the governance gap risks deepening, leaving large parts of the world vulnerable to digital exploitation, exclusion, and regulatory imposition.

Closing this gap will require inclusive multilateral mechanisms, capacity-building in the Global South, and a shift toward shared accountability in shaping a fair, secure, and interoperable global digital order.

7. Toward Pluralistic and Inclusive Digital Sovereignty

In an increasingly fragmented digital world, the idea of digital sovereignty can no longer be approached through rigid, uniform models. Rather than imposing a one-size-fits-all governance framework, the future of digital sovereignty may lie in pluralistic, layered, and interoperable systems that respect national agency while fostering global cooperation.

This pluralistic approach envisions a modular and flexible architecture of governance, where different actors and levels of engagement coexist and complement each other. Key components include:

Regional regulatory compacts: Initiatives like the European Union's digital strategy (including the GDPR, Digital Services Act, and Digital Markets Act) and ASEAN's digital frameworks are examples of region-specific governance models that promote data protection, digital trade facilitation, and platform accountability, while respecting regional values and economic priorities. These frameworks allow regional blocs to assert collective digital agency without total isolation from global norms.

Bilateral and trilateral interoperability accords: Countries are increasingly forming data transfer agreements and digital trade pacts-such as Japan–EU, U.S.–Japan–South Korea, or India–UAE–France digital trilaterals-to enable trusted cross-border data flows, cybersecurity collaboration, and regulatory alignment. These smaller-scale, plurilateral arrangements offer a pragmatic middle path in the absence of comprehensive global consensus.

Multi-stakeholder governance models: Inclusive digital sovereignty requires broad input from civil society, academia, technical communities, and the private sector. Multi-stakeholder engagement ensures that governance frameworks are not only state-centric but also ethically grounded, technologically sound, and socially accountable. Examples include the Internet Governance Forum (IGF) and the Global Digital Compact, which aim to democratize the rule-making process across diverse voices.

In this evolving ecosystem, digital sovereignty must be reimagined not as isolationist control, but as the empowerment of local actors to shape their digital futures within a cooperative and interconnected global order.

It should prioritize normative pluralism-the acceptance that different societies may define privacy, security, and data ownership in varied ways-while upholding core principles of transparency, fairness, and interoperability.

Ultimately, the path forward lies in embracing layered sovereignty-where national, regional, and global digital governance coexist, adapting to the realities of a multipolar digital landscape.

8. Conclusion:

The evolving discourse on digital sovereignty is more than a matter of data localization or tech regulation-it reflects a profound geopolitical contest over the values, norms, and institutions that will shape the future global digital order. As cyberspace becomes central to governance, commerce, defense, and identity, the stakes have risen far beyond infrastructure. What we are witnessing is a struggle over who gets to define the rules of engagement, whose values prevail in the design of algorithms, and which actors will hold norm-setting authority in the digital realm.

The fragmentation of cyberspace into competing regulatory ecosystems-the so-called Splinternet-has brought into focus divergent approaches to digital governance. Whether cyberspace evolves into a battleground of ideological control, marked by state surveillance and techno-nationalism, or a cooperative domain, governed by inclusive multilateralism and shared norms, will profoundly influence the nature of 21st-century geopolitics.

Navigating this transformation requires a delicate balance:

Cooperation without compromising autonomy: Nations must find ways to collaborate across borders on cybersecurity, digital trade, and internet governance, while maintaining strategic control over their digital infrastructure and protecting their citizens' rights.

Innovation without marginalization: Ensuring that technological advancement does not widen the gap between digital haves and have-nots-particularly across the Global South-will be essential to fostering a more equitable digital future.

Sovereignty without isolation: Digital sovereignty must not become an excuse for digital protectionism or censorship, but rather a framework for responsible self-determination that remains open to interoperability, pluralism, and shared values.

Ultimately, the politics of data will define not only who gains economic advantage, but also who sets the rules, controls the narratives, and wields influence over digital infrastructures that underpin modern life. The choices made today-by governments, corporations, civil society, and international institutions-will shape whether cyberspace serves as a platform for empowerment and collaboration, or a domain of division and dominance.

The path forward demands both vision and vigilance-to ensure that the digital future is not only powerful, but also inclusive, accountable, and just.

CHAPTER FOURTEEN

Global Health Geopolitics Post-COVID-19

1. Introduction: Health Security as National Security

The COVID-19 pandemic transformed global health from a humanitarian priority into a cornerstone of national security strategy. In an era of hyperconnectivity, infectious diseases are now seen as threats not just to individual lives but to the economic stability, political legitimacy, and strategic autonomy of nations. The crisis exposed fragile public health infrastructures, disrupted global supply chains, and fueled diplomatic tensions, elevating health security as a key domain in geopolitical calculus.

Health is no longer confined to the margins of global governance-it is now central to how nations project power, build alliances, and shape global norms.

- Vaccine Diplomacy and Strategic Competition
- The Geopolitics of Vaccine Distribution

Vaccines emerged as powerful tools of soft power during the COVID-19 pandemic, where states used medical aid not solely for public health, but to extend geopolitical influence. Countries with advanced biotech and pharmaceutical capabilities-most notably the United States, China, Russia, and India-converted vaccine production and distribution into instruments of strategic outreach, especially across the Global South.

China's "Health Silk Road": As part of its broader Belt and Road Initiative, China launched a health-focused diplomacy campaign. Through the large-scale delivery of Sinopharm and Sinovac vaccines, Beijing deepened its presence in Africa, Southeast Asia, and Latin America. This initiative complemented its "mask diplomacy" and aimed at shaping narratives around China as a benevolent global leader.

Russia's Use of Sputnik V: The Sputnik V vaccine became a key element of Moscow's foreign policy. Delivered to countries like Argentina, Iran, and Serbia, it served as a symbol of scientific prowess and diplomatic goodwill, especially where Western vaccines were delayed or politicized.

India's "**Vaccine Maitri**" and Domestic Vaccination Success

Launched in January 2021, "Vaccine Maitri" (Vaccine Friendship) marked India's bold pivot from pandemic responder to global health leader. Through this initiative, India supplied approximately 162.9 million doses to 96 countries by February 2022-around 14.3 million gifted outright, 107.1 million sold commercially, and 41.5 million channeled through the COVAX facility (en.wikipedia.org). Facing a severe domestic COVID wave in spring 2021, India suspended exports to prioritize local needs, underscoring the delicate balance between vaccine diplomacy and public health responsibility.

Concurrently, India orchestrated a monumental domestic vaccination campaign, reflecting both logistical prowess and community engagement. As of March 2023:

Over 2.20 billion total doses have been administered (en.wikipedia.org, dashboard.cowin.gov.in)

Fully vaccinated individuals (two doses) numbered 952 million, covering approximately 70% of India's population aged 12 and above (pmc.ncbi.nlm.nih.gov)

An additional 22.7 million booster doses have been distributed as of dashboard.cowin.gov.in.

By January 16, 2022, 93% of adults had received at least one shot, with 70% fully vaccinated (pmc.ncbi.nlm.nih.gov).

This achievement stemmed from a massive immunization infrastructure effort: the Co-WIN digital platform, extensive mobile vaccination clinics, and grassroots mobilization through Accredited Social Health Activists (ASHAs), particularly in remote regions like Uttarakhand, where 100% of eligible adults in some districts received their first dose by late 2021 (dashboard.cowin.gov.in)

This dual-track accomplishment-exporting millions of vaccine doses while simultaneously fully immunizing nearly the entire adult population-illustrates India's ability to leverage its pharmaceutical manufacturing strength. It also highlights the challenges of balancing global solidarity with national health security during a crisis, and affirming its role as both the "pharmacy of the world" and a country meeting the vaccination needs of its citizens.

This vaccine diplomacy not only shaped bilateral ties but also exposed fault lines in global health equity and governance. The World Health Organization's COVAX platform struggled to ensure equitable distribution, as wealthy nations secured doses through pre-purchase agreements, fueling accusations of "vaccine nationalism."

Case Study: COVAX and the Politics of Equity

The COVAX facility-a global vaccine-sharing initiative co-led by the World Health Organization (WHO), the Global Alliance for Vaccines and Immunization (Gavi), and the Coalition for Epidemic Preparedness Innovations (CEPI)-was established to ensure equitable access to COVID-19 vaccines across all countries, regardless of income level.

However, its founding principle of solidarity was soon tested by the rise of vaccine nationalism. High-income countries, prioritizing their domestic populations, pre-ordered and stockpiled large quantities of vaccines through advance purchase agreements (APAs) directly with pharmaceutical companies. This monopolized early supplies and left low- and middle-income countries (LMICs) dependent on delayed COVAX shipments.

Although COVAX eventually delivered over 1.8 billion doses globally, significant distribution delays and supply shortfalls meant many vulnerable nations faced extended pandemic waves without sufficient immunization. Countries in Sub-Saharan Africa and parts of Southeast Asia received vaccines months after richer countries had already launched booster campaigns.

This highlighted deep-rooted structural inequalities in global health governance, where decision-making power, production capacity, and intellectual property rights remain concentrated in the Global North. The COVAX experience exposed the limitations of voluntary multilateralism in the face of geopolitical self-interest, prompting renewed calls for a legally binding pandemic treaty and a more resilient, decentralized health infrastructure for future crises.

2. Global Institutions under Strain: WHO and Beyond

The COVID-19 pandemic significantly challenged the effectiveness and credibility of global health institutions, particularly the World Health Organization (WHO)-the UN's primary authority for international public health coordination.

Key Criticisms of WHO Performance:

Delayed response and transparency concerns: WHO was criticized for its slow initial response to the outbreak in Wuhan, China, and its reluctance to independently verify early outbreak data. This exposed the organization's structural dependence on member state disclosures under the International Health Regulations (IHR 2005), which lack enforceable compliance mechanisms.

Geopolitical vulnerability: WHO became a flashpoint in the U.S.–China rivalry, with former U.S. President Donald Trump suspending U.S. funding in 2020, accusing the organization of bias toward China. Although the Biden administration reinstated funding, the episode underscored the institution's political fragility in a multipolar world order.

Reform Proposals:

Reform discussions have focused on three main areas:

Independent investigative capacity: Enhancing WHO's authority to conduct on-the-ground verification missions without waiting for national consent could improve early outbreak response.

Financial independence: WHO relies heavily on voluntary contributions (over 80% of its budget), often earmarked for donor priorities. Diversifying and increasing assessed contributions (mandatory funding by member states) could boost impartiality and flexibility.

Governance reform: Improving transparency, accountability, and decision-making procedures has been advocated to ensure timely responses and depoliticize pandemic declarations and travel advisories.

Role of Other Institutions:

During the pandemic, other multilateral actors gained prominence:

The Global Fund to Fight AIDS, Tuberculosis, and Malaria expanded its mandate to assist in COVID-19 diagnostics, therapeutics, and health system strengthening.

The Coalition for Epidemic Preparedness Innovations (CEPI), launched in 2017, played a key role in funding early-stage vaccine development, particularly through the COVAX facility.

Gavi, the Vaccine Alliance, managed vaccine procurement and distribution in lower-income countries under COVAX, despite facing logistical and supply challenges.

Fragmented Coordination:

Despite the involvement of multiple agencies, the overall global response remained fragmented, revealing gaps in coordination, data-sharing, and equitable resource distribution. The Global Preparedness Monitoring Board (GPMB) warned in multiple reports that systemic reform is needed to avoid similar failures in future pandemics.

The pandemic thus underscored the urgent need for a reimagined global health architecture-one that balances state sovereignty with transnational responsiveness, integrates equity-focused financing, and is resilient to geopolitical shocks.

3. Health Security and Geostrategic Realignments

1. Health as a Foreign Policy Tool

The COVID-19 pandemic transformed health diplomacy from a niche concern into a key pillar of foreign and security policy. Major powers and regional blocs have integrated health cooperation into their broader geostrategic frameworks, using it to deepen alliances, expand influence, and build resilience.

United States: Under its Indo-Pacific Strategy, the U.S. has elevated health security as a regional priority. Through initiatives like the Global Health Security Agenda (GHSA) and the QUAD Vaccine Partnership, Washington aims to counterbalance China's influence while supporting disease surveillance, emergency preparedness, and vaccine distribution in Asia and the Pacific.

China: As part of its expanded Health Silk Road-a health-focused extension of the Belt and Road Initiative (BRI)-China has invested in building hospitals, training medical personnel, and supplying digital health platforms (such as AI-based diagnostics) across Asia, Africa, and Latin America. These efforts enhance China's soft power while embedding its health infrastructure into local systems.

African Union: In a landmark move toward health sovereignty, the African Union (AU) has prioritized regional vaccine production and regulatory capacity. The creation of the African Medicines Agency (AMA) in 2021 marks a critical step toward harmonizing pharmaceutical regulations across Africa, reducing dependence on external suppliers, and strengthening continental response capabilities.

Broader Strategic Impacts:

Health partnerships are now embedded in regional integration agendas, trade negotiations, and security dialogues. For example:

EU–Africa health pacts include provisions for pharmaceutical manufacturing and workforce development.

ASEAN has adopted pandemic response protocols as part of its regional security frameworks.

Health diplomacy is increasingly featured in free trade agreements (e.g., IP rules for vaccines) and bilateral summits.

This growing intersection of health and geopolitics underscores that global health security is no longer just a humanitarian concern-it is a lever of strategic realignment and diplomatic capital.

2. India's G20 Presidency and Global Health Diplomacy

India's presidency of the G20 in 2023 marked a significant moment in the evolution of global health governance, particularly in the post-COVID-19 landscape. Drawing on its successful domestic vaccine production and global outreach during the pandemic, India used its leadership role to push for a more inclusive, resilient, and equitable Global Health Architecture. This strategic pivot positioned India not just as a stakeholder but as a normative leader in shaping future health diplomacy.

A. Global Digital Health Initiative (GDHI):

One of the flagship proposals during India's presidency was the Global Digital Health Initiative, aimed at leveraging India's experience with platforms like CoWIN (COVID Vaccine Intelligence Network) and Ayushman Bharat Digital Mission (ABDM). The GDHI called for:

Interoperable digital health systems across the G20 and partner countries.

Secure health data sharing protocols respecting digital sovereignty.

Promotion of open-source health tech platforms for disease surveillance, vaccine delivery, and telemedicine.

India's emphasis on Digital Public Infrastructure (DPI) was central to this vision. Drawing parallels with its success in financial inclusion through the India Stack, India proposed a similar stack for digital health services, designed to be scalable, affordable, and customizable for use across the Global South.

B. Decentralized Vaccine Production in the Global South:

India advocated for regional vaccine manufacturing hubs, particularly in Africa, Latin America, and Southeast Asia. This push stemmed from its pandemic-era experience as the "pharmacy of the world," supplying vaccines to over 90 countries under the Vaccine Maitri initiative.

Key elements of the proposal included:

Technology transfer and IP sharing, especially for mRNA platforms.

Investment in cold-chain logistics and regulatory harmonization.

Encouraging public-private partnerships (PPPs) to boost local production.

This vision was aligned with broader calls for health sovereignty in the Global South and addressed concerns raised during the COVAX shortfalls and vaccine inequity during the early waves of COVID-19.

C. Inclusive and Equitable Health Systems:

India's G20 agenda emphasized "One Earth, One Health", a holistic view that connects human health with environmental sustainability and socio-economic equity. In line with this theme, India promoted:

Resilient primary healthcare systems are accessible to marginalized communities.

Investments in pandemic preparedness and emergency response mechanisms.

Mainstreaming traditional systems of medicine, such as Ayurveda, through global dialogues on integrative health.

By doing so, India positioned itself as a bridge between the Global North and Global South, promoting models that respect local contexts while adhering to global standards.

D. Elevating the Global South's Voice in Health Diplomacy:

India invited countries like Egypt, Nigeria, and Bangladesh to the G20 Health Working Group discussions-amplifying Global South perspectives on vaccine equity, financing, and health data governance. It also backed the African Union's membership in the G20, marking a step toward democratizing global health decision-making.

India's stance was rooted in strategic pluralism-resisting Western monopolization of health norms while avoiding full alignment with authoritarian health models (e.g., China's surveillance-heavy health systems).

Conclusion: India's Norm-Setting Role

India's G20 presidency became a defining moment for global health diplomacy. By fusing technological innovation, developmental pragmatism, and normative leadership, India reshaped key conversations on digital health, vaccine equity, and inclusive governance. Rather than merely responding to global health trends, India actively influenced their direction, positioning itself as a credible, compassionate, and capable architect of a post-pandemic global order.

4. The Weaponization of Health and Biosecurity Risks

The COVID-19 pandemic elevated global attention toward the weaponization of health and emerging biosecurity threats, redefining how states perceive and prepare for future biological crises.

A. Biosecurity and Bioweapon Concerns:

The outbreak renewed fears of biological warfare, particularly amid speculative claims about a lab-origin theory in Wuhan. Though unproven, such claims strained diplomatic ties between China and Western powers, leading to heightened scrutiny of global biosafety protocols.

Many governments now view dual-use biological research-scientific work that could be repurposed for harmful outcomes-as a potential national security threat. Technologies like CRISPR-Cas9 gene editing, while revolutionary for medicine, also pose risks of misuse in developing genetically modified pathogens.

B. Intelligence and Pathogen Surveillance:

National intelligence agencies and defence departments across the U.S., China, the EU, and India have integrated bio-surveillance into their strategic frameworks. This includes monitoring:

Zoonotic spillover events (where diseases jump from animals to humans),

Synthetic biology advances, and

Gain-of-function research, which alters viruses to study transmissibility or virulence.

Agencies like the U.S. National Center for Medical Intelligence (NCMI) and equivalents in other major powers now classify emerging pathogens under non-traditional security threats.

C. Cyberbiosecurity and Hybrid Threats:

The pandemic also exposed vulnerabilities in health infrastructure through cyberattacks. Hospitals, pharmaceutical firms, and vaccine research institutions faced ransomware attacks, data breaches, and intellectual property theft. For example, multiple Western intelligence reports accused state-linked hackers of targeting vaccine developers like Pfizer and Moderna.

This convergence of biological and cyber threats-termed cyberbiosecurity-highlights the need for integrated protection of digital and biomedical systems, especially as health technologies become increasingly data-dependent.

D. Defence and Strategic Doctrines:

In response, countries have formally incorporated biosecurity into national defence strategies. The U.S. National Defense Authorization Act (NDAA), China's Biosecurity Law (2021), and India's growing investments in bio-defence preparedness reflect this strategic shift.

Militaries are now training for CBRN (Chemical, Biological, Radiological, and Nuclear) scenarios with health-specific protocols, and several nations are developing strategic stockpiles of vaccines, PPE, and diagnostics for future pandemics.

Conclusion:

The pandemic transformed health from a sectoral concern into a core element of national and global security. As biological and digital domains converge, the line between natural health emergencies and weaponized threats becomes increasingly blurred, necessitating cross-sectoral, transnational approaches to bio-preparedness, ethics, and governance.

5. Governance Gaps and the Future of Global Health Cooperation

The COVID-19 pandemic exposed critical governance deficits in the global health architecture, prompting widespread calls for a comprehensive and enforceable pandemic treaty. However, progress has been slow and contentious due to diverging national interests and institutional limitations.

A. Sovereignty vs. Global Health Security:

At the heart of negotiations lies the tension between national sovereignty-a state's right to independently manage its affairs-and the need for binding global obligations to ensure pandemic preparedness. Many nations remain reluctant to cede decision-making authority to international institutions, even in the face of global health threats.

This has led to disputes over the scope of a future treaty-.whether it should impose legally binding protocols on outbreak reporting, information sharing, and emergency response coordination under the World Health Organization (WHO).

B. Transparent Early Warning and Surveillance Mechanisms:

The absence of effective, independent early warning systems was a major shortfall during COVID-19. Current frameworks rely heavily on self-reporting by states, which may delay or obscure the real-time sharing of critical health data.

Reform efforts emphasize the need for transparent biosurveillance systems, potentially modeled on climate monitoring frameworks, with authority granted to multilateral institutions to conduct field investigations without state approval during global health emergencies.

C. Equitable Access to Health Technologies:

A cornerstone of future cooperation is the guarantee of equitable access to vaccines, diagnostics, and therapeutics-collectively referred to as "medical countermeasures"-during health crises. COVID-19 highlighted disparities, where high-income countries hoarded doses while many low- and middle-income countries were left behind.

Proposals for technology transfer mechanisms, waivers on intellectual property (IP) rights (such as under the WTO's TRIPS Agreement), and the regional manufacturing of vaccines aim to address these inequities, but remain politically divisive.

D. Regulation of Dual-Use Biological Research:

Another challenge is regulating dual-use research of concern (DURC)-scientific studies intended for public health benefit but that could be repurposed for bioterrorism or biological warfare. There are no globally harmonized guidelines on gain-of-function (GOF) research or synthetic biology, both of which raise risks if misused.

The proposed treaty seeks to incorporate bioethics protocols, transparency requirements, and oversight mechanisms to manage DURC responsibly, but countries differ on enforcement and disclosure thresholds.

E. Pandemic Fund and Institutional Innovations:

The creation of the Pandemic Fund-launched in 2022 under the World Bank and endorsed by the G20-is a step toward sustainable financing for pandemic prevention, preparedness, and response (PPR). It supports countries in building resilient health systems, expanding surveillance infrastructure, and training health workforces.

However, without inclusive governance structures, equitable funding distribution, and accountability mechanisms, the fund risks becoming a symbolic gesture rather than a transformative tool.

Conclusion:

To build a resilient global health order, the world must move beyond voluntary frameworks and develop binding, inclusive, and enforceable norms. The challenge lies in reconciling state autonomy with the collective action imperative of pandemic security. Whether the world learns from the COVID-19 crisis-or repeats its mistakes-will depend on how these governance gaps are addressed in the years ahead.

6. Conclusion: Health as a Core Pillar of Geopolitical Stability

The COVID-19 pandemic has fundamentally reshaped the global understanding of health, not merely as a technical or humanitarian concern, but as a strategic variable in international relations. Health security now intersects with critical domains such as national defence, economic sustainability, technological sovereignty, and global diplomacy. In this transformed landscape, the capacity to prevent, detect, and respond to health threats has become a core metric of state capability and global influence.

From Reactive to Strategic: Health in Foreign Policy

Where once health featured peripherally in diplomatic agendas, it is now a geopolitical currency. Nations that demonstrated agility in managing the pandemic, through vaccine development, resilient supply chains, or global health outreach, enhanced their soft power, legitimacy, and bilateral leverage. Initiatives like vaccine diplomacy, health infrastructure investments, and digital health platforms have become tools of strategic engagement, especially across the Global South.

India's leadership through the Global Digital Health Initiative, China's Health Silk Road, and U.S. involvement in ACT-Accelerator partnerships demonstrate how health is being woven into the fabric of international cooperation and competition alike.

Health as a Driver of Economic and Technological Competitiveness

Beyond crisis response, health systems are increasingly tied to economic performance and technological innovation. The pandemic accelerated investment in biotechnology, telemedicine, digital health records, and AI-driven diagnostics-sectors poised to shape the future global economy. Countries that lead in health innovation ecosystems will not only safeguard their populations but also command emerging markets and influence international standards.

Moreover, resilient health infrastructure is now a prerequisite for uninterrupted global trade, tourism, and mobility, making health a cross-cutting enabler of economic globalization.

The Imperative for Reforming Global Health Governance

Despite the urgency, current global health institutions remain fragmented, underfunded, and politically constrained. The World Health Organization (WHO), though central to coordination, lacks enforcement powers and financial independence. Mechanisms like COVAX revealed structural inequities and exposed the limitations of voluntary frameworks in crisis conditions.

To safeguard against future pandemics, the global community must co-create a robust multilateral framework built on:

Binding commitments to transparency and data sharing

Equitable access to medical countermeasures

Oversight of dual-use biomedical research

Sustainable financing for low- and middle-income countries

Inclusive governance that empowers the Global South

The Risk of Geopolitical Fragmentation

If these challenges go unaddressed, future health emergencies may not unite the world, but divide it further. Vaccine nationalism, intellectual property barriers, and surveillance disputes could widen North-South inequities and erode trust in multilateralism. Health could become a vector of geopolitical fragmentation, mirroring trends seen in AI, cyber governance, and climate diplomacy.

Health as Existential Diplomacy

Ultimately, building a resilient, inclusive, and accountable global health order is not just about disease control-it is about future-proofing the international system. The next pandemic, bioterrorism event, or antimicrobial resistance crisis could test the very fabric of global cooperation. In that context, health governance becomes an existential imperative, akin to climate security and nuclear non-proliferation.

A world that fails to embed health solidarity into the architecture of global governance risks repeating the catastrophic missteps of the COVID-19 era. But a world that succeeds may not only prevent pandemics, but also chart a more cooperative, equitable, and secure geopolitical future.

Key References:

Kickbusch, I. (2021). The Geopolitics of Global Health. Lancet Global Health.

WHO. (2021). Independent Panel for Pandemic Preparedness and Response: COVID-19 Make it the Last Pandemic.

Katz, R. (2019). Pandemic Preparedness and the Politics of Global Health Security. Journal of Global Health.

United Nations. (2022). Our Common Agenda: Health for All.

Fidler, D. (2020). The Return of Health as Geopolitics. Council on Foreign Relations.

CHAPTER FIFTEEN

Maritime Geopolitics and the Blue Economy

1. Introduction: Oceans as Strategic Space

Throughout history, maritime domains have been central to global power projection-whether through colonial expansion, naval supremacy, or dominance over critical sea trade routes. In today's geopolitical landscape, the oceans are once again emerging as pivotal arenas of competition and cooperation. Regions like the South China Sea, known for its contested territorial claims, and the Arctic, now increasingly accessible due to climate change, exemplify how maritime frontiers are becoming flashpoints of strategic interest.

A crucial new dimension is the rise of the Blue Economy-a concept that refers to the sustainable use of ocean resources for economic growth, improved livelihoods, and jobs, while preserving the health of ocean ecosystems. This framework links economic ambition with ecological responsibility and is now influencing national strategies and international policies alike.

Modern maritime geopolitics goes beyond traditional naval security. Oceans today are vital for energy exploration (e.g., offshore oil and gas), food security (through fisheries and aquaculture), digital infrastructure (via undersea data cables), and global logistics (with over 90% of trade moving through maritime routes). They also serve as strategic buffers and defense zones, especially in an era of expanding great power rivalries.

Thus, the seas are no longer just spaces of commerce or conflict-they are critical theatres where national interests, regional influence, environmental sustainability, and global security intersect. As countries increasingly turn seaward for economic and strategic leverage, the maritime domain is being redefined as both a resource base and a geopolitical battleground of the 21st century.

2. South China Sea: Geopolitical Flashpoint

The South China Sea is one of the world's most contested and strategically vital maritime regions. China asserts sweeping sovereignty over nearly the entire sea using its controversial "Nine-Dash Line"-a demarcation first published in 1947 that overlaps with the exclusive economic zones (EEZs) of several Southeast Asian nations, including the Philippines, Vietnam, Malaysia, Brunei, and Taiwan.

At the heart of the conflict are high-stakes interests:

Maritime trade: Over $3.4 trillion in global commerce transits this sea annually, making it a vital artery of international shipping.

Energy resources: The region holds significant untapped oil and natural gas reserves, especially around the Spratly and Paracel Islands, attracting competition over future energy security.

Fisheries: Home to rich fishing grounds, the South China Sea supports the livelihoods of millions across coastal Southeast Asia.

Military-strategic control: Dominance over this waterway ensures influence across the Indo-Pacific, a region increasingly central to global geopolitics.

China has intensified its presence through land reclamation and militarization of disputed features-transforming reefs like Fiery Cross Reef and Subi Reef into fortified outposts equipped with runways, missile systems, and radar installations. These actions have provoked regional tension and led to Freedom of Navigation Operations (FONOPs) by powers like the United States, Australia, and Japan, aimed at challenging China's expansive maritime claims.

A landmark legal decision in 2016 by the Permanent Court of Arbitration (PCA) in The Hague ruled in favor of the Philippines (Philippines v. China), stating that China's nine-dash claims had no legal basis under the United Nations Convention on the Law of the Sea (UNCLOS). However, China rejected the ruling and has continued its activities unabated-illustrating how power politics can override international legal norms in today's maritime disputes.

The South China Sea thus stands as a symbol of 21st-century maritime geopolitics-where legal rulings, environmental concerns, economic interests, and military strategy collide in a contested space with global implications.

2.2 The Arctic: The New Maritime Frontier

Accelerated climate change is dramatically transforming the Arctic-melting long-standing sea ice and unlocking previously inaccessible maritime routes and natural resources. Chief among these emerging pathways is the Northern Sea Route (NSR), a shipping lane along Russia's Arctic coast that significantly shortens transit time between Europe and Asia compared to traditional routes like the Suez Canal.

This environmental shift is reshaping the Arctic into a strategic geopolitical corridor, leading to renewed interest and competition among regional and global powers.

Key developments include:

Russia's Arctic Militarization: As the country with the largest Arctic coastline, Russia has taken the lead in asserting control by establishing new military bases, radar installations, and airstrips, alongside operating the world's largest fleet of nuclear-powered icebreakers. These efforts are aimed at securing its energy assets and asserting sovereignty over the Northern Sea Route, which Moscow treats as internal waters.

China's "Near-Arctic State" Strategy: Although geographically distant, China has declared itself a "Near-Arctic State" to justify its inclusion in Arctic affairs. Through its Polar Silk Road initiative, China is investing in Arctic infrastructure, scientific research, and joint ventures in mining, energy, and port development-especially in Iceland, Greenland, and Russia's Yamal LNG project.

NATO's Strategic Reorientation: In response to increased Russian and Chinese presence, NATO has intensified its focus on the "High North"-a term referring to the Arctic regions of Northern Europe. Member states, including the U.S., Norway, and Canada, have ramped up naval patrols, joint exercises, and surveillance to ensure freedom of navigation and deter potential militarization.

While the United Nations Convention on the Law of the Sea (UNCLOS) provides a legal framework for maritime rights and continental shelf claims, the Arctic presents unique challenges. Multiple countries-Russia, Canada, Denmark (via Greenland), and Norway-have submitted overlapping claims to extend their exclusive economic zones (EEZs) based on seabed geology. However, the absence of a dedicated Arctic governance body akin to an Arctic Treaty leaves room for strategic ambiguity and future conflict.

In sum, the Arctic is no longer just a frozen wilderness-it is rapidly emerging as a new frontier of geopolitical competition, where environmental change intersects with military buildup, energy security, and global trade realignments.

3. Maritime Connectivity and Indo-Pacific Realignments

The Indo-Pacific region has become the strategic heart of 21st-century maritime geopolitics. Encompassing the Indian and Pacific Oceans, this vast zone is central to global trade, energy flows, and great power competition-particularly between the U.S.-led rules-based maritime order and China's expanding strategic presence through the Belt and Road Initiative (BRI).

At the forefront of democratic cooperation is the Quadrilateral Security Dialogue (QUAD), comprising the United States, India, Japan, and Australia. The QUAD promotes a free, open, and inclusive Indo-Pacific by focusing on maritime domain awareness, joint naval drills like Exercise Malabar, humanitarian assistance, and the protection of undersea data cables, which form the backbone of global internet and financial systems.

India, as a rising maritime power, has advanced its regional vision through the SAGAR doctrine-"Security and Growth for All in the Region." This framework emphasizes inclusive development, maritime stability, and cooperative engagement with littoral states. New Delhi's strategic port investments, such as Chabahar Port in Iran (linking India to Afghanistan and Central Asia) and Sittwe Port in Myanmar (under the Kaladan project), reflect its bid to strengthen regional connectivity and naval access.

In contrast, China's "String of Pearls" strategy involves a series of civilian and dual-use port developments across the Indian Ocean Region (IOR)-notably in Gwadar (Pakistan), Hambantota (Sri Lanka), Djibouti, and Kyaukpyu (Myanmar). These maritime nodes provide logistical depth, refueling stations, and potential military utility, enabling the People's Liberation Army Navy (PLAN) to sustain longer deployments and safeguard its energy corridors.

The competition intensifies around Sea Lines of Communication (SLOCs)-critical maritime chokepoints such as the Strait of Malacca, Bab el-Mandeb, and the Suez Canal. These narrow waterways are vital for the movement of oil, goods, and data, and have become flashpoints in the strategic calculus of global powers seeking to ensure uninterrupted access and influence.

In essence, the Indo-Pacific is not just a geographic space-it is a geopolitical construct where connectivity, competition, and cooperation converge, redefining maritime power and shaping the contours of a new global order.

4. Blue Economy and Maritime Sustainability

4.1 The Promise and Perils of the Blue Economy

The Blue Economy refers to the sustainable use of oceanic resources to drive economic growth, improve livelihoods, and ensure environmental health. Globally valued at over $3 trillion annually, it spans a diverse array of sectors that balance development with ecological responsibility.

Key sectors include:

Sustainable fisheries and aquaculture: These support global food security and employ millions, particularly in coastal and island economies. However, overfishing and illegal, unreported, and unregulated (IUU) fishing are depleting critical fish stocks.

Offshore renewable energy: Technologies like wind turbines, tidal generators, and wave energy systems are rapidly expanding, offering low-carbon alternatives to fossil fuels and helping meet climate targets.

Marine biotechnology: The exploration of marine genetic resources for pharmaceuticals, enzymes, and biofuels is a growing field with vast potential, especially in sectors like health and industrial production.

Eco-tourism and ocean-based carbon capture: Ocean-friendly tourism promotes economic sustainability and conservation awareness, while innovations in blue carbon (e.g., mangroves, seagrass beds) help sequester atmospheric CO_2 , playing a role in climate mitigation.

Yet, the Blue Economy is not without risk:

Overexploitation of marine life endangers biodiversity and disrupts ecosystems, undermining long-term food supply chains.

Marine pollution, especially from plastic waste, chemical runoff, and oil spills, poses serious threats to ocean health, impacting marine species and coastal communities alike.

The rise of seabed mining-targeting minerals like cobalt, nickel, and rare earths from ocean floors-raises alarms over the irreversible ecological damage it could inflict on fragile deep-sea environments due to limited regulation and scientific understanding.

The United Nations Sustainable Development Goal (SDG) 14: Life Below Water calls for the conservation and sustainable use of oceans, seas, and marine resources. However, enforcement remains weak, with fragmented governance, limited international coordination, and inadequate monitoring systems.

In sum, the Blue Economy holds immense promise, but realizing its full potential requires robust policy frameworks, global cooperation, and a commitment to balancing economic ambition with environmental stewardship.

4.2 Seychelles as a Model Blue Economy State

The Seychelles, a small island developing state (SIDS) in the Indian Ocean, has emerged as a global exemplar of sustainable ocean governance. Despite its limited military and economic clout, Seychelles has become a "norm entrepreneur"-a country that champions new ideas and practices on the international stage-especially in the realm of the Blue Economy.

Key innovations include:

Blue Bond Initiative: In 2018, Seychelles issued the world's first sovereign Blue Bond-a financial instrument designed to raise capital for marine conservation and sustainable fisheries. Backed by the World Bank and the Global Environment Facility, it raised $15 million to support marine projects while promoting economic resilience.

Marine Protected Areas (MPAs): Seychelles has designated over 30% of its Exclusive Economic Zone (EEZ)-an area spanning 1.4 million square kilometers-as MPAs, safeguarding coral reefs, fish habitats, and biodiversity while enabling controlled eco-tourism and research.

International Partnerships: The country has successfully partnered with global NGOs, such as The Nature Conservancy, and multilateral institutions like the World Bank, to implement innovative tools such as debt-for-nature swaps. In such arrangements, part of the national debt is restructured or forgiven in exchange for commitments to environmental protection.

Seychelles' leadership illustrates how small island states, often at the frontline of climate vulnerability and ocean degradation, can exercise moral authority and diplomatic creativity to influence global norms around ocean governance and sustainable development.

In essence, Seychelles demonstrates that marine sustainability and economic innovation are not just the purview of large powers-even microstates can lead in shaping the future of the Blue Economy.

5. Maritime Law, Governance, and Power Asymmetries

The United Nations Convention on the Law of the Sea (UNCLOS), adopted in 1982, serves as the foundational legal framework for global maritime governance. Often referred to as the "constitution of the oceans," UNCLOS regulates sovereign rights, freedom of navigation, resource access, and dispute resolution mechanisms in maritime zones.

Key provisions include:

Territorial Sea: Extends 12 nautical miles from a country's coastline, granting it full sovereignty-similar to its land territory-over airspace, waters, and seabed.

Exclusive Economic Zone (EEZ): Extends 200 nautical miles from the baseline, giving the coastal state special rights to explore, exploit, conserve, and manage natural resources-from fisheries to offshore oil.

High Seas and Freedom of Navigation: Beyond national jurisdictions, UNCLOS safeguards the rights of all states-especially for commercial shipping and military passage-in international waters.

Despite its wide acceptance, power asymmetries distort its application:

United States: While it follows UNCLOS principles as customary international law, the U.S. has not ratified the treaty, limiting its ability to formally influence interpretation or partake in certain dispute forums.

China: A party to UNCLOS, China has been criticized for selective interpretation-notably in the South China Sea, where it asserts historic claims that conflict with UNCLOS-based rulings, such as the 2016 Permanent Court of Arbitration decision in favor of the Philippines.

Enforcement Challenges: Bodies like the International Tribunal for the Law of the Sea (ITLOS) and UNCLOS arbitration panels offer legal recourse but lack binding enforcement authority. Compliance is often contingent on political will, rendering decisions difficult to implement against major powers.

Moreover, the current legal framework is ill-equipped to address emerging threats, including:

Climate-related disputes (e.g., sea-level rise affecting maritime boundaries).

Non-state actors such as piracy networks, maritime militias, and private security contractors.

Technological shifts, including undersea data cables, autonomous vessels, and seabed mining, which fall into legal grey zones.

As maritime disputes intensify and ocean governance becomes more complex, there is growing consensus on the need for updated, inclusive, and enforceable legal frameworks that reflect 21st-century realities.

6. Conclusion: Oceans as Arenas of Convergence and Contestation

In today's shifting geopolitical landscape, the oceans are no longer passive highways of commerce-they have become dynamic spaces of strategic competition, environmental urgency, and multilateral cooperation. Maritime domains now intersect hard security concerns (such as naval rivalries and military posturing), economic priorities (like trade and resource extraction), and climate-related vulnerabilities (rising sea levels, ecosystem degradation).

Modern maritime geopolitics weaves together multiple threads:

Naval security and deterrence in contested waters like the South China Sea or the Arctic.

Ecological sustainability through the promotion of the Blue Economy, which balances economic use with conservation.

Legal frameworks, particularly the United Nations Convention on the Law of the Sea (UNCLOS), that attempt to codify rights, responsibilities, and dispute resolution mechanisms among states.

To safeguard the maritime commons-shared ocean spaces beyond any single nation's jurisdiction-21st-century governance must be proactive and integrated. This entails:

Establishing crisis-management and naval de-escalation mechanisms in maritime flashpoints to avoid miscalculation and unintended conflict.

Accelerating investments in sustainable Blue Economy models, particularly for small island developing states (SIDS) and coastal economies reliant on ocean-based livelihoods.

Building inclusive and adaptive maritime governance regimes that reconcile national sovereignty with global environmental stewardship-ensuring equitable access, ecosystem protection, and rule-based conduct.

Left unmanaged, the maritime domain risks becoming a fragmented space of zero-sum rivalries and environmental collapse. But if governed wisely, the oceans can be a platform for cooperation, driving economic inclusion, ecological resilience, and strategic stability for generations to come.

Key References:

- United Nations Convention on the Law of the Sea (UNCLOS), 1982.
- Chatham House (2021). *Maritime Security and the Future of the Indo-Pacific.*
- European Union Institute for Security Studies (2020). *Blue Economy and Geopolitical Rivalry.*
- World Bank. (2017). *The Potential of the Blue Economy.*
- Scott, D. (2018). *The Indo-Pacific in U.S. Grand Strategy: Changing Geopolitical Settings.* Journal of Maritime Affairs.

CHAPTER SIXTEEN

Religion, Ideology, and Civilizational Politics

1. Introduction: Faith, Identity, and Power in Global Affairs

Despite earlier assumptions that modernization and secularization would marginalize religion in global affairs, the 21st century has instead witnessed the resurgence of religious, ideological, and civilizational identities as powerful forces in international politics. Far from being relegated to the private sphere, religion now actively shapes statecraft, diplomacy, national identity, and political legitimacy.

Religious and ideological factors are visible across multiple domains:

In state policy, where governments adopt theocratic laws, invoke majoritarian religious narratives, or forge alliances based on shared faith, as seen in the Iran–Saudi rivalry or evangelical influence in U.S. foreign policy.

In transnational movements, where actors like ISIS, the Muslim Brotherhood, or Christian Zionist networks operate across borders with ideological coherence that often bypasses traditional state structures.

In populist politics, where leaders mobilize support by appealing to religious nationalism, such as Hindutva in India, Buddhist majoritarianism in Myanmar, or Orthodox-Christian identity in Russia.

This chapter investigates how religious belief systems, civilizational narratives, and ideological frameworks function not only as tools of soft power but also as strategic levers in conflict, diplomacy, and national image-building.

It also revisits Samuel Huntington's "Clash of Civilizations" thesis, not as an absolute prediction, but as a provocative lens through which to examine current global tensions. Huntington argued that future conflicts would be driven less by ideology or economics and more by cultural and civilizational divides. While widely debated, this framework continues to influence how policymakers and scholars interpret geopolitical fault lines-especially along religio-cultural boundaries such as Islam vs. the West, China's Confucian revival, or Orthodox Eurasianism.

Ultimately, this chapter highlights that in a multipolar and identity-conscious world, faith and ideology are not relics of the past, but active agents of power, resistance, and transformation in global affairs.

2. Religion and the Nation-State: Strategic Alignments

2.1 Political Islam and Transnational Networks

Since the late 20th century, Islam has become a central force in geopolitical strategy, particularly through its integration with statecraft, ideological outreach, and transnational activism. This trend, often referred to as Political Islam, involves the instrumental use of Islamic identity and religious legitimacy to shape foreign policy, regional alliances, and domestic governance.

Key players within the Muslim world have developed distinct models of Islamic influence, leading to both ideological divergence and strategic rivalry:

Iran promotes a Shia Islamist model, rooted in the 1979 Iranian Revolution, which fused theocracy with anti-imperialist ideology. Tehran projects its influence across the region by supporting Shia militias and proxy groups-notably Hezbollah in Lebanon, Hashd al-Shaabi in Iraq, and the Houthis in Yemen. This "Axis of Resistance" frames itself as opposing Western interventionism and Israeli expansionism, using religion to legitimize geopolitical posture.

Turkey, under President Recep Tayyip Erdoğan, has embraced a form of Sunni Islamist populism, intertwined with neo-Ottomanism-a vision that seeks to revive Turkey's leadership in the Muslim world by invoking the cultural and political legacy of the Ottoman Empire. Through political Islam, soft power (e.g., religious education, media), and regional assertiveness (e.g., involvement in Syria, Libya, and the Caucasus), Turkey positions itself as a civilizational bridge and Sunni leader.

Saudi Arabia, custodian of Islam's two holiest cities-Mecca and Medina, wields immense religio-political influence. Through the global export of Wahhabi doctrine and its strategic deployment of petrodollars, Riyadh has shaped Islamic discourse from Pakistan to North Africa, funding religious institutions, media networks, and charitable fronts. The kingdom also leverages its religious status to maintain leadership within institutions like the Organisation of Islamic Cooperation (OIC).

These competing visions of Islamic authority-Shia revolutionary Islam (Iran), Sunni political Islam (Turkey), and Wahhabi conservatism (Saudi Arabia)-have produced significant intra-Islamic contestation. Their rivalry plays out across proxy wars, media narratives, and diplomatic alignments, particularly in volatile regions like the Middle East, North Africa, and South Asia.

Thus, Political Islam today is not a monolith, but a geopolitical mosaic-where religious identity serves as both a unifying force and a source of sectarian and strategic fragmentation on the global stage.

2.2 Christian Nationalism and Western Conservatism

In the contemporary West, Christian nationalism has re-emerged as a potent force, shaping populist movements, identity-based politics, and foreign policy agendas. Rooted in the belief that national identity is intrinsically linked to a particular Christian heritage, this trend merges religious symbolism with political ideology, particularly in the United States, Russia, and parts of Eastern and Central Europe.

In Russia, President Vladimir Putin has positioned the Russian Orthodox Church as a pillar of national identity and geopolitical legitimacy. This alignment forms part of a broader Orthodox civilizational narrative-framing Russia as the spiritual heir to "Holy Rus," an idea that sacralizes Russian control over regions like Ukraine, Belarus, and Crimea. By casting Russia as a guardian of traditional Christian values in contrast to Western secular liberalism, the Kremlin justifies both its neo-imperial ambitions and its cultural confrontation with the West.

In the United States, evangelical Christian communities have become a powerful political bloc, especially within the Republican Party. This base has significantly influenced foreign policy positions-such as unwavering support for Israel, opposition to global climate agreements perceived as anti-growth, and advocacy against reproductive rights and gender equality policies at international forums like the United Nations. These stances are often justified through biblical prophecy, moral absolutism, or the notion of American exceptionalism rooted in a divine mandate.

In both contexts, Christian identity is weaponized not just for domestic political consolidation, but to reshape global alignments. Whether through anti-globalist rhetoric in Europe, anti-LGBTQ+ legislation in Hungary and Poland, or resistance to liberal international norms, Christian nationalism reflects a broader backlash against secular cosmopolitanism, reinforcing cultural sovereignty as a strategic posture.

Thus, the fusion of faith and conservatism in Western geopolitics is not simply ideological-it is strategic, offering both a domestic rallying point and a framework for global differentiation and power assertion.

3. Civilizational Politics: Between Cultural Pride and Geostrategic Rivalry

3.1 The Huntington Thesis Revisited

In his influential work The Clash of Civilizations (1996), Samuel Huntington argued that future global conflicts would stem not from ideological or economic rivalries, but from deep-rooted cultural and religious divides among major "civilizations." These included the Western, Islamic, Sinic (Chinese), Hindu, Orthodox, African, and Latin American worlds. His thesis sparked intense debate, with critics warning against civilizational essentialism and the oversimplification of identity.

Yet, in today's multipolar landscape, elements of Huntington's framework continue to echo:

China has increasingly portrayed itself as a Sinic civilization, rooted in Confucian ethics, Han cultural identity, and a modernized Communist political system. Under Xi Jinping, Beijing promotes "discourse power"—a strategy to challenge Western liberal norms and assert a distinct Chinese worldview through institutions like the Belt and Road Initiative, the Global Civilization Initiative, and Confucius Institutes worldwide.

India, under the Bharatiya Janata Party (BJP), has blended realpolitik with civilizational diplomacy. Its foreign policy increasingly references Hindu cultural heritage, drawing upon Vedic philosophy, Indic knowledge systems, and civilizational exceptionalism. This "civilizational state" framing reinforces narratives of cultural sovereignty, especially in response to Western critiques on human rights, secularism, or caste.

In parts of the Islamic world, there is a growing emphasis on ummatic identity-the notion of a unified Muslim community (ummah) that transcends the Westphalian state system. This sentiment often underpins pan-Islamic solidarity movements in defense of causes like Palestine, Kashmir, or global Islamophobia, and influences the foreign policy discourse of states such as Turkey, Iran, Pakistan, and Malaysia.

These civilizational postures increasingly shape:

Domestic policies, such as cultural education, religious law, or censorship.

Diaspora politics, where national and civilizational loyalties intertwine across borders.

Regional alignments, as states form partnerships not only based on interest, but shared cultural-historical identities.

While Huntington's binary framing often overlooks intra-civilizational conflicts and hybrid identities, the strategic invocation of civilizational narratives in global affairs today suggests that culture and identity are no longer peripheral-they are core drivers of geopolitical imagination and alignment.

4. Case Studies in Civilizational Geopolitics

Case Study A: India's Cultural Diplomacy and Strategic Hindutva

India's global engagement has increasingly drawn on civilizational soft power-leveraging its ancient cultural heritage to promote a distinct identity on the world stage. Initiatives like International Yoga Day, Sanskrit language promotion, Ayurveda diplomacy, and spiritual tourism position India as a spiritual superpower, rooted in Hindu philosophical traditions.

Concurrently, under the leadership of the Bharatiya Janata Party (BJP), India's domestic and foreign policy narratives have moved toward a Hindutva-centric worldview. Hindutva-an ideology asserting that India's national identity is fundamentally Hindu-reimagines the Indian polity as a "civilizational state" rather than a secular, pluralist democracy. This shift influences internal policies such as:

The Citizenship Amendment Act (CAA) and National Register of Citizens (NRC).

Debates on minority rights, particularly affecting Muslims and Christians.

Recasting history and education through a Hindu nationalist lens.

On the international front, this identity politics affects India's diplomatic calculus-leading to selective solidarity with Islamic countries (e.g., UAE and Saudi Arabia), cautious engagement with the Western liberal order, and strategic cultivation of the Hindu diaspora, particularly in the United States,

UK, and Canada. The result is a dual-track diplomacy: combining inclusive cultural outreach with majoritarian ideological assertiveness.

Case Study B: China's Sinocentric Soft Power

China's global narrative is increasingly framed through the lens of civilizational revivalism, emphasizing its 5,000-year-old heritage as a source of legitimacy and moral leadership. This Sinocentric worldview is embedded in initiatives such as:

Confucius Institutes, which promote Chinese language and Confucian ethics as a counterbalance to Western liberal education.

The Belt and Road Initiative (BRI), framed not just as infrastructure investment but as a modern "Silk Road of cooperation" rooted in historical connectivity and civilizational harmony.

Traditional Chinese Medicine (TCM) diplomacy and cultural exchanges that reinforce China's narrative of holistic, indigenous wisdom.

President Xi Jinping's "China Dream" encapsulates this vision-promising the "great rejuvenation of the Chinese nation", the restoration of civilizational dignity, and resistance to Western hegemony. In this narrative, China is not merely rising-it is returning to its rightful place as the moral and cultural center of global order.

However, this identity-driven soft power frequently clashes with Western liberal values, especially in:

Xinjiang (Uighur rights and re-education camps).

Hong Kong (autonomy and democratic freedoms).

The South China Sea (territorial sovereignty and international law).

In these flashpoints, civilizational rhetoric is used to justify domestic control and reject foreign criticism as cultural imperialism. Thus, China's soft power is deeply intertwined with strategic narrative-building, aimed at constructing a post-Western global order centered on authoritarian modernity and civilizational pride.

5. Religion in Conflict and Peacebuilding

Religion often plays a dual role in global affairs-while it can intensify ethno-political divisions and justify violence, it also serves as a powerful instrument for diplomacy, reconciliation, and peacebuilding.

The Holy See (Vatican) exemplifies the role of religious diplomacy. As a sovereign entity and spiritual authority, it conducts quiet, behind-the-scenes mediation, such as its pivotal role in facilitating the Cuba–U.S.

rapprochement (2014) and efforts to mediate in conflicts across Central Africa. The Vatican's moral credibility and global Catholic network allow it to act as a neutral intermediary in otherwise intractable conflicts.

Faith-based NGOs-such as World Vision (Christian), Islamic Relief (Muslim), and Caritas (Catholic)-operate on the frontlines of humanitarian assistance. These organizations often enjoy local trust and cultural legitimacy, enabling them to deliver aid, support post-conflict trauma healing, and mediate between warring communities in regions where secular or foreign actors may lack influence.

Interfaith dialogue platforms, such as the United Nations Alliance of Civilizations (UNAOC), promote cross-religious understanding, counter-extremism, and confidence-building between diverse groups. These forums create diplomatic spaces where religious leaders, civil society, and state actors can address shared concerns-from hate speech to minority rights-in a spirit of pluralism and mutual respect.

These initiatives underscore religion's ambivalence but enduring relevance: it can both fuel sectarianism and forge peace, depending on how it is mobilized. When leveraged constructively, religious institutions and belief systems offer unique pathways to healing, solidarity, and long-term conflict transformation, especially in divided or post-war societies.

6. Conclusion: Faith, Identity, and Global Strategy

The re-emergence of religion and civilizational identity as central pillars of international relations challenges the secular assumptions that have historically guided diplomacy, development, and international law. Far from fading in the modern era, religion now functions as a source of ideology, cultural authority, and institutional influence, shaping everything from foreign policy alignments to public diplomacy narratives.

In today's global order, religion manifests in multiple dimensions:

As identity, it reinforces national belonging and distinguishes civilizational blocs.

As ideology, it legitimizes state policies, resistance movements, or geopolitical ambitions.

As institutional power, it drives transnational networks, influences diaspora communities, and interfaces with global governance bodies.

Understanding religious and civilizational politics requires recognizing their dual nature-capable of fueling sectarian divisions, culture wars, and geopolitical rivalry, but also of enabling dialogue, peacemaking, and moral leadership.

Crucially, strategic cultures-the enduring ways in which states perceive and pursue power-are not only built on military capabilities or economic interests, but are deeply informed by:

Spiritual histories (e.g., religious narratives embedded in national myths).

Sacred geographies (e.g., contested holy sites, pilgrimage routes).

Moral imaginaries (e.g., visions of justice, salvation, or divine mission).

In this evolving landscape, engaging with religion not as a relic, but as a strategic variable, is essential for interpreting contemporary geopolitics and designing more inclusive, culturally attuned frameworks for conflict resolution, diplomacy, and global cooperation.

Key References:

Huntington, S. (1996). The Clash of Civilizations and the Remaking of World Order.

Juergensmeyer, M. (2019). Terror in the Mind of God: The Global Rise of Religious Violence.

Mandaville, P. (2022). Islam and Politics.

Snyder, T. (2018). The Road to Unfreedom: Russia, Europe, America.

Fox, J. (2007). Religion and International Relations Theory. Oxford University Press.

CHAPTER SEVENTEEN

Strategic Culture and National Identity in Foreign Policy

1. Introduction: Beyond Rational Choice in International Relations

Mainstream theories in international relations-such as realism, liberalism, and neoliberal institutionalism-have traditionally explained state behavior through the lenses of rational choice, material self-interest, and the balance of power. While analytically useful, these approaches often neglect the ideational dimensions that shape how states interpret their environment, define threats, and pursue goals.

This is where the concept of strategic culture becomes essential. Unlike models that assume states act purely on cost-benefit calculations, strategic culture emphasizes the influence of:

Collective historical memory (e.g., traumas, victories, colonial experiences),

National identity narratives (e.g., exceptionalism, victimhood, civilizational pride),

Institutional habits and military traditions, and

Enduring belief systems and cultural norms.

These elements are not simply rhetorical-they inform perception, guide threat assessments, and shape foreign policy doctrines over time. Strategic culture thus operates as a cognitive framework through which states understand the world and react to it, often unconsciously and across generations.

This chapter explores how strategic culture and national identity interact to shape geopolitical behavior. Through comparative case studies-such as the U.S. doctrine of exceptionalism, Russia's Orthodox-Eurasian worldview, or China's Confucian-Communist synthesis-we analyze how different nations' foreign policies are rooted as much in cultural memory and civilizational outlooks as in realpolitik considerations.

By moving beyond rationalist paradigms, this inquiry offers a more holistic and historically grounded understanding of international relations-where ideas, identities, and strategic narratives matter as much as capabilities and alliances.

2. Defining Strategic Culture

2.1 Origins and Theoretical Foundations

The concept of strategic culture emerged during the Cold War, as scholars sought to explain why the United States and the Soviet Union-despite possessing similar nuclear capabilities-exhibited distinct strategic preferences, particularly in their doctrines of deterrence and use of force.

One of the earliest articulations came from Jack Snyder (1977), who argued that the Soviet Union's nuclear posture could not be fully understood through rational actor models alone. He introduced the idea that deep-seated historical experiences, ideological values, and cultural norms shaped how nations interpret and respond to threats. Later scholars like Colin Gray, Ken Booth, and Alastair Iain Johnston further developed the concept, linking it to security studies, political psychology, and constructivist IR theory.

Strategic culture refers to the enduring set of beliefs, assumptions, traditions, and symbolic narratives that guide a nation's approach to security and statecraft. It influences how states:

Perceive threats and adversaries,

Define strategic interests, and

Choose military or diplomatic tools.

Key components of strategic culture include:

Civilizational legacy and national myths: Foundational stories of origin, trauma, or triumph-such as China's "Century of Humiliation," the U.S. belief in manifest destiny, or Russia's historical experience with encirclement—help shape national worldview.

Political ideology and regime type: Whether a state is democratic, authoritarian, theocratic, or hybrid affects how it balances civil liberties, security, and power projection.

Civil-military relations and doctrinal preferences: The structure of military institutions, their relationship with political leadership, and favored military doctrines (e.g., offensive realism vs. strategic restraint) all reflect cultural orientations toward war and peace.

Societal attitudes toward risk, force, and morality in war: Public perceptions of military sacrifice, just war principles, and acceptable levels of civilian casualties play a crucial role in legitimizing-or constraining-strategic behavior.

Rather than being fixed, strategic culture evolves gradually, shaped by historical turning points, leadership change, and generational memory. However, its influence remains long-term and path-dependent, making it a vital lens for understanding the distinct strategic identities of states.

2.2 Intersection with National Identity

National identity refers to the collective understanding a nation holds about its history, values, purpose, and place in the international system. This identity acts as a psychological and cultural lens through which states interpret global events, construct their interests, and legitimize strategic decisions.

National identity can manifest in different postures:

Defensive (victimhood): Nations that emphasize a legacy of colonization, invasion, or marginalization-such as China's "Century of Humiliation" or post-World War II Germany-often pursue non-expansionist, stability-seeking strategies or, conversely, use historical grievance to justify assertiveness.

Assertive (exceptionalism): Countries like the United States often view themselves as morally unique and globally destined to lead or democratize, which supports interventionist foreign policies and expansive security doctrines.

Restorative (revanchism): States like Russia or Turkey invoke historical grandeur or lost territories, seeking to revive civilizational status or regain influence in former imperial zones-a mindset often linked to revisionist geopolitics.

In this context, strategic culture serves as the operational expression of national identity-it translates abstract self-perceptions into tangible security policies, military doctrines, and diplomatic behavior. For example:

A nation with a victimhood identity may prioritize territorial integrity, build defensive alliances, and emphasize sovereignty norms.

An exceptionalist identity may lead to doctrines promoting unilateralism, humanitarian intervention, or global norm-setting.

A revanchist identity may manifest in territorial claims, military modernization, and a rejection of international constraints.

Thus, strategic culture and national identity are not separate phenomena-they are mutually reinforcing constructs. Identity gives strategic culture its emotional and symbolic depth, while strategic culture institutionalizes identity into long-term policy habits and security behavior.

3. Comparative Case Studies of Strategic Culture

Case Study A: The United States – Exceptionalism and Forward Engagement

The strategic culture of the United States is deeply rooted in a narrative of moral exceptionalism-the belief that the U.S. has a unique responsibility and capacity to lead the world toward democracy, liberalism, and global stability. This worldview stems from formative historical experiences, including:

Victories in World Wars I and II, which positioned the U.S. as the savior of the free world,

The Cold War triumph over the Soviet Union, reinforcing the binary of freedom vs. authoritarianism, and

The post-9/11 global security posture, which amplified a pre-emptive doctrine underpinned by homeland security concerns.

Key features of U.S. strategic culture include:

Pre-emption over reaction: Rather than waiting for threats to materialize, the U.S. often pursues preventive or anticipatory action, as seen in the Bush Doctrine and interventions in Iraq and Afghanistan. This reflects a belief in shaping, rather than adapting to, the global order.

Power projection through global alliances: The U.S. maintains a vast network of military bases, defense partnerships, and multilateral security alliances (e.g., NATO, AUKUS, QUAD), enabling it to sustain a forward presence in nearly every region of the world.

Missionary approach to liberal internationalism: From the Marshall Plan to democracy promotion efforts, the U.S. frequently aligns its strategic interests with a normative agenda, framing interventions as acts of global public good.

Even during moments of strategic retrenchment-as witnessed under the Trump administration's "America First" policy-the underlying cultural expectation of U.S. global leadership remains strong within both the foreign policy establishment and popular imagination.

Thus, American strategic culture blends military primacy, ideological conviction, and a civilizational narrative of global stewardship-making it one of the most proactive and enduringly influential strategic cultures in the international system

Case Study B: Russia – Fortress Mentality and Strategic Depth

Russia's strategic culture is profoundly shaped by its historical experience of repeated invasions-from the Mongol yoke, to Napoleon's march on Moscow, to Hitler's Operation Barbarossa. These events embedded a deep-seated "fortress mentality"-a perception of encirclement and vulnerability that prioritizes defensive buffers and territorial depth.

The collapse of the Soviet Union in 1991 intensified this cultural psychology, leading to a post-imperial identity crisis. Under President Vladimir Putin, Russia has reconstituted its strategic culture around a blend of:

Neo-imperial nostalgia-celebrating the Soviet and Tsarist legacies,

Orthodox civilizational identity-positioning Russia as the Third Rome and protector of Slavic and Christian values, and

Great power revanchism-challenging the U.S.-led unipolar order and reclaiming influence in its "near abroad."

Key features of Russian strategic culture include:

Fear of NATO encroachment: The eastward expansion of NATO is viewed not as benign enlargement but as an existential threat. This drives Russia's efforts to militarize border regions, form counter-blocs (e.g., CSTO, BRICS), and assert a sphere of influence in Eastern Europe and Central Asia.

Hybrid warfare doctrine: Russia employs non-linear strategies that combine cyberattacks, disinformation, proxy militias, and conventional force-as seen in Georgia (2008), Crimea (2014), and the ongoing war in Ukraine. These methods reflect a preference for asymmetric tools that exploit ambiguity and undermine Western cohesion.

Valorization of sacrifice and resistance: Russian national narratives glorify heroism, suffering, and military endurance-especially during the Great Patriotic War (World War II). This ethos justifies high tolerance for prolonged conflict and strategic attrition, bolstering domestic support for military campaigns framed as defensive or sacred missions.

In this context, Russia's strategic culture is not only a security doctrine but a geopolitical worldview-anchored in historical grievance, civilizational exceptionalism, and a restorative agenda. It legitimizes aggressive revisionism under the guise of protecting identity, restoring balance, and defending sovereignty against perceived Western intrusion

Case Study C: China – Middle Kingdom Legacy and Strategic Patience

China's strategic culture is rooted in the dual influences of Confucian thought and the historical legacy of imperial decline and foreign subjugation, particularly during the "Century of Humiliation" (mid-19th to mid-20th century). These foundational experiences shape a worldview defined by caution, dignity, and long-term national rejuvenation.

At the core lies the "Middle Kingdom" mentality-a civilizational self-perception that sees China as the natural center of regional, if not global, order. This legacy informs its strategic patience, subtle assertiveness, and gradual accumulation of influence rather than abrupt confrontation.

Key elements of China's strategic culture include:

Preference for long-term strategic planning: Guided by Confucian emphasis on stability, harmony, and hierarchy, China adopts a cumulative approach to power-prioritizing economic statecraft, institutional engagement, and incremental military modernization. Its grand strategies, such as the Belt and Road Initiative (BRI), are designed to expand influence across decades, not election cycles.

Emphasis on asymmetric and psychological warfare: Drawing from Sun Tzu's principles of deception and indirect force, China favors tools like cyber operations, influence campaigns, grey-zone tactics, and legal warfare ("lawfare"). These methods seek to undermine adversaries' will and cohesion without direct confrontation.

Centrality of sovereignty and non-interference: Shaped by memories of colonial-era foreign incursions, China is deeply sensitive to territorial integrity. Issues such as Taiwan, Xinjiang, and the South China Sea are framed not as foreign policy matters, but as core national interests tied to historical injustice and internal unity.

China's global posture-exemplified by the BRI, the militarization of the South China Sea, and diplomatic firmness on Taiwan-is thus not necessarily about imperial expansion, but about restoring historical status, achieving developmental security, and asserting civilizational sovereignty.

In this framework, strategic culture acts as both a temporal lens and behavioral compass-guiding China's patient but resolute ascent, while avoiding the pitfalls of direct conflict unless core interests are threatened.

Case Study D: India – Strategic Ambiguity and Civilizational Continuity

India's strategic culture is shaped by a complex interplay of postcolonial sensitivities, civilizational consciousness, and a historical commitment to non-alignment and strategic autonomy. Drawing from its ancient philosophical traditions (e.g., Kautilya's Arthashastra, Gandhian ethics), as well as its experience of colonial subjugation, India's approach to geopolitics has traditionally been marked by caution, restraint, and flexibility.

At the core is the idea of "strategic ambiguity"-a deliberate posture that allows India to navigate major power rivalries without being bound by rigid alliances, while preserving decision-making independence in times of crisis.

Key elements of India's strategic culture include:

Strategic autonomy over alliance entanglements: Since the Nehruvian era, India has avoided joining military blocs like NATO or becoming a client state of any superpower. Instead, it promotes multi-alignment-simultaneously engaging with the U.S., Russia, France, Japan, and others, while advancing national interest on a case-by-case basis.

Ambiguity in nuclear doctrine and foreign alignment: India's nuclear policy, articulated in its "No First Use" (NFU) doctrine, reflects a desire for moral restraint combined with credible minimum deterrence. In foreign policy, it avoids overt bandwagoning-whether in the U.S.-China rivalry, or on contentious issues like Russia–Ukraine, maintaining a principled, interest-based stance.

Soft power as a strategic tool: India leverages its diaspora networks, cultural diplomacy (e.g., International Yoga Day), spiritual traditions, and educational exchanges to shape perceptions and build goodwill globally. This approach underscores the civilizational continuity that connects India's ancient past with its global aspirations.

In recent years, especially after the 1998 nuclear tests and under the leadership of the Bharatiya Janata Party (BJP), India's strategic culture has become more assertive. Themes of Hindu civilizational pride, calls for Atmanirbharta (self-reliance), and increased emphasis on maritime power and Indo-Pacific partnerships (e.g., QUAD, SAGAR doctrine) signal a shift toward a more proactive and security-conscious posture.

Yet, even within this evolution, India continues to balance realpolitik with values-driven diplomacy, retaining its identity as a civilizational state that seeks global leadership through pluralism, dialogue, and strategic independence.

4. Strategic Culture in Practice: Defence and Diplomacy

Strategic culture shapes how states conceive and implement their security and foreign policy choices, going beyond abstract doctrines to influence the operational structure of militaries, diplomatic alignments, and crisis behavior.

Rather than being uniform, strategic responses are filtered through deep-rooted historical experiences, institutional habits, and threat perceptions, resulting in varied state behavior-even under comparable circumstances.

Key domains where strategic culture manifests include:

Force structure and military modernization: A state's investment in specific military capabilities often reflects its strategic worldview. For instance, China prioritizes cyber warfare, anti-access/area denial (A2/AD) systems, and ballistic missile development over traditional blue-water naval supremacy, indicating a continental defense mindset focused on regional dominance and deterrence.

Military doctrines and operational principles: National doctrines often encode historical memory and existential priorities. Israel's Begin Doctrine, which endorses preemptive strikes against potential nuclear threats, exemplifies a survivalist strategic culture shaped by regional hostility and the trauma of past wars.

Alliances and security arrangements: Strategic culture also dictates how and why states form alliances. Japan's pacifist orientation, rooted in its post-World War II constitution, leads to a defensive military posture and a reliance on the U.S.-Japan security alliance for extended deterrence-reflecting a culture of demilitarization and normative restraint.

Crisis management and escalation behavior: States with revanchist or assertive strategic cultures-such as Russia or Turkey-are more inclined toward escalation, unilateral action, or hybrid tactics in regional disputes, whereas others with status quo or institutionalist cultures (e.g., Canada, Germany) may prioritize mediation, multilateralism, and rules-based diplomacy.

Ultimately, understanding strategic culture is essential for anticipating state behavior, avoiding strategic miscalculations, and designing more effective deterrence, engagement, and conflict prevention strategies. It explains why similar threats elicit different responses and why diplomacy often fails when cultural assumptions are misread or ignored.

5. Critiques and Evolving Paradigms

While strategic culture offers valuable insights into a nation's geopolitical behavior, it is not without limitations. Scholars and analysts have raised several critiques regarding its analytical scope and methodological application:

Risk of cultural determinism: Strategic culture can sometimes overemphasize historical and ideational continuity, leading to the assumption that a state's behavior is unchangeable or preordained by its past. This risks downplaying the role of contemporary material factors, such as economic constraints, technological innovations, or shifting power dynamics.

Assumption of homogeneity: The framework often treats states as monolithic actors, ignoring internal pluralism, elite competition, or regime transitions. For instance, democratic turnovers or authoritarian leadership shifts can significantly alter a country's strategic priorities, challenging the notion of a singular cultural trajectory.

Retrospective rationalization: There is a tendency for strategic culture analyses to become post-facto narratives-explaining actions after they occur rather than offering predictive power. This weakens its empirical robustness unless paired with forward-looking indicators and comparative analysis.

However, when integrated with broader international relations theories-such as:

Realism (emphasizing power, security, and state interest), or

Constructivism (highlighting identity, norms, and ideational factors),

-strategic culture serves as a contextual and path-dependent lens, explaining why states define threats and opportunities differently, even within similar structural conditions.

Moreover, strategic culture is not static. It evolves through:

Globalization and digital communication: Exposure to transnational discourses, diaspora networks, and real-time information ecosystems reshapes national narratives and influences policymaking.

Changing regimes and leadership styles: Strategic preferences often shift with new administrations, ideological agendas, or external shocks (e.g., wars, economic crises, pandemics).

Institutional learning and adaptation: States can recalibrate their strategic identities through military reform, diplomatic reorientation, or normative shifts, leading to hybrid or transitional cultures over time.

Thus, while critiques are valid, strategic culture remains a vital interpretive tool when used dynamically-anchored in history but responsive to change.

6. Conclusion: Identity as a Strategic Asset and Risk

Strategic culture and national identity are dynamic constructs, shaped by a nation's historical traumas, civilizational narratives, leadership transitions, and external shocks such as wars, economic crises, or technological revolutions. Far from being fixed, they evolve over time-yet they remain deeply embedded in how states perceive threats, define interests, and prioritize responses.

These ideational frameworks are more than background context-they are strategic assets that inform a state's diplomatic posture, defence planning, and alliance behavior. At the same time, they can become strategic liabilities when they breed exceptionalism, revanchism, or misperceptions that drive conflict escalation.

Understanding strategic culture enables:

Predictive insight: By analyzing a state's worldview, historical memory, and security ethos, analysts can better anticipate how it might behave in a crisis or interpret external actions.

Empathetic engagement: In a fragmented and multipolar international system, grasping the cultural and identity-driven motivations behind state behavior is crucial for designing credible deterrents, sustainable alliances, and constructive diplomacy.

In a world increasingly shaped by asymmetric threats, normative contestations, and civilizational reassertions, the study of strategic culture offers a bridge between material capabilities and symbolic meaning-helping to decode why states act not just as rational actors, but as storied communities with distinct strategic logics.

For policymakers, ignoring these deeper currents risks strategic miscalculation. For peacemakers, engaging them thoughtfully can be the key to preventing conflict and fostering enduring cooperation.

Key References:

Snyder, J. (1977). The Soviet Strategic Culture: Implications for Limited Nuclear Options. RAND.

Gray, C. (1999). Modern Strategy. Oxford University Press.

Johnston, A. I. (1995). Cultural Realism: Strategic Culture and Grand Strategy in Chinese History. Princeton University Press.

Mahbubani, K. (2019). Has the West Lost It?.

Katzenstein, P. (Ed.). (1996). The Culture of National Security: Norms and Identity in World Politics.

CHAPTER EIGHTEEN

The Global South and the Quest for Strategic Autonomy

1. Introduction: Reimagining Agency in a Multipolar World

The emergence of the Global South-encompassing nations across Africa, Latin America, South Asia, and Southeast Asia-marks a transformative shift in global geopolitics. Historically positioned as aid recipients, developmental peripheries, or arenas of Cold War proxy conflict, these countries are now reasserting themselves as sovereign actors with strategic agency.

In the context of a declining unipolar order and the fragmentation of global hegemony, states of the Global South are no longer content with binary alignments between major powers such as the United States and China. Instead, they are pursuing strategic autonomy-a foreign policy orientation that emphasizes self-determined interests, non-alignment, and issue-based coalitions.

This new posture is visible in three critical ways:

Agenda-setting: Whether in climate negotiations, trade reform, or vaccine equity, Global South nations are pushing to reshape multilateral forums like the WTO, UN, G20, and BRICS+ from within.

Norm entrepreneurship: These countries advocate for inclusive global norms around sovereignty, development finance, digital governance, and resource justice, often diverging from both Western liberal and authoritarian models.

Coalition-building: Through South-South cooperation, platforms like the Non-Aligned Movement, and new multilateral groups such as IBSA or the African Union, these states are forming horizontal partnerships that reflect pluralism, not bloc politics.

Ultimately, the Global South's pursuit of strategic autonomy represents a reimagining of global governance-centered not just on power-balancing, but on equity, mutual respect, and diversified diplomacy in a truly multipolar world.

2. Historical Foundations: From Bandung to BRICS

2.1 Bandung and the Non-Aligned Movement

The 1955 Bandung Conference marked a pivotal moment in postcolonial geopolitics, where leaders from 29 Asian and African nations gathered to assert their political independence and collective agency during the Cold War. This summit laid the groundwork for the Non-Aligned Movement (NAM), which formally emerged in 1961 as a coalition rejecting alignment with either the U.S.-led capitalist bloc or the Soviet communist bloc.

Rooted in principles of sovereignty, anti-colonialism, non-intervention, and South-South cooperation, NAM became the moral and diplomatic voice of the Third World. Although its political influence declined after the collapse of bipolarity in 1991, its ideological legacy-emphasizing strategic autonomy, global equity, and decolonial solidarity-continues to shape the foreign policy of many Global South nations today.

2.2 BRICS and the Rise of Plurilateralism

The formation of BRICS in 2009 (initially as BRIC, with South Africa joining in 2010) reflects a modern iteration of Global South cooperation-one focused not only on diplomacy but on institution-building and economic governance reform. Unlike NAM's normative orientation, BRICS emphasizes plurilateralism-collaboration among a select group of emerging powers to influence global institutions without forming rigid alliances.

Key initiatives include:

The New Development Bank (NDB): A multilateral bank designed to fund infrastructure and sustainable development projects in emerging and developing economies, providing an alternative to the World Bank.

The Contingent Reserve Arrangement (CRA): A financial safety net to offer liquidity support to member states during balance-of-payments crises, countering reliance on the International Monetary Fund (IMF).

Advocacy for UN Security Council (UNSC) reform and enhanced Global South representation in Bretton Woods institutions (IMF and World Bank), challenging the Western-centric structure of global decision-making.

Together, Bandung and BRICS underscore the continuity and evolution of Global South efforts to reclaim voice and agency in world affairs-shifting from ideological non-alignment to pragmatic multilateralism and institutional autonomy within a multipolar order.

3. Strategic Autonomy in Action: Case Studies

India's Balancing Act

Under the decisive leadership of Prime Minister Narendra Modi and the strategic stewardship of External Affairs Minister Dr. S. Jaishankar, India has redefined strategic autonomy not as neutrality, but as purposeful, self-confident engagement with the world on its own terms. India's foreign policy today reflects a blend of principled realism, developmental ambition, and civilizational self-assurance, making it a pivotal player in a multipolar global order.

Key dimensions of this reoriented global posture include:

Multi-alignment with Strategic Clarity: India has deepened its role in the QUAD, actively contributing to a shared vision of a free and open Indo-Pacific, while simultaneously safeguarding its longstanding defence and energy ties with Russia. Despite Western pressure during the Russia–Ukraine conflict, India under Modi held firm on an interest-based neutrality, with Jaishankar articulating India's position globally: "Europe's problems are not the world's problems." This rhetorical clarity has reinforced India's image as a sovereign decision-maker, immune to bloc politics.

Global South Advocacy at the G20 Presidency (2023): India's G20 presidency, championed by Modi as a "People's Presidency," placed the Global South at the center of global governance. India led calls for debt restructuring, climate justice, and the global scaling of Digital Public Infrastructure (DPI)-drawing from its domestic success with Aadhaar, UPI, and CoWIN. Jaishankar's diplomatic engagements ensured India emerged as both a voice and a bridge between developed and developing economies.

Shaping a Multipolar Asia in Response to China: Confronting Chinese assertiveness, particularly after the Galwan Valley clash, India has sharpened its Indo-Pacific strategy. Modi's government has strengthened ties with ASEAN, Japan, Australia, and Gulf nations, while initiating new formations like I2U2 (India-Israel-UAE-USA). India's Indo-Pacific Oceans Initiative and Act East Policy signal a vision of Asian multipolarity where no single power dominates-a doctrine repeatedly emphasized in Jaishankar's speeches at global forums.

Together, Modi's visionary diplomacy and Jaishankar's intellectual and strategic precision have elevated India's global standing. They have demonstrated that strategic autonomy in the 21st century is not passive non-alignment, but assertive, agenda-setting leadership-rooted in civilizational confidence, national interest, and a commitment to a fairer global order.

African Agency and Continental Diplomacy

In the evolving multipolar order, Africa is no longer a passive periphery-it is emerging as a cohesive geopolitical actor, exercising continental agency through institutions like the African Union (AU) and landmark initiatives such as the African Continental Free Trade Area (AfCFTA). These frameworks signal a pan-African shift toward economic integration, diplomatic self-determination, and a reimagining of Africa's global role.

Key expressions of this growing strategic confidence include:

Institutional Assertiveness: The African Union, representing 55 member states, has become a central platform for articulating collective African priorities-from climate finance and vaccine equity to digital transformation and peacebuilding. The AfCFTA, launched in 2021, is one of the world's largest free trade zones by participating countries and aims to boost intra-African trade, industrialize economies, and reduce external dependency.

Diplomatic Leadership in Conflict Mediation: Nations like South Africa, Nigeria, Kenya, and Ethiopia frequently play mediation roles in regional crises, including in Sudan, the Sahel, and the Horn of Africa. These efforts reflect the continent's evolving capacity for regional security governance and homegrown conflict resolution mechanisms, diminishing reliance on external peacekeepers.

Global Representation and Normative Confidence: African leaders are increasingly vocal about reforming global governance structures. The African Union's permanent membership in the G20 (2023) and calls for permanent African representation on the UN Security Council (UNSC) reflect rising normative confidence-grounded in demands for equity, historical redress, and shared sovereignty in global rule-making.

Recalibrating Relations with China and Beyond: While China remains a major investor through its Belt and Road Initiative, African governments are increasingly renegotiating loan terms, demanding technology transfer, and seeking economic diversification beyond Sino-centric dependencies. This reflects a broader diplomatic shift toward multi-alignment, engaging partners from India, the EU, Turkey, and the Gulf to maximize strategic leverage.

Africa's diplomatic evolution represents not just continental consolidation but a global repositioning-from a site of intervention to a source of initiative, from aid-dependence to policy influence, and from regional fragmentation to continental coherence.

Latin America and Post-Hegemonic Regionalism

Latin America's foreign policy landscape is increasingly defined by post-hegemonic regionalism—a strategic reorientation that seeks to decenter U.S. dominance and forge autonomous paths of cooperation rooted in regional solidarity, multipolar engagement, and issue-based diplomacy.

Key institutional expressions of this trend include:

CELAC (Community of Latin American and Caribbean States): A regional bloc that excludes the United States and Canada, CELAC serves as a platform for collective dialogue, political coordination, and South-South collaboration, reinforcing the region's quest for diplomatic self-reliance.

UNASUR (Union of South American Nations): Though currently fragmented, UNASUR was founded on principles of continental integration, conflict prevention, and independent defence cooperation, reflecting Latin America's broader aspiration for sovereign-led multilateralism.

Brazil's Return to Global Stage under Lula

Under President Luiz Inácio Lula da Silva, Brazil has reclaimed its role as a champion of Global South diplomacy, advancing South-South coalitions, deepening BRICS cooperation, and taking leadership on climate governance. Lula's foreign policy emphasizes:

A multipolar vision of international order.

Strong advocacy for UN reform and climate justice.

Revitalization of regional development banks and environmental pacts, including Brazil's stewardship of the Amazon rainforest as a global ecological asset.

Middle Powers with Strategic Soft Power

Countries like Mexico and Chile are increasingly leveraging middle power diplomacy to shape global discourse:

Mexico has used its G20 presence, migration policy leadership, and historical legacy of non-intervention (Estrada Doctrine) to assert regional influence and negotiate on North-South asymmetries-particularly on issues of border governance and narcotics trade.

Chile, known for its stable democratic institutions and human rights advocacy, advances climate diplomacy, digital governance, and cultural diplomacy through its global cultural exports and participation in forums like the OECD and Escazú Agreement (Latin America's regional environmental treaty).

In sum, Latin America is redefining its global engagement not through Cold War alignments or dependency frameworks, but through a pluralistic, post-hegemonic regionalism that prioritizes strategic autonomy, developmental sovereignty, and a values-driven multilateralism

4. Key Themes Driving Southern Autonomy

4.1 Development Sovereignty

A central pillar of the Global South's quest for strategic autonomy is development sovereignty-the right of nations to determine their own developmental trajectories, free from external conditionalities, neoliberal prescriptions, and donor-driven agendas. This marks a conscious departure from the traditional Washington Consensus model that emphasized privatization, austerity, and deregulation.

Key manifestations of this shift include:

South-Led Financial Institutions: The rise of institutions like the Asian Infrastructure Investment Bank (AIIB) and the New Development Bank (NDB) under BRICS reflects the Global South's commitment to alternative development financing. These banks prioritize infrastructure, sustainability, and inclusive growth, often with less intrusive conditionalities than those imposed by the IMF or World Bank.

Technology Transfer and Indigenous Innovation: Southern countries are actively advocating for equitable access to technology and the establishment of local innovation ecosystems. This includes not just digital technologies but also advancements in healthcare, agriculture, and green energy-areas critical for self-reliant and context-specific development.

TRIPS Reform for Public Health Equity: The Global South continues to push for reform of the WTO's Trade-Related Aspects of Intellectual Property Rights (TRIPS) regime, particularly in the wake of the COVID-19 pandemic. Developing countries argue that patent protections should not override public health imperatives, calling for waivers and flexibility that would enable affordable access to vaccines, diagnostics, and life-saving medicines.

In essence, development sovereignty is not just about rejecting dependency-it is about reclaiming agency, reshaping global development norms, and ensuring that growth models are just, inclusive, and reflective of local priorities and realities.

4.2 Digital and Climate Justice

The Global South increasingly champions equity-driven frameworks in two critical arenas of contemporary geopolitics-climate governance and digital sovereignty. These intersecting domains are no longer seen as technical or sectoral issues, but as fundamental to development rights, geopolitical voice, and global justice.

Key initiatives and demands include:

Climate Justice and Loss & Damage Financing: At the heart of climate diplomacy is the Global South's call for historical accountability. Countries most vulnerable to climate change-particularly small island nations, African states, and South Asian economies-have successfully placed Loss and Damage on the global agenda. The creation of a Loss and Damage Fund at COP27 and further operationalization at COP28 reflects recognition of the climate debt owed by industrialized nations for their disproportionate emissions.

Just Energy Transitions and Green Industrialization: The Global South emphasizes the need for fair and inclusive energy transitions. This includes access to finance, technology, and capacity building to support renewable energy adoption, while also safeguarding economic stability, employment, and energy security. Initiatives like South Africa's Just Energy Transition Partnership (JETP) serve as blueprints for equitable decarbonization aligned with developmental imperatives.

Digital Sovereignty and AI Governance: In the digital sphere, Southern nations are asserting data sovereignty-the right to store, regulate, and monetize their citizens' data locally rather than relying on Global North-dominated platforms and cloud services. From data localization laws (e.g., in India and Brazil) to proposals for AI ethics frameworks that reflect cultural and developmental contexts, the South is increasingly vocal in shaping rules for platform governance, algorithmic accountability, and inclusive digital economies.

These efforts-often advanced through Southern-led coalitions in forums like the G77, G20, and COP-underscore a transformative shift: the move from aid-seeking participation to norm-setting leadership in global sustainability and digital futures.

4.3 Neutrality and Multipolar Engagement

In a global order marked by intensifying great power rivalries-particularly between the United States, China, and Russia-many Global South nations are pursuing a strategy of pragmatic multi-alignment, also known as strategic hedging. Rather than aligning ideologically or permanently with one bloc, these states adopt issue-based partnerships across geopolitical divides to maximize autonomy, security, and developmental gain.

This posture reflects a realist recalibration-not the Cold War-era ideological non-alignment, but a flexible and interest-driven engagement strategy suited for a multipolar world.

Examples include:

ASEAN's Centrality in Indo-Pacific Diplomacy: The Association of Southeast Asian Nations (ASEAN) plays a balancing role in regional geopolitics, promoting inclusive regional architecture through platforms like the East Asia Summit and the ASEAN Regional Forum (ARF). Despite U.S.-China tensions, ASEAN continues to engage both powers while advancing its own vision of a "rules-based, open, and inclusive Indo-Pacific."

Gulf States' Geopolitical Equidistance: Countries like Saudi Arabia, the UAE, and Qatar exemplify strategic equidistance, maintaining robust economic and security partnerships with the U.S., deepening infrastructure and energy cooperation with China, and even collaborating defensively and diplomatically with Russia (e.g., through OPEC+ energy coordination). This reflects their intent to diversify alliances, reduce dependency, and project regional influence on their own terms.

Africa's Diversified Engagement: African states increasingly adopt polycentric diplomacy-engaging a wide range of external partners in trade, defence, technology, and infrastructure development. While China, the EU, and the U.S. remain key actors, African countries are also building ties with India, Turkey, Brazil, and the Gulf states, fostering competitive multipolarism to enhance bargaining power and developmental choice.

This approach represents a shift from passive neutrality to active multi-vector diplomacy. It enables Global South countries to navigate geopolitical fault lines, retain policy independence, and shape global outcomes without being trapped in binary choices.

5. Barriers to Autonomy

While the Global South is increasingly vocal and active in asserting strategic autonomy, significant systemic and structural constraints continue to hinder its full realization. These barriers stem from historical inequalities, external dependencies, and internal fragmentation, creating persistent vulnerabilities despite the region's rising geopolitical visibility.

Key challenges include:

Structural Economic Dependency: Many Southern economies remain embedded in commodity-based export models, heavily reliant on volatile global markets and foreign direct investment (FDI). This is further exacerbated by sovereign debt burdens, with several countries facing debt distress, capital flight, and currency volatility-limiting fiscal space for domestic priorities and reinforcing dependency on institutions like the IMF, World Bank, and credit rating agencies.

Technological Asymmetries and Platform Reliance: A lack of indigenous technological infrastructure leaves much of the Global South dependent on Western and Chinese digital ecosystems, from cloud computing and AI platforms to cybersecurity tools. This digital dependency undermines efforts at data sovereignty, digital industrialization, and strategic competitiveness in emerging tech domains.

Weak Regional Integration and Political Fragmentation: Despite initiatives like AfCFTA, UNASUR, or SAARC, intra-South regionalism often suffers from institutional fragility, intra-regional rivalries, and lack of implementation capacity. This limits the ability of regional blocs to act as collective bargaining platforms, weakening the South's leverage in multilateral forums.

External Geopolitical Pressures: Traditional powers-particularly the U.S., EU, and increasingly China-continue to exert pressure on Global South states to align with their strategic frameworks, whether through military partnerships, aid conditionalities, or diplomatic influence. This often forces smaller states into constrained choices, undermining their ability to maintain equidistant or multi-aligned postures.

Yet, despite these constraints, the Global South is actively negotiating its space in world affairs. The rise of intra-South cooperation mechanisms, normative innovation (e.g., development as a sovereign right, climate justice), and growing institutional assertiveness (e.g., BRICS+, G77, AU's G20 entry) are gradually rebalancing the global order in favor of greater equity and plurality.

6. Conclusion: A Pluralist Global Order?

The Global South's determined quest for strategic autonomy is not just altering global power dynamics-it is redefining the architecture of international relations. Moving beyond the logic of Cold War-era alliances and unipolar dominance, the emerging world order is increasingly characterized by multipolarity, distributed influence, and a demand for equity-based governance.

At the forefront of this shift stands India, whose ascent as a global power symbolizes the broader transformation underway. Under strong and purposeful leadership, India has positioned itself as a bridge between the developed and developing worlds, advocating for reforms in global institutions while amplifying the voice of the Global South. From leading climate diplomacy and digital public infrastructure dialogues to hosting the G20 with a pro-South agenda, India exemplifies the kind of developmental leadership that blends national interest with global stewardship.

India's foreign policy under Prime Minister Narendra Modi, articulated through External Affairs Minister Dr. S. Jaishankar, reflects a doctrine of multi-alignment, strategic clarity, and principled pragmatism. India engages with the U.S., Russia, China, and the EU on its terms, while championing issues like debt justice, technology equity, and inclusive growth on behalf of the wider Global South. Its civilizational ethos and democratic credentials add normative weight to its geopolitical role.

The broader future of the international order-in areas such as trade, security, technology governance, and climate justice-will increasingly be shaped by how effectively the Global South, with India as a key leader, can:

- Mobilize collective agency across regions.
- Institutionalize cooperation through plurilateral platforms like BRICS+, G20, ISA, and IPEF.

- Reform global governance frameworks to reflect new power realities and plural values.

In this transformation, the Global South is not merely a counterweight to Western hegemony-it is an architect of alternative global visions, with India emerging as a pivotal force in crafting a more inclusive, resilient, and democratic world order.

Key References:

Acharya, A. (2018). The End of American World Order.

Kornegay, F., & Bohler-Muller, N. (Eds.). (2021). The Global South and BRICS in a Multipolar World.

Thakur, R. (2019). The United Nations, Peace and Security: From Collective Security to the Responsibility to Protect.

Hopewell, K. (2021). Breaking the WTO: How Emerging Powers Disrupted the Neoliberal Project.

UNCTAD (2023). South-South Cooperation Report: Transforming Global Partnerships.

CHAPTER NINETEEN

India's Strategic Rise in the Emerging Global Order

1. Introduction: From Regional Actor to Global Shaper

India's journey from a newly independent post-colonial nation, grappling with poverty, partition, and institutional fragility, to a decisive actor in global affairs represents one of the most compelling arcs of the 21st century. Historically committed to non-alignment and domestic consolidation, India today is no longer a hesitant bystander in world affairs-it is a deliberate, confident, and often catalytic force in reshaping the emerging global order.

This transformation has not occurred overnight, nor is it simply a byproduct of economic growth or demographic size, though India's $3.7 trillion economy and 1.4 billion-strong population do offer undeniable heft. Rather, India's rise stems from a strategic recalibration rooted in self-assurance, institutional maturity, and an ability to engage across ideological, regional, and technological divides.

Under Prime Minister Narendra Modi, India has infused its foreign policy with both civilizational depth and geopolitical agility. Strategic autonomy has evolved from a passive non-alignment into an active doctrine of multi-alignment, allowing India to maintain robust relations with the United States, Russia, Europe, the Middle East, and the Indo-Pacific, without being subsumed by any singular power bloc. This nuanced diplomacy, underpinned by national interest, is what positions India as a credible and respected global player.

In a world characterized by geopolitical fragmentation, decaying multilateralism, and the return of great power rivalry, India has positioned itself across multiple dimensions:

A Bridge-Builder Between North and South: India champions the concerns of the Global South, advocating for fairer development finance, climate justice, and equitable access to resources. Its G20 presidency in 2023 symbolized this balancing act, giving voice to nations historically excluded from decision-making tables.

A Technology-First Democracy: Through initiatives like the India Stack and UPI, India has demonstrated how digital public infrastructure can be a global public good. Unlike surveillance-driven tech ecosystems, India's model of open, inclusive, and scalable digital governance offers a compelling alternative for developing nations.

A Norm Entrepreneur in Global Governance: India's response to the COVID-19 pandemic, particularly through the Vaccine Maitri initiative, showcased its role in global health equity. Its consistent calls for WTO reform, United Nations restructuring, and democratized global decision-making further cement its status as a reform-minded power.

A Security Stakeholder in the Indo-Pacific: India's military modernization, enhanced maritime presence, and deepening security partnerships-through mechanisms like the QUAD, Malabar exercises, and bilateral defense ties-underscore its commitment to maintaining a free, open, and rules-based regional order.

A Sustainability Leader: Through the International Solar Alliance, Mission LiFE (Lifestyle for Environment), and its bold clean energy goals, India is also shaping the climate diplomacy narrative-not just as a petitioner of aid, but as a provider of solutions.

India's ascent is thus defined by agency, not alignment; by strategic purpose, not reactive positioning. Whether it is facilitating dialogue in a polarized multilateral setting, asserting its red lines on national security, or innovating governance models fit for the digital age, India is steadily transitioning from being a regional actor to a norm-setting global shaper.

This rise is not without friction. India faces challenges-strategic frictions with China, Western skepticism about its assertiveness, and pressures to pick sides in global rivalries. But it is precisely through navigating these complexities with calibrated clarity that India is reinforcing its global standing.

As Powerplay contends, the future of geopolitics will be written not just by the largest powers but by those who can act with strategic coherence, moral clarity, and adaptive leadership. India, more than any other rising actor, embodies this triad. It is not just adapting to the global order-it is helping draft its next chapter.

2. Dimensions of India's Rise

2.1 Economic Weight and Digital Leadership

India's rise on the world stage is underpinned by a dual engine: its expanding economic footprint and its pioneering approach to digital governance. Together, these forces are reshaping not only India's domestic landscape but also its international standing as a developmental model, innovation hub, and strategic actor.

Economic Power: From Scale to Sophistication

With a nominal GDP now surpassing $4 trillion, India has risen to become the fourth-largest economy in the world, trailing only the United States, China, and Germany. It also ranks third globally by purchasing power parity (PPP)-a metric that adjusts for the relative cost of living and real output. This ascent is not merely a numerical milestone; it signals a deeper structural transformation in how India participates in global capital flows, production networks, and consumption markets. From being a back-office services hub, India is evolving into a diversified economic engine, integrating scale with increasing sophistication across industries.

The Indian economy is no longer limited to back-office outsourcing or low-end manufacturing. Today, India boasts a vibrant services sector (accounting for over 50% of GDP), a robust startup ecosystem (with over 100 unicorns), and a growing footprint in high-tech manufacturing, green energy, and pharmaceuticals. Its demographic dividend-with a median age of under 30-fuels not only domestic consumption but also makes India an attractive investment destination for supply chain diversification, especially in the post-COVID, China-plus-one era.

India's foreign direct investment (FDI) flows have remained resilient, and its ambitious production-linked incentive (PLI) schemes aim to make the country a global hub for electronics, semiconductors, and renewable technologies. The digital economy, projected to exceed $1 trillion by 2030, will increasingly shape how India contributes to global growth and governance.

But beyond economic size lies something more consequential: strategic autonomy through economic resilience. By diversifying its trade partners, securing energy relationships, and boosting indigenous manufacturing under Atmanirbhar Bharat, India is creating buffers against global shocks and policy coercion-hallmarks of a maturing power.

Digital Public Infrastructure: A New Development Paradigm

Where India has truly broken new ground is in its creation of Digital Public Infrastructure (DPI)-a model that departs from Silicon Valley-style tech capitalism and instead treats core digital services as public goods accessible to all, especially the marginalized. This approach has redefined what digital transformation means in the Global South.

Some flagship DPI platforms include:

Aadhaar: The world's largest biometric identity system, covering over 1.3 billion people, which enables real-time verification and targeted delivery of subsidies, pensions, and social benefits. It has dramatically reduced leakages and identity fraud in welfare schemes.

Unified Payments Interface (UPI): A transformative, real-time digital payments system developed by the National Payments Corporation of India. UPI enables seamless peer-to-peer and peer-to-merchant transactions across banks and platforms, processing over 10 billion transactions per month (as of 2025). It has revolutionized financial inclusion, bringing millions into the formal economy.

Co-WIN: The COVID-19 vaccination registration and tracking platform, which efficiently coordinated one of the world's largest vaccination drives. It was later offered to other countries as part of India's digital diplomacy, positioning India not only as the pharmacy of the world, but also as a provider of health governance solutions.

DigiLocker, e-Sign, and Account Aggregator frameworks: These support digital documentation, verified signatures, and data portability while enhancing citizen control over personal data.

Impact: Techno-Democracy as Soft Power

India's DPI model is generating global interest-not only as a technical toolkit, but as a governance philosophy. It challenges the binary between Western liberal tech platforms and authoritarian surveillance states, offering a third path grounded in inclusion, transparency, scalability, and public accountability.

Countries in Africa, Southeast Asia, and Latin America are now adopting or adapting Indian DPI components to modernize their administrative systems. India's launch of the Global Digital Public Infrastructure Repository during its G20 presidency further demonstrated its willingness to act as a norm entrepreneur—exporting not just software, but values and frameworks around ethical, people-first digitization.

In doing so, India is redefining what digital sovereignty looks like in the developing world. It is no longer just a user of Western technologies-it is a creator of platforms, standards, and protocols that serve as a blueprint for the future of digital governance.

In summary, India's economic weight gives it a seat at the high table of global power. But it is its digital leadership-rooted in inclusive innovation and techno-sovereignty-that sets it apart as a force not just of scale, but of strategic imagination. This convergence of economic and digital strength forms a foundational pillar of India's ascent in the emerging global order.

- **Reference**: World Bank Digital Economy Report (2023); NITI Aayog (2022)

2.2 Geostrategic Location and Maritime Reach

India's rise as a global power is anchored not only in economic and technological strength but also in the geopolitical centrality of its maritime geography. Strategically situated at the confluence of major international sea lanes, India serves as a natural gateway between the East and the West. Its location in the Indian Ocean Region (IOR)-home to nearly 80% of global maritime oil trade and 90,000 commercial vessels annually-gives New Delhi a commanding vantage point over the world's most critical trade arteries.

With a coastline stretching over 7,500 kilometers, 1,200 islands, and a string of naval bases from Gujarat to the Andaman and Nicobar Islands, India's physical geography is both a security asset and a geopolitical lever. It is adjacent to three strategic chokepoints:

The Strait of Hormuz, through which nearly one-fifth of global oil passes.

The Bab el-Mandeb, connecting the Red Sea to the Arabian Sea, and vital for trade with Europe and Africa.

The Strait of Malacca, a key conduit linking the Indian and Pacific Oceans, is crucial for the economies of East and Southeast Asia.

In essence, India sits at the fulcrum of the Indo-Pacific-a region that has become the new epicenter of global power play. Its ability to influence maritime flows, secure sea lanes, and act as a first responder in regional crises gives it unique strategic weight in shaping the future of maritime governance.

SAGAR: A Doctrine of Cooperative Maritime Order

Recognizing the transformative potential of its geography, India articulated the vision of SAGAR-Security and Growth for All in the Region. Far from being a rhetorical slogan, SAGAR is a strategic doctrine rooted in inclusive security, regional capacity building, and shared prosperity.

Its pillars include:

Promoting regional peace and stability through multilateral engagement and confidence-building measures.

Enhancing humanitarian assistance and disaster response (HADR), particularly for smaller island and littoral nations vulnerable to climate risks.

Ensuring freedom of navigation and unimpeded commerce, aligned with international law, especially UNCLOS (United Nations Convention on the Law of the Sea).

Supporting smaller Indian Ocean states-like the Maldives, Seychelles, and Mauritius-through grants, training, satellite surveillance, and port development.

This vision positions India not as a hegemon, but as a net security provider-a trusted and stabilizing maritime actor that fosters regional resilience while protecting its strategic interests.

Operationalizing Maritime Diplomacy

India's maritime engagement has moved beyond doctrinal declarations to tangible strategic architecture:

Logistics Exchange Agreements (LEMOA) with countries like the United States, France, Australia, and Japan allow for reciprocal use of naval bases, enabling long-range deployments and sustaining blue-water capabilities.

Trilateral and minilateral dialogues-such as the India-France-Australia trilateral-enhance strategic coordination, maritime domain awareness, and alignment on the Indo-Pacific rules-based order.

Naval exercises further solidify India's role:

Malabar Exercise (with the U.S., Japan, and Australia) enhances high-end interoperability and deterrence in the Indo-Pacific.

Varuna (with France) and JIMEX (with Japan) reflect deeper maritime convergence with key partners.

India's leadership in the Indian Ocean Naval Symposium (IONS) underscores its convening power among regional navies.

These initiatives collectively extend India's operational reach, enhance naval readiness, and project power across a vast maritime arc-from the eastern African coast to the western Pacific.

Impact: A Maritime Power with Strategic Intent

India's expanding maritime posture reflects a broader shift in its strategic identity-from a land-focused regional actor to a comprehensive Indo-Pacific power. As China militarizes the South China Sea and deepens port investments across the IOR (e.g., Gwadar in Pakistan and Hambantota in Sri Lanka), India's maritime diplomacy offers a democratic, rules-based alternative rooted in transparency, sovereignty, and mutual respect.

India's Andaman and Nicobar Command-its only tri-service command-sits at the gateway to the Malacca Strait, symbolizing both strategic deterrence and logistical depth. Plans to enhance naval infrastructure in Lakshadweep and Mauritius, coupled with submarine acquisitions and indigenous aircraft carrier deployment (e.g., INS Vikrant), indicate a long-term maritime ambition.

India's emphasis on maritime security is not just about safeguarding trade or deterring rivals-it is about shaping the normative and operational architecture of the Indo-Pacific. Its commitment to open seas, regional capacity building, and multilateral engagement has earned it the image of a responsible maritime stakeholder and a preferred security partner for both Western powers and smaller Indian Ocean states.

In conclusion, India's geostrategic location is not merely a geographic blessing-it is a strategic asset actively leveraged through doctrine, diplomacy, and deterrence. In the evolving power matrix of the Indo-Pacific, India is not just guarding its maritime frontiers-it is helping define the rules of maritime engagement in the 21st century.

- **Reference**: Indian Navy Maritime Doctrine (2022); Carnegie India

2.3 Political Identity and Strategic Autonomy

India's rising global stature in 2025 is deeply rooted in its dual identity as the world's largest democracy and an ancient civilizational state-a rare synthesis that offers it both institutional legitimacy and historical depth. This combination grants India a unique normative appeal, positioning it between the ideological extremes of Western liberalism and authoritarian state-led capitalism, particularly that of China.

India's model, grounded in constitutional pluralism, federalism, and democratic resilience, promotes a vision of the world anchored in sovereignty, non-intervention, multipolarity, and inclusive development. These principles form the core of its enduring doctrine of strategic autonomy-a stance that enables India to pursue diversified partnerships without being locked into permanent alliances or ideological blocs.

Within this framework, India advances:

Pluralistic and decentralized governance, upholding diversity as a strength in both domestic politics and international engagement.

South–South solidarity, focused on capacity-building, development partnerships, and technology sharing-seen in initiatives like the International Solar Alliance and the Global South summits hosted by India.

A reformed, rules-based international order that recognizes the legitimacy of varied development models and civilizational values.

Impact:

In a polarized and post-hegemonic world order, India is increasingly seen by emerging economies as a credible model of "democratic development," where electoral democracy, inclusive governance, and economic modernization can coexist. Its ability to maintain democratic norms while navigating global power politics enables it to act as a moral and strategic anchor for many countries seeking autonomy from great power rivalries.

India's normative leadership now extends across a range of global issues-digital governance, climate justice, development financing, and multilateral reform-where it advocates not just for representation, but for rebalancing the very rules of global engagement. As a result, India is no longer just a balancing power in the strategic sense-it is emerging as a civilizational voice and ethical force in the reimagining of the global order.

- **Reference**: Shivshankar Menon, *Choices* (2016); Foreign Affairs (2023)

3. Impact on Global Order

3.1 Reforming Global Institutions

India has been a consistent advocate for reforming global governance structures to make them more representative, democratic, and inclusive. It argues that institutions like the United Nations Security Council (UNSC), International Monetary Fund (IMF), and World Trade Organization (WTO) remain anchored in post-World War II power dynamics, sidelining the voices and priorities of emerging economies, particularly those from the Global South.

India's demand includes:

A permanent seat at the UNSC, reflecting its demographic size, economic weight, and peacekeeping contributions.

Greater voting rights and representation for developing countries in financial institutions like the IMF and World Bank.

Reforming WTO rules to support development-friendly trade policies, especially in agriculture, health, and technology.

Case Study – India's G20 Presidency (2023):
During its landmark presidency, India championed the cause of Global South representation by successfully pushing for the African Union (AU) to be granted permanent membership in the G20. This unprecedented move not only enhanced the legitimacy of the G20 but also positioned India as a bridge-builder between continents and a voice for underrepresented regions in global decision-making.

Impact: India's push for multilateral reform reflects its strategic aim to reshape global institutions to reflect 21st-century realities, where power is more diffused, economic influence is shared, and regional leadership from Asia, Africa, and Latin America is acknowledged.

- **Reference**: G20 New Delhi Leaders' Declaration (2023)

3.2 Vaccine Maitri and Health Diplomacy

1. India's Mass Vaccination Drive (Domestic)

Launched on January 16, 2021, India's COVID-19 vaccination drive has been one of the largest and most rapid in the world (en.wikipedia.org)

As of early June 2025, over 2.2 billion doses have been administered:

Around 1.03 billion first doses

Approximately 952 million second doses

Nearly 229 million booster doses (pib.gov.in)

2. Vaccine Maitri: India's International Outreach

Operational since 20 January 2021, Vaccine Maitri distributed roughly 162.9 million doses to 96 countries by 21 February 2022 (en.wikipedia.org)

Gifts/grants: ~14.3 million doses to 98 countries

Commercial exports: ~107.1 million doses

COVAX contributions: ~41.5 million doses, newyorker.com, en.wikipedia.org, pib.gov.in.

As of November 29, 2021, a total of 72.3 million doses had been supplied to 94 countries and 2 UN entities (ourworldindata.org).

By late May 2021, over 66.4 million doses had been exported-10.7 million as grants-to more than 95 nations (en.wikipedia.org)

3. Role in COVAX

Through Serum Institute of India, about 19.8 million doses of Covishield were delivered to COVAX (en.wikipedia.org)

Between January and April 2021, India sent 60+ million doses to countries worldwide, including via COVAX, covering more than 90 nations (newyorker.com)(en.wikipedia.org)

Key Takeaways

?? Domestic Impact: Successfully administered over 2.2 billion vaccine doses, achieving broad coverage at home.

- Global Outreach: Funded or sold more than 160 million doses to 96 countries, boosting global access.
- COVAX Support: Contributed over 41 million doses via COVAX, helping less affluent nations.

Summary Table

Initiative Number of Doses (approx.)Purpose

Domestic Vaccinations 2.2 billion+First, second, and booster doses
Vaccine Maitri (Total)162.9 million Grants, commercial exports, COVAX
– Grants14.3 millionFree donations to ~98 countries
– Commercial Exports107.1 millionSold internationally
– Via COVAX41.5 millionProvided to the global COVAX programme

Through its monumental domestic vaccination campaign and extensive Vaccine Maitri efforts-including direct country donations and support to COVAX-India not only safeguarded its citizens but also solidified its reputation as the "pharmacy of the world" and a trusted global humanitarian leader.

- **Reference**: The Lancet (2022); Ministry of External Affairs (2021)

3.3 Strategic Balancing in a Multipolar World

India's foreign policy is increasingly defined by a doctrine of multi-alignment-a nuanced approach where it actively engages with diverse and even competing blocs such as the QUAD (Quadrilateral Security Dialogue), BRICS (Brazil, Russia, India, China, South Africa), SCO (Shanghai Cooperation Organisation), and I2U2 (India-Israel-UAE-USA) to advance its strategic interests. Simultaneously, India maintains robust defence cooperation with Russia, its longstanding partner, while deepening economic, technological, and investment ties with Western democracies, including the United States and the European Union.

Impact: This reflects India's strategic commitment to flexible alignment-a practice that avoids rigid ideological camps and instead champions strategic autonomy. By refusing to be bound by Cold War-era binaries, India leverages issue-based partnerships to amplify its global agency, preserve policy independence, and position itself as a responsible, pragmatic actor in the evolving multipolar order.

- **Reference**: Brookings India; C. Raja Mohan (2024)

4. Case Study: Indo-Pacific Strategy and Maritime Doctrine

India's Indo-Pacific strategy—rooted in freedom of navigation, respect for sovereignty, and open trade-has gained global resonance.

- **Initiatives**:
    - **QUAD participation** (with the U.S., Japan, Australia)
    - **Indo-Pacific Oceans Initiative**
    - **Chabahar Port development** in Iran
    - **Information Fusion Centre – Indian Ocean Region (IFC-IOR)** for maritime surveillance
- **Reference**: Observer Research Foundation (ORF); Ministry of External Affairs (2023)

5. Constraints and Challenges

Despite its growing stature, India faces several internal and external limitations:

- **Border tensions** with China and Pakistan (e.g., Galwan Valley, 2020)
- **Demographic challenges**, urban-rural divides, and environmental stress
- **Democracy concerns** cited by some Western observers
- **Technological dependency** in semiconductors and AI
- **Reference**: Freedom House (2023); Human Rights Watch (2024); NITI Aayog Competitiveness Report (2023)

6. Strategic Outlook: India as a Civilizational Power

India's ascent in the global hierarchy is not a replication of Western great power trajectories, nor an attempt to dominate through force or dependency. Instead, it is deeply rooted in India's civilizational ethos, which offers an alternative paradigm for power-one that harmonizes sovereignty with solidarity, modernity with tradition, and national interest with global responsibility.

At the heart of this worldview lies the principle of "Vasudhaiva Kutumbakam"-a Sanskrit maxim meaning "the world is one family." This ancient idea forms the moral spine of India's contemporary strategic thinking. It reframes international engagement not merely as a pursuit of advantage, but as a responsibility to co-create a more inclusive and cooperative world order. India does not seek to impose its will, but to offer a model of power rooted in coexistence, pluralism, and developmental equity.

This approach has profound implications in today's fractured geopolitical climate. Where many actors are retreating into nationalism or aggressive unilateralism, India is projecting quiet strength through consensus-building, strategic patience, and multilateral initiatives. It does not fill the global vacuum with dominance, but with dialogue, balance, and representation.

India's civilizational identity also enables it to transcend traditional binaries:

East and West: By engaging both the liberal West and non-Western coalitions, India builds bridges across ideological divides.

North and South: While increasingly integrated into G7 economies, India continues to lead the Global South in reforming multilateralism, advocating climate justice, and enabling South–South cooperation.

Tradition and Modernity: India's digital innovation, space exploration, and economic liberalization coexist with its deep-rooted spiritual, cultural, and philosophical legacies, offering a holistic model of progress.

Democracy and Development: India demonstrates that democratic governance and developmental priorities can advance simultaneously without sacrificing political pluralism.

This civilizational approach is evident in India's leadership on the global stage-from hosting the G20 presidency with a Global South focus, to advancing digital public goods for other developing countries, and promoting sustainable lifestyles through initiatives like Mission LiFE (Lifestyle for Environment). These are not isolated policy moves; they are expressions of a strategic worldview grounded in ethical statecraft.

In an age where many powers seek to command, India seeks to convince and co-create. Its model of power is neither status-quoist nor revolutionary-it is constructive, adaptive, and values-driven. As global norms continue to shift and power becomes more diffuse, India's civilizational outlook offers a much-needed moral compass and stabilizing force for a world in flux.

India is not just rising-it is reimagining leadership itself, not through dominance but through dignity, diplomacy, and deeply rooted cultural wisdom. This is not only a strategy-it is a statement of who India is, and how it seeks to shape the world.

- **Reference**: Amitav Acharya, *The End of American World Order* (2017); External Affairs Minister S. Jaishankar's speeches (2021–2024)

7. Conclusion: A Plural Pole in a Multiplex World

India's rise is increasingly recognized not as a mere shift in global rankings but as the emergence of a new kind of power-one that refrains from imitating past hegemonies and instead presents a distinctive, values-driven model rooted in democracy, diversity, and development. Rather than asserting dominance through hard coercion or rigid alliances, India leverages consensus-building, capacity-sharing, and civilizational soft power to shape global discourse.

In a fragmented global landscape marked by competing technologies, contested ideologies, and fractured identities, India stands out as a plural, pragmatic, and principled pole-one capable of navigating complexity without capitulating to it. Its ability to engage with a wide range of actors-from Silicon Valley to sub-Saharan Africa, from QUAD security partners to BRICS reformers-underscores its versatility and rising credibility.

Yet, the path ahead demands more than visibility-it requires conversion of normative leadership into tangible global influence. To do so, India must reinforce its democratic institutions, sustain inclusive growth, and continue offering scalable solutions in areas like climate action, digital governance, and development finance.

If successful, India's ascent will do more than elevate South Asia-it will help redefine what global leadership looks like in a post-Western, post-hegemonic world. As a plural pole in a multiplex system, India has the potential not just to balance global power but to recalibrate it.

References

- Acharya, A. (2017). *The End of the American World Order*. Polity Press.
- Indian Navy. (2022). *Maritime Security Strategy Document*.
- Jaishankar, S. (2023). Selected Speeches and Addresses. Ministry of External Affairs.
- Ministry of External Affairs. (2021). *Vaccine Maitri Overview Report*.
- NITI Aayog. (2022). *Digital India at Scale: Impact Evaluation Report*.
- ORF. (2023). *India's Maritime Power in the Indo-Pacific*.
- Shivshankar Menon. (2016). *Choices: Inside the Making of India's Foreign Policy*. Penguin.
- The Lancet. (2022). "India's Vaccine Diplomacy and Public Health."
- World Bank. (2023). *Digital Economy Profile: India*.
- Freedom House. (2023). *Freedom in the World: India Report*.

CHAPTER TWENTY

Gendered Perspectives in Global Power and Security

1. Introduction: Why Gender Matters in Geopolitics

Traditionally, geopolitics has been framed through a masculinized lens, emphasizing military strength, territorial control, and state-centric power dynamics, often sidelining the role of social structures and identity politics. This gender-blind approach overlooked how international power and security are shaped by deeply embedded gender norms and inequalities.

In recent decades, however, there has been a paradigm shift: gender is now recognized as a core analytical lens in global affairs. From examining the disproportionate impact of war and displacement on women and girls to analyzing the transformative role of feminist foreign policies, such as those adopted by Sweden, Canada, and Mexico, gendered perspectives have expanded the scope of international relations.

They help unpack how power is constructed (who holds it), enacted (how it is used), and resisted (through activism or diplomacy) across lines of identity. Whether it's in peacebuilding, counterterrorism, or development aid, integrating gender in geopolitics leads to more inclusive, sustainable, and just global outcomes.

2. Gender and Security: From Marginalization to Mainstreaming

2.1 Women, Peace, and Security Agenda (UNSCR 1325)

Adopted in 2000, United Nations Security Council Resolution (UNSCR) 1325 was a landmark shift in the global security discourse, formally recognizing the gendered impact of armed conflict and the agency of women in peace processes. It emphasized three key pillars:

The disproportionate impact of war and violence on women and girls-including sexual violence, displacement, and socio-economic marginalization.

The essential role of women as active agents in conflict prevention, peace negotiations, peacebuilding, and post-conflict reconstruction-not merely as victims.

The imperative for gender-sensitive approaches in peacekeeping operations, policymaking, and security governance.

In response, over 100 countries have adopted National Action Plans (NAPs) to institutionalize the Women, Peace, and Security (WPS) agenda across defense, diplomacy, and development sectors. However, mainstreaming gender into security remains a work in progress. Implementation is often hindered by tokenism, inadequate political will, insufficient funding, and structural barriers that prevent women's full and meaningful participation in decision-making. The challenge now is to move beyond symbolic inclusion and ensure that gender perspectives shape the core architecture of global peace and security.

2.2 Gender-Based Violence as a Weapon of War

Gender-based violence (GBV)-especially sexual violence-has increasingly been recognized not as incidental, but as a systematic and strategic weapon of war. In many conflict zones, rape, sexual slavery, forced pregnancy, and other forms of violence are deliberately deployed to terrorize populations, ethnically cleanse communities, and destroy social fabric.

In Bosnia (1990s), during the ethnic conflict, mass rape camps were established as part of a campaign of genocide and ethnic cleansing-targeting women as carriers of cultural identity.

In the Democratic Republic of Congo, widespread sexual violence by militias and armed groups has been used to instill fear, punish communities, and exert control over contested territories.

In Myanmar's Rohingya crisis, the military's campaign included acts of gendered violence against women and girls, aimed at both persecution and population displacement of the minority Rohingya community.

Framing such acts as tactical instruments of war, rather than unintended consequences or collateral damage, is essential to understanding modern conflict dynamics. It also plays a critical role in shaping transitional justice mechanisms, such as war crimes tribunals, truth commissions, and reparative frameworks, which now increasingly include gender justice as a core component of accountability and post-conflict healing.

3. Feminist Foreign Policy: A New Paradigm

3.1 Definition and Principles

Feminist Foreign Policy (FFP) represents a transformative shift in how nations approach diplomacy, global governance, and international engagement. It challenges the traditional, often militarized and male-dominated frameworks of foreign policy by centering gender justice, equity, and human rights in both goals and practices.

At its core, FFP emphasizes:

Human security over military security-prioritizing the safety, dignity, and well-being of individuals and communities rather than focusing solely on state sovereignty or military dominance.

Inclusion and intersectionality in decision-making-ensuring diverse voices, especially those of women, LGBTQ+ individuals, and marginalized groups, are integrated across all levels of foreign policy formulation and implementation.

Redistribution of power, both globally and within institutions-aiming to dismantle hierarchies that perpetuate inequality in international systems and create space for more equitable multilateral engagement.

A rights-based approach to peacebuilding, trade agreements, development aid, climate policy, and humanitarian interventions-grounded in international human rights law and gender equality norms.

Sweden launched the world's first official Feminist Foreign Policy in 2014, setting a precedent that was later adopted by countries including Canada, Mexico, France, Germany, and Chile. These governments have incorporated FFP principles through concrete steps such as:

Internal gender audits of foreign ministries and diplomatic institutions.

Gender-responsive budgeting to ensure resources are equitably allocated.

Reorientation of development assistance and diplomatic priorities to support feminist movements, women peacebuilders, and inclusive governance in partner countries.

FFP is not just a policy stance-it is a normative and operational framework aimed at building a more just, peaceful, and inclusive international order.

3.2 Case Study: Sweden's Feminist Foreign Policy

Sweden's FFP led to:

Increased support for reproductive health and women's rights organizations abroad.

Gender mainstreaming in peace mediation and arms export decisions.

Reframing of national interest to include equity and dignity.

Though Sweden formally retired the term in 2022, its legacy has inspired a growing global conversation on values-based foreign engagement.

4. Militarism, Masculinities, and Strategic Culture

National strategic cultures-the deeply embedded beliefs and norms guiding a state's approach to security and foreign policy-are often shaped by hegemonic masculinities. These dominant gender norms idealize traits such as aggression, dominance, competition, and control, which are valorized in military doctrines and national defense narratives.

Feminist scholars critique this militarized framing for reinforcing a gendered hierarchy of values that:

Marginalizes diplomacy, empathy, and reconciliation-traits often culturally coded as feminine-by framing them as signs of weakness or naïveté in contrast to the perceived strength of forceful action.

Legitimizes hyper-militarization and security exceptionalism, where extraordinary threats are used to justify excessive military spending, surveillance, and the erosion of civil liberties, often at the expense of human rights and development priorities.

Excludes alternative leadership models and diverse voices, particularly those of women, peace activists, and marginalized communities, from security policymaking and strategic dialogue.

This gendered strategic culture is evident in how certain policy choices are interpreted. For instance:

Nuclear deterrence is seen as "rational" and credible because it is rooted in threats, retaliation, and control-hallmarks of masculinized power.

In contrast, nuclear disarmament or pacifist approaches are often dismissed as idealistic, emotional, or unrealistic, due to their association with cooperation, care, and non-violence-traits linked with femininity.

By exposing the gendered assumptions underlying strategic behavior, feminist analysis calls for a reimagining of global security that values inclusive leadership, sustainable peace, and human-centered policies-challenging the notion that force is the ultimate guarantor of safety.

Case Study: Women in Conflict Resolution Roles

In Liberia, women's mobilization under the Women of Liberia Mass Action for Peace helped end a brutal civil war in 2003. In Colombia, female negotiators shaped inclusive provisions in the 2016 peace accord. These cases show that women are not just victims-they are architects of peace and resilience.

5. Global Challenges through a Gender Lens

5.1 Climate Change and Gendered Vulnerability

Climate change is not gender-neutral-it exacerbates existing social inequalities, disproportionately impacting women, especially in the Global South. These women often bear the brunt of environmental degradation due to structural and systemic factors that compound their vulnerability:

Economic dependency on climate-sensitive sectors such as subsistence agriculture, fishing, and forest-based livelihoods makes women particularly susceptible to erratic weather patterns, droughts, and crop failures.

Socially ascribed roles-including responsibility for fetching water, securing food, and caring for children and the elderly-mean that climate-related disruptions place additional, unpaid labor burdens on women and girls.

Exclusion from climate governance and limited access to climate adaptation financing and policy platforms results in their voices being absent from critical decisions on mitigation and resilience-building.

In response, feminist climate justice frameworks advocate for:

The integration of indigenous and local ecological knowledge, often held by women, into formal climate strategies.

The adoption of gender-responsive budgeting to ensure that climate financing addresses the differentiated needs and priorities of women and other marginalized groups.

The establishment of gender-sensitive disaster risk reduction and recovery systems, ensuring that emergency response plans are inclusive and equitable.

By viewing climate challenges through a gender lens, policymakers can build more resilient, inclusive, and socially just environmental strategies, recognizing that gender equity is not only a human rights imperative but also a climate resilience multiplier.

5.2 COVID-19 and the Gendered Face of Crisis

The COVID-19 pandemic not only triggered a global health emergency but also exposed and deepened existing gender inequalities across sectors. Far from being an equalizer, the crisis revealed how gender roles, labor segmentation, and structural discrimination shape the experiences and outcomes of crises for women and marginalized groups.

Women comprised nearly 70% of the global health and care workforce, serving as doctors, nurses, community health workers, and caregivers. Despite their critical frontline role, they were subjected to greater exposure to infection, faced shortages in protective equipment, and continued to earn systematically lower wages than their male counterparts-highlighting entrenched gender wage gaps and occupational vulnerabilities.

The world witnessed a sharp rise in gender-based violence, especially domestic violence, as lockdowns and mobility restrictions confined women with abusers, often without access to support services. UN Women termed this the "shadow pandemic", pointing to the failure of crisis response systems to integrate protection and justice mechanisms for survivors.

Women-led businesses, especially in micro, small, and informal sectors, experienced disproportionate economic fallout due to market closures, reduced demand, and limited access to digital infrastructure or stimulus packages. In many regions, female informal workers were the first to lose livelihoods and the last to regain them-exposing the fragility of women's economic participation in global supply chains and informal economies.

These gendered impacts underscore a vital lesson: global crises act as force multipliers of inequality. However, they also provide an opportunity to reimagine recovery through inclusive, intersectional, and gender-responsive frameworks-ones that promote care economies, social protection, and equitable representation in pandemic preparedness, economic rebuilding, and health governance.

6. The Role of Institutions and Intersectionality

International institutions such as UN Women, the OECD, and the World Bank have increasingly recognized the importance of mainstreaming gender analysis into global frameworks of security, economic development, and governance. This includes efforts to integrate gender indicators into policy evaluations, expand gender-disaggregated data collection, and promote women's participation in leadership, peacebuilding, and economic recovery.

However, progress has often been undermined by tokenistic inclusion and technocratic approaches-where gender equality is reduced to box-checking exercises, quotas, or superficial representation. Such practices fail to address the structural power imbalances that perpetuate inequality and can obscure the deeper transformation needed in institutional cultures, priorities, and funding mechanisms.

To move beyond symbolic gestures, institutions must adopt intersectional approaches-an analytical framework that examines how various forms of identity and oppression (such as race, class, caste, sexuality, disability, and migration status) interact to shape people's lived experiences. Without intersectionality, gender-focused policies risk essentializing "women" as a monolithic group, ignoring the layered vulnerabilities and privileges that shape different women's realities.

An intersectional lens ensures that policy interventions are context-sensitive, inclusive, and justice-oriented-enabling institutions to address root causes of inequality and design programs that empower the most marginalized, not just the most visible. True transformation lies in institutional accountability, redistribution of power, and the centering of voices that have historically been excluded from decision-making spaces.

7. Conclusion: Gender as a Lens for Global Transformation

Viewing global power through a gendered lens is not a matter of simply inserting women into existing diplomatic and security structures-it is about redefining the very foundations upon which those structures are built. Gender perspectives interrogate the hierarchies, norms, and binaries-such as public vs. private, hard vs. soft power, rational vs. emotional-that have historically shaped geopolitical thought and practice through a masculinized framework.

The rise of feminist foreign policy, inclusive peacebuilding processes, and gender-responsive governance models signals a shift toward a transformative vision of global leadership. These approaches reject zero-sum notions of power and instead emphasize collaborative security, shared prosperity, and human dignity as cornerstones of international engagement.

Incorporating gender is not about appeasing progressive agendas or fulfilling diversity metrics. It is about building a more resilient, equitable, and human-centered global order-one that recognizes how inequalities intersect and seeks to dismantle them through structural change. In doing so, it moves us closer to a geopolitics of justice, empathy, and sustainable peace, rather than one dominated by coercion, exclusion, and perpetual conflict.

Key References:

Enloe, C. (2014). Bananas, Beaches and Bases: Making Feminist Sense of International Politics.

Hudson, V., Ballif-Spanvill, B., Caprioli, M., & Emmett, C. (2009). Sex and World Peace.

True, J. (2013). The Political Economy of Violence Against Women.

Shepherd, L. J. (2017). Gender, Violence and Security: Discourse as Practice.

UN Women (2020). WPS Agenda: 20 Years of Impact.

CHAPTER TWENTY-ONE

Displacement, Migration, and the Weaponization of Borders

1. Introduction: Migration as a Strategic Fault Line

Migration is often framed as a humanitarian or economic issue. Yet in the 21st century, displacement and migration have become deeply geopolitical phenomena, shaped by conflict, climate, inequality, and the strategic decisions of states. From refugee flows weaponized in war zones to borders manipulated for political leverage, human mobility is now at the heart of global power plays.

Migration, traditionally viewed through humanitarian or economic lenses, has increasingly emerged as a strategic fault line in global geopolitics. In the 21st century, patterns of displacement and cross-border mobility are no longer just byproducts of conflict or poverty-they are actively shaped, manipulated, and politicized by states and non-state actors alike.

Driven by a complex mix of armed conflict, climate change, socio-economic inequality, ethnic persecution, and authoritarian governance, large-scale human displacement has become a tool of geopolitical strategy. For example, refugee flows are weaponized-used deliberately to destabilize neighboring countries or extract concessions in diplomatic negotiations. Similarly, border regimes are securitized, turning physical and administrative boundaries into instruments of exclusion, deterrence, and political posturing.

As human mobility becomes entangled with statecraft, migration is no longer a peripheral concern-it sits at the nexus of national security, foreign policy, and global order, revealing the power dynamics of who moves, who is stopped, and who decides.

2. Patterns and Drivers of Contemporary Displacement

2.1 Conflict and Fragility

Armed conflict continues to be the most significant and persistent driver of forced displacement in the contemporary world. According to the UNHCR, by 2024, more than 117 million people were forcibly displaced globally-an unprecedented figure reflecting the scale and severity of ongoing crises.

This displacement is fueled by a combination of active warfare, political repression, ethnic persecution, and the collapse of state institutions. Major source countries include:

Syria, where over a decade of civil war has displaced millions internally and externally.

Afghanistan, where regime instability and Taliban resurgence have led to renewed refugee flows;

Sudan, gripped by internal strife and militia violence;

Venezuela, plagued by economic collapse and authoritarian governance.

Ukraine, affected by Russia's ongoing invasion and hybrid warfare tactics;

Myanmar, where ethnic cleansing and military crackdowns continue to displace Rohingya and other minorities.

In fragile states such as Yemen and Somalia, displacement is compounded by state failure, food insecurity, and the breakdown of public infrastructure, leading to high levels of internal displacement alongside outward migration.

These population movements frequently spill across porous borders, placing immense pressure on neighboring states—economically, socially, and politically. Host countries often struggle with limited resources, security concerns, and political tensions, while regional dynamics are reshaped through demographic shifts, cross-border militancy, and competing narratives of responsibility.

In this context, conflict-induced displacement is not only a humanitarian emergency but a strategic disruptor, altering power balances, testing international solidarity, and challenging the adequacy of the global refugee protection regime.

2.2 Climate-Induced Migration

Climate change has emerged as a powerful and accelerating force behind human displacement, transforming the global landscape of migration. No longer a distant threat, its impacts-rising sea levels, extreme weather events, prolonged droughts, desertification, and ecosystem degradation-are already undermining livelihoods, food security, water access, and the habitability of entire regions, particularly in the Global South.

The regions most vulnerable include:

Small Island Developing States (SIDS) are facing existential threats due to submersion risks;

South Asia, where monsoon variability, glacier melt, and coastal erosion imperil millions;

The Sahel region, suffering from chronic droughts, land degradation, and agricultural collapse.

Projections suggest that by 2050, tens of millions could become climate migrants, forced to relocate due to environmental stressors. These migrations may be internal (within countries) or transboundary, creating new patterns of mobility and vulnerability.

Despite this growing crisis, international refugee law-particularly the 1951 Refugee Convention-does not formally recognize climate-induced migrants as "refugees", leaving them outside the scope of legal protection. This normative gap hampers global governance, as affected individuals often fall through bureaucratic cracks, with no clear legal status or access to resettlement rights and humanitarian aid.

Climate-driven migration also acts as a conflict multiplier:

It heightens competition over scarce resources such as water, land, and jobs.

It contributes to urban overcrowding and infrastructure strain in receiving regions.

It can provoke xenophobic, nationalist backlash in host communities, leading to social polarization and political instability.

In short, climate-induced displacement sits at the intersection of environmental change, human rights, development, and security. Addressing it requires a multidimensional strategy-combining climate resilience, legal reform, and inclusive urban and migration planning-to protect the most vulnerable and uphold human dignity in an era of ecological upheaval.

3. Borders as Tools of Power and Control

3.1 The Securitization of Migration

In recent decades, migration has been increasingly securitized-framed by states not as a humanitarian or developmental issue, but as a threat to national security, sovereignty, and cultural cohesion. Governments across the globe have linked migration to terrorism, transnational crime, demographic anxiety, and identity-based fear, reshaping public discourse and policy around risk and control rather than rights and protection.

This securitization has led to the expansion of militarized border regimes characterized by:

Advanced surveillance systems, including biometric data collection, facial recognition, and drones, are being used to monitor and deter migrants.

Pushback operations, where migrants are intercepted and returned without access to asylum procedures, often in violation of the principle of non-refoulement.

Detention infrastructures, such as migrant holding centers and offshore processing facilities, notably seen in Australia's "Pacific Solution", which relocates asylum seekers to remote islands to avoid domestic legal accountability.

Physical border walls and barriers have also proliferated as symbols of sovereignty and deterrence:

The U.S.–Mexico border wall has been reinforced under successive administrations.

The India–Bangladesh border, heavily fenced and patrolled.

The Greece–Turkey fence, aiming to block migration routes into Europe;

The Israel–West Bank barrier, controversial for both its geopolitical and humanitarian implications.

These measures are often justified as tools of territorial integrity and public order, but they undermine international human rights norms, erode access to asylum, and heighten the precarity of displaced individuals. Migrants are frequently left in legal limbo-vulnerable to exploitation, abuse, and statelessness-while the humanitarian obligations of host countries are sidelined in favor of deterrence-based governance.

Ultimately, the securitization of migration reflects a deeper instrumentalization of borders as tools of geopolitical power, shaping who is allowed to move, who is excluded, and how global inequalities are reinforced in the name of national interest.

3.2 Case Study: Belarus-Poland Border Crisis (2021)

In 2021, the Belarus–Poland border crisis emerged as a stark example of the weaponization of migration as a tool of geopolitical coercion. Following the imposition of EU sanctions on the Belarusian regime led by President Alexander Lukashenko, Belarus was accused of deliberately engineering migrant flows from conflict-affected regions in the Middle East and Africa, including Iraq, Syria, and Yemen, toward the eastern borders of the European Union, particularly Poland, Lithuania, and Latvia.

The Belarusian government reportedly eased visa regimes, facilitated flights, and transported migrants to border areas as part of a calculated retaliatory strategy, using human mobility as asymmetric leverage against the EU. Thousands of migrants and asylum seekers became trapped in a legal and humanitarian "gray zone"-denied entry by EU border guards, yet unable to return or receive protection within Belarus.

These individuals faced extreme cold, physical abuse, food insecurity, and medical neglect, while both sides engaged in pushback operations that violated international law, particularly the 1951 Refugee Convention and the principle of non-refoulement. EU member states invoked emergency powers, fortified their borders, and reframed the incident as a hybrid attack, blurring the lines between humanitarian crisis and national security threat.

This crisis highlights how migration has evolved into a geopolitical instrument, where authoritarian regimes exploit human vulnerability to destabilize rival states, test regional cohesion, and erode the legitimacy of international norms. It also exposed the fragility of EU solidarity, as frontline states demanded stronger border defenses while others criticized the erosion of asylum rights.

Ultimately, the Belarus–Poland episode underscores the urgent need for robust, rights-based, and coordinated global responses to migration governance-ones that resist manipulation, uphold humanitarian obligations, and prevent the erosion of ethical principles in the face of geopolitical gamesmanship.

4. Refugee Diplomacy and International Bargaining

4.1 Turkey and the EU: Conditional Cooperation

The 2016 EU–Turkey Deal marked a turning point in refugee diplomacy, establishing a model of conditional cooperation that linked migration management to geopolitical bargaining. Under the agreement, the European Union committed over €6 billion in financial aid to support the needs of over 3.6 million Syrian refugees hosted by Turkey, along with promises of visa liberalization, the reopening of EU accession talks, and enhanced political engagement.

In exchange, Turkey agreed to prevent irregular migration to Europe by increasing border security and accepting the return of asylum seekers who crossed into Greece unlawfully. The deal significantly reduced migrant arrivals to the EU, particularly via the eastern Mediterranean route, and was hailed by some EU leaders as a successful containment strategy.

However, the agreement also conferred substantial geopolitical leverage to Ankara. The Turkish government has since used the threat of "opening the gates"-that is, allowing refugee flows into Europe-as a strategic pressure tactic, especially in moments of diplomatic friction. This tactic has been employed in response to EU criticism of Turkey's domestic authoritarianism, military interventions in Syria, and tensions in the Eastern Mediterranean.

Critics argue that the deal effectively externalized the EU's border control responsibilities, outsourcing protection obligations to a non-EU state with a contested human rights record. It also raised serious concerns about the commodification of refugees-treating displaced people as bargaining chips in foreign policy negotiations, rather than as rights-bearing individuals.

The EU–Turkey case illustrates how refugee governance has become entangled in international power dynamics, where humanitarian obligations are often subordinated to realpolitik. It highlights the risks of transactional migration diplomacy, which may achieve short-term containment but undermines long-term accountability, ethical coherence, and the universality of refugee rights.

4.2 Jordan, Lebanon, and Fragile Host States

Frontline host countries such as Jordan and Lebanon play a critical but often underappreciated role in the global refugee regime. Despite their limited economic capacity and fragile political environments, these states have hosted millions of displaced people, particularly from Syria, Palestine, and Iraq, shouldering disproportionate humanitarian and infrastructural burdens with inadequate international support.

In response, these host countries have developed strategies of refugee diplomacy, using their hosting role as both a bargaining asset and a means of navigating domestic and regional complexities. Key aspects include:

Leveraging refugee populations to attract donor funding from international organizations, development banks, and Western governments. Aid is often contingent upon their continued willingness to host refugees, making displacement management a tool of foreign aid mobilization and development financing.

Controlling refugee access to public services, legal protections, and formal employment as a means to manage domestic political tensions and mitigate societal backlash. This often results in policies of semi-formal containment, where refugees remain in legal limbo-neither fully integrated nor forcibly removed.

Using refugee hosting to gain geopolitical relevance, especially concerning regional diplomatic negotiations. For example:

Jordan positions itself as a stabilizing actor in Israel–Palestine diplomacy and Syrian peace talks, emphasizing its role as a buffer state.

Lebanon, with its historically delicate sectarian balance, uses refugee dynamics to influence international political discourse around power-sharing, reconstruction aid, and regional security arrangements.

This approach reveals how fragile host states navigate the intersection of humanitarian responsibility and strategic calculus. While often portrayed as passive recipients of crisis, countries like Jordan and Lebanon actively instrumentalize refugee governance to enhance their foreign policy leverage, domestic control mechanisms, and international visibility-a reflection of how migration is embedded within broader geopolitical and institutional negotiations.

5. Migration, Nationalism, and Global Governance Challenges

5.1 The Rise of Anti-Immigration Politics

In recent years, migration has become a lightning rod for nationalist and populist politics, reshaping political discourse and electoral behavior across many liberal democracies. Rather than being addressed through balanced policy debate, migration is increasingly framed as a threat to national identity, cultural cohesion, and economic stability, fueling fear-based narratives and exclusionary ideologies.

In the United Kingdom, the 2016 Brexit referendum was significantly influenced by anti-immigration sentiment, particularly concerns over freedom of movement within the European Union, the perceived strain on public services, and anxieties about cultural integration. The Leave campaign's slogans around "taking back control" were deeply tied to border sovereignty and national autonomy.

In the United States, migration policy became a core pillar of political polarization during the Trump administration, which introduced highly controversial measures such as the "Muslim Ban", heightened deportations, and efforts to build a border wall with Mexico. These policies reflected a broader nativist narrative that depicted immigrants, especially from Muslim-majority and Latin American countries, as existential threats to American values and security.

Across Europe, far-right and ultranationalist parties have capitalized on migration fears to gain political ground:

Germany's Alternative für Deutschland (AfD) used the 2015 refugee crisis to advance anti-Islam rhetoric and critique the Merkel government's asylum policies.

France's Rassemblement National (RN) under Marine Le Pen has long leveraged anti-immigration platforms to promote French cultural nationalism.

Hungary's Fidesz party, led by Viktor Orbán, has implemented hardline anti-migration policies and built a political identity around "illiberal democracy" and ethno-nationalism.

These developments reveal how migration is no longer just a policy issue-it has become deeply entwined with domestic identity politics, often serving as a proxy for wider debates around globalization, multiculturalism, economic inequality, and sovereignty.

The politicization of migration contributes to rising polarization, the erosion of democratic norms, and the mainstreaming of xenophobic discourse. It also poses challenges to global migration governance, as nationalist governments resist multilateral cooperation and retreat from human rights commitments, complicating efforts to build a fair, coordinated, and humane international migration regime.

5.2 Failures and Fractures in Global Migration Governance

Despite high-profile initiatives such as the Global Compact for Safe, Orderly and Regular Migration (2018) and the Global Compact on Refugees, the international governance of migration remains deeply fragmented, non-binding, and unevenly implemented. These compacts represent important normative milestones-emphasizing principles like shared responsibility, human rights, and international cooperation-yet they lack legal enforceability and universal consensus.

One of the critical gaps lies in the absence of binding frameworks for equitable burden-sharing, especially in responding to mass displacement and climate-induced migration. While the compacts encourage voluntary pledges and policy harmonization, they stop short of compelling states to accept asylum seekers, contribute resources, or accommodate those displaced by environmental degradation and slow-onset disasters-a growing and urgent category of forced migrants.

Resistance to global governance mechanisms is also driven by concerns over national sovereignty and domestic political backlash. Countries such as the United States (under the Trump administration) and Hungary openly rejected the Global Compact on Migration, portraying it as an infringement on their right to control borders and determine who enters their territory. This reflects a broader trend of sovereigntist populism, where multilateral cooperation is reframed as a threat rather than a solution.

Even within regional frameworks, governance mechanisms have proven fragile. The European Union's Dublin Regulation, which assigns responsibility for asylum claims to the first country of entry, has repeatedly collapsed under the weight of major refugee inflows, particularly during the 2015 crisis. This system has led to asymmetrical burdens on frontline states like Greece and Italy, exposing the lack of solidarity within the EU and sparking intra-regional disputes.

The consequence of these fractures is a global landscape marked by ad hoc, reactive, and crisis-driven responses to displacement, characterized by closed borders, deterrence strategies, and humanitarian shortfalls. Without a coherent, rights-based, and enforceable system, migration governance risks normalizing exceptionalism, undermining long-term solutions, and perpetuating human insecurity for the world's most vulnerable populations.

6. Alternative Models and Human-Centered Approaches

Amid widespread securitization and deterrence-driven migration policies, several countries and communities have pioneered inclusive, rights-based models that offer human-centered alternatives to conventional approaches. These models prioritize dignity, integration, and social cohesion, showing that migration governance can balance sovereign interests with global solidarity and humanitarian commitments.

Canada's community sponsorship program stands out as a leading example of civil society-driven refugee resettlement. Under this model, private citizens, faith groups, and local organizations co-sponsor refugees by providing financial support and integration assistance. This decentralized and participatory system not only builds public ownership over refugee protection but also fosters social trust and community engagement, demonstrating how local actors can play a central role in global displacement solutions.

In Colombia, the government took a bold and unprecedented step by granting temporary protected status to over 1.7 million Venezuelan migrants fleeing economic and political collapse. Rather than criminalizing or marginalizing displaced populations, Colombia implemented a large-scale regularization policy that allows access to education, health care, and formal employment. This regional leadership model offers a pragmatic and humane template for mass displacement management in Latin America and beyond.

Uganda's refugee policy is widely regarded as one of the most progressive in Africa. Refugees are granted freedom of movement, the right to work, and even access to land for cultivation, enabling self-reliance and reducing dependency on humanitarian aid. Crucially, Uganda integrates refugees into national development plans, rather than isolating them in camps, reflecting a vision of inclusion over containment.

These approaches illustrate that migration governance need not be rooted in fear, exclusion, or emergency responses. Instead, solidarity-based models can promote mutual benefit, where host communities and migrants co-create solutions that uphold rights while addressing development, demographic, and labor needs. They demonstrate the viability of long-term, humane, and sustainable strategies, reinforcing the idea that security and compassion are not mutually exclusive, but can coexist in well-designed migration systems.

7. Case Study: The Rohingya Displacement and South Asia's Migration Faultline

One of the most critical, yet underexamined, migration crises in South Asia is the cross-border displacement of Rohingya Muslims from Myanmar-first into Bangladesh, and subsequently into India. What began as a humanitarian emergency has evolved into a regional geopolitical challenge, reflecting the convergence of statelessness, identity politics, and strategic hesitations in migration governance.

Denied citizenship under Myanmar's 1982 nationality law and subjected to decades of institutional persecution, the Rohingyas are among the most persecuted and stateless communities in the world. The 2017 military crackdown by the Myanmar junta-marked by mass killings, sexual violence, and the burning of villages-forced over 750,000 Rohingyas to flee into Bangladesh, joining earlier waves that date back to the 1970s.

While Bangladesh became the primary host, sheltering over 1.1 million Rohingyas in camps such as Cox's Bazar, a significant number-estimated in lakhs-have entered and settled illegally in various parts of India, exploiting porous borders across West Bengal, Assam, and the Northeast. Their presence has increasingly become a security and governance concern, particularly in urban clusters like Jammu, Delhi, Hyderabad, and other states. Numerous reports from law enforcement and intelligence agencies have linked individuals from the Rohingya community to criminal networks, forged identity documents, illegal encroachments, and in some cases, suspected links to extremist elements, prompting heightened surveillance and periodic detentions by security forces. This has intensified political and public debates on the need for stricter border controls, refugee regulation, and national security safeguards.

India's Response: Between Security and Statelessness

India, despite its history of accommodating refugee communities, has refused to grant refugee status to the Rohingyas, citing its non-signatory status to the 1951 Refugee Convention and portraying the group as a national security risk. The government has linked the Rohingya presence to potential radicalization and demographic imbalance, especially in politically sensitive regions.

This has resulted in:

- Detention and deportation campaigns without formal asylum hearings.
- Denial of access to basic services, legal documentation, and education.
- Political rhetoric that often paints Rohingyas as illegal infiltrators.

India's approach reflects a broader trend of securitization of migration, where human vulnerability is subsumed under narratives of threat, law and order, and identity protection.

Geopolitical Tensions and Strategic Calculations-

The Rohingya crisis also highlights the triangular strategic tensions between India, Bangladesh, and Myanmar:

India has strategic interests in Myanmar under its Act East Policy, and has been cautious not to alienate the military junta, even in the face of international condemnation.

In its bilateral engagement with Bangladesh, India walks a tightrope-supporting refugee relief in Cox's Bazar but resisting burden-sharing and remaining silent on pathways to long-term resettlement.

Meanwhile, Myanmar's continued intransigence, refusal to guarantee safe repatriation, and denial of Rohingya citizenship ensure that the crisis remains unresolved.

This scenario underscores how refugee diplomacy operates within geopolitical hierarchies, with states choosing strategic silence or transactional engagement over durable protection solutions.

Internal Polarization and Politicization in India-

Domestically, the presence of Rohingyas has become a focal point in India's evolving nationalist political discourse, closely tied to electoral strategies, internal security narratives, and citizenship reforms. The ruling party, driven by its nationalist ideology, has consistently maintained that illegal immigration, particularly from Muslim-majority regions, poses a demographic, security, and sovereignty challenge. In this context, measures such as the Citizenship Amendment Act (CAA) and the proposed National Register of Citizens (NRC) are positioned not merely as administrative exercises but as efforts to safeguard India's cultural identity, territorial integrity, and national interests.

The Rohingyas, viewed by the government as illegal immigrants rather than legitimate refugees, are considered particularly problematic due to their stateless status and alleged involvement in unlawful activities. Their case has come to symbolize the broader challenge of border management and undocumented migration, where identity-based scrutiny is framed as a legitimate tool of statecraft rather than an exclusionary measure. This reflects the ruling party's emphasis on nation-first governance, where migration policy is tightly linked to internal security, demographic balance, and the assertion of India's sovereign right to determine who belongs within its borders.

Broader Implications for Migration Governance-

The Rohingya displacement into India highlights the urgent need for migration governance that prioritizes national security, legal integrity, and the rights of Indian citizens above all else. In the absence of a binding regional refugee protection mechanism under platforms like SAARC, countries like India are left to independently manage complex cross-border inflows, often in challenging security and demographic contexts.

India's decision not to adopt a blanket domestic refugee law is rooted in its pragmatic recognition of regional volatility, security vulnerabilities, and the need for case-by-case discretion. A one-size-fits-all asylum framework could compromise the nation's ability to filter threats, protect borders, and uphold the rights of legal citizens.

Global compacts, such as the Global Compact for Refugees, lack legal enforceability and often overlook the sovereign concerns of middle-income nations like India. These non-binding instruments cannot compel states to accept unchecked migration, especially when national interests, social cohesion, and citizen welfare are at stake.

Moreover, the Rohingya situation reveals how statelessness and forced migration are increasingly weaponized for political or diplomatic leverage. India, therefore, must retain the strategic autonomy to distinguish between genuine refugees and those who may pose a risk to internal stability or exploit legal and welfare loopholes. The priority remains clear: citizen rights first, national security first, and legal accountability above all.

Implication: The Rohingyas and India's Sovereign Right to Security and Order

The handling of the Rohingya situation by India reflects a firm and necessary assertion of national sovereignty in the face of complex cross-border challenges. While global discourses often emphasize shared responsibility for stateless populations, India maintains that any response must be grounded in the primacy of national security, legal citizenship, and the welfare of its people.

In an era where migration is increasingly used as a geopolitical tool, the Rohingya crisis highlights the urgent need for clear, enforceable norms that respect a nation's right to control its borders, vet entrants, and protect its socio-political fabric. The onus of responsibility cannot be disproportionately shifted onto frontline states like India, especially when the displaced enter illegally and without an international mandate.

Rather than being viewed as a test of regional moral responsibility alone, the Rohingya issue is a litmus test for strategic clarity, internal stability, and rule-of-law enforcement. India's position remains unequivocal: while humanitarian values matter, they must not override the constitutional obligation to uphold the rights, safety, and security of Indian citizens.

A truly effective regional response must begin by respecting each nation's sovereign authority to decide who qualifies for protection, under what conditions, and without compromising internal harmony or legal order.

8. Conclusion: Human Mobility and the New Geopolitical Faultlines

In the 21st century, displacement and migration have emerged as pivotal elements of global geopolitics, no longer confined to humanitarian margins but directly influencing national security, strategic stability, and geopolitical alignments. From border control and demographic management to refugee diplomacy and climate-induced displacement, migration today sits at the crossroads of human vulnerability and calculated statecraft.

As climate change accelerates, conflicts persist, and economic disparities widen, the global contest over borders, identity, and belonging will only intensify. In this evolving environment, migration governance must be shaped not by abstract ideals but by grounded national priorities, rooted in legality, sovereignty, and internal security.

India's position remains clear: while it acknowledges humanitarian concerns, the protection of its borders, its legal citizens, and its socio-political cohesion must come first. Any global or regional framework on migration must respect the sovereign right of nations to determine who enters, who stays, and under what terms.

The real test ahead is not simply about embracing shared responsibility, but about ensuring that international mechanisms do not dilute national will, nor impose asymmetric burdens on states like India. In this context, India's approach to migration will increasingly define its role as a stable, decisive, and security-conscious global power-one that safeguards its citizens while engaging with the world on its terms.

Key References:

Betts, A. & Collier, P. (2018). Refuge: Transforming a Broken Refugee System.

UNHCR (2023). Global Trends: Forced Displacement in 2022.

IOM (2022). World Migration Report.

Crawley, H., & Skleparis, D. (2018). Refugees, Migrants, Neither, Both: Categorical Fetishism and the Politics of Bounding in Europe's Migration Crisis.

Zaiotti, R. (2011). Cultures of Border Control: Schengen and the Evolution of European Frontiers.

CHAPTER TWENTY-TWO

Reimagining Global Order in a Fragmented World

1. Introduction- The end of Certainity

The post-World War II international system-further refined in the aftermath of the Cold War-was underpinned by a powerful triad: Western dominance, liberal institutionalism, and the belief in the progressive universalization of democracy and free-market capitalism. At its core, this global framework operated on the assumption that nations, regardless of history or culture, would ultimately converge under the stewardship of a U.S.-led, rules-based international order.

For decades, this model shaped global diplomacy, trade regimes, and security architectures. Institutions like the United Nations, Bretton Woods financial bodies, NATO, and the World Trade Organization were seen as pillars of global stability. The narrative was one of linear progress, in which liberal democracy and globalization would gradually displace authoritarianism, protectionism, and conflict.

Today, that certainty has unraveled.

The international order is no longer anchored in a singular vision. Instead, we are witnessing a polycentric world in flux, marked by competing power centers, contested norms, and the erosion of universal ideological consensus. The return of great power rivalry-between the U.S., China, and Russia-the assertiveness of middle powers like Turkey, Iran, and Brazil, and the resurgence of civilizational, regional, and technological blocs have redrawn the strategic map.

At the forefront of this transformation stands India, emerging as a decisive global player, not just demographically but economically, militarily, and diplomatically. With its robust economic growth, increasing global influence in forums like the G20, BRICS, QUAD, and SCO, and its enhanced defense capabilities, India is asserting its position as a civilizational power that champions strategic autonomy, pluralism, and rule-based multilateralism-on its terms. India is no longer a balancing actor; it is a shaping force in the evolving global order.

Rather than a steady march toward convergence, the contemporary world is defined by fragmentation, fluidity, and hybrid alignments. Alliances are now transactional, norms are selectively applied, and power is exercised not just through military might or economic clout, but also through narrative control, cyber influence, and technological sovereignty.

This transition does not signal the collapse of global order-it signifies its transformation. The emerging paradigm is not post-liberal, but post-unipolar. Power is increasingly distributed, legitimacy is contested, and strategic autonomy-once a luxury-is now a necessity for states navigating multiple, overlapping spheres of influence.

As explored throughout this book, the current era demands a reimagination of global governance, one that reflects multipolarity, diversity of political models, and plural civilizational values. This is not just a geopolitical shift-it is an epistemological one, redefining how we understand legitimacy, leadership, and order itself in a world where certainty is no longer a given.

2. The Multipolar Mosaic - Beyond Bipolar Templates:

The current global constellation defies the simplistic binaries of the past. While the U.S.–China rivalry continues to dominate global headlines-framing narratives around trade wars, tech decoupling, and ideological competition-the broader geopolitical reality is far more complex. We are now situated in a polycentric, multipolar world, where power is diffuse, issue-specific, and context-dependent.

The United States retains unmatched military supremacy, a sprawling network of strategic alliances (NATO, AUKUS, QUAD), and global financial influence through institutions like the IMF and World Bank. Yet, it faces domestic political polarization, rising protectionist tendencies, and a decline in normative leadership, particularly on issues such as climate justice, multilateralism, and human rights consistency.

China has rapidly risen as a techno-industrial behemoth, leading in 5G infrastructure, electric vehicles, AI ecosystems, and Belt and Road investments. However, it grapples with demographic decline, shrinking global trust, and growing resistance to its authoritarian model and territorial assertiveness in regions like the South China Sea, the Himalayas, and the Taiwan Strait.

The European Union presents a powerful model of regulatory influence, soft power, and climate diplomacy, particularly through its Green Deal, digital privacy regulations (like GDPR), and normative leadership on sustainability. Yet, it struggles with internal fragmentation, limited hard power projection, and slow institutional agility in responding to crises like Ukraine, Middle East instability, and migration surges.

Meanwhile, a set of rising powers and regional coalitions are increasingly asserting strategic autonomy and multi-alignment, reshaping global norms without aligning rigidly with any one pole:

India, with its massive population, robust democracy, and accelerating economic growth, is emerging as a decisive global power across military, diplomatic, and technological domains. India blends civilizational identity with pragmatic statecraft-engaging simultaneously with QUAD, BRICS, SCO, I2U2, and G20-while advocating for a reformed multilateral order that reflects Global South priorities. Its indigenous technological advances, expanding defense capacity, and leadership in digital public infrastructure further solidify its strategic profile.

Brazil, South Africa, Indonesia, and Mexico are also gaining prominence in climate negotiations, trade diplomacy, and regional peacekeeping, while platforms like ASEAN and the African Union are asserting collective agency in economic integration, crisis response, and development pathways.

Multipolarity today is uneven, dynamic, and multidimensional-it operates not just along military or economic lines, but also in technology governance, data regulation, cultural influence, and development finance. The old Cold War template of binary alignments has been replaced by a mosaic of fluid coalitions, issue-based alignments, and shifting priorities.

This strategic decentralization creates new opportunities for diplomatic innovation, flexible partnerships, and plural leadership, but it also injects greater uncertainty, contested norms, and institutional stress into global governance. States like India now navigate a landscape that demands balance without alignment, voice without bloc loyalty, and agility in response to shifting fault lines.

3. From Hegemony to Inclusive Governance

Legacy institutions-the United Nations, IMF, World Bank, WTO, and NATO-increasingly appear as outdated frameworks, products of a post–World War II era that no longer reflect contemporary geopolitical, economic, and demographic realities. Their structures and decision-making mechanisms are often shaped by historical privilege, leaving emerging powers and the Global South underrepresented in agenda-setting, leadership roles, and financial influence.

Yet the world today faces polycrises-from climate change and global health insecurity to digital sovereignty, cyber threats, and mass displacement-that transcend national borders and require inclusive, agile, and decentralized responses.

Reform of multilateral institutions is no longer optional-it is imperative. The next generation of global governance must prioritize equity, responsiveness, and legitimacy, moving beyond the inertia of permanent vetoes, donor-driven conditionalities, and Western-centric mandates. India, among other rising powers, has repeatedly advocated for this shift, calling for restructured global institutions that mirror 21st-century power configurations and demographic weight.

Platforms such as BRICS+, the G20, and new regional architectures (like the International Solar Alliance, ISA, and I2U2) are emerging as laboratories of institutional innovation. These groupings promote multi-alignment, issue-based coalitions, and a more pluralistic model of cooperation that expands the space for diverse leadership beyond traditional power blocs.

The complexity of today's global challenges demands cross-sectoral governance. Cities, civil society organizations, technology communities, academia, and non-state actors must be integrated into decision-making ecosystems. From pandemic response to climate resilience and data governance, these actors bring local knowledge, technical expertise, and grassroots legitimacy that traditional states alone cannot deliver.

What is needed is a new global governance ethos-one that is rooted not merely in power balancing but in shared responsibility, practical problem-solving, inclusive legitimacy, and ethical leadership. Such a shift would empower nations like India and others from the Global South to shape agendas not as rule-takers but as co-creators of a more accountable and participatory international order.

In this reimagined world, inclusivity becomes strength, and governance is not an extension of dominance but a collective enterprise in managing common futures.

4. Redefining Security in a Complex Age

In today's interconnected world, security can no longer be confined to traditional military definitions. The 21st-century landscape demands a holistic, multidimensional approach that addresses the full spectrum of threats, many of which lie beyond borders and bombs. This expanded view of security recognizes that resilience, equity, and human well-being are as vital to global stability as deterrence and defense.

A modern conception of security must include:

Health Security: The COVID-19 pandemic underscored the fragility of global health systems and the inequalities in vaccine access. Future frameworks must prioritize universal healthcare preparedness, supply chain sovereignty, and vaccine equity. India, with its role in Vaccine Maitri and as the "pharmacy of the world," has already demonstrated leadership in health diplomacy and humanitarian outreach.

Ecological Security: From biodiversity collapse and extreme weather events to water scarcity and desertification, environmental degradation now poses existential risks. India's push for climate action through the International Solar Alliance (ISA) and its growing investment in green hydrogen and sustainable infrastructure positions it as a proactive player in global ecological resilience.

Digital and Data Security: As cyberwarfare, surveillance capitalism, and algorithmic manipulation reshape geopolitics, nations must safeguard data sovereignty, digital infrastructure, and AI governance. India, through initiatives like Digital India and its advocacy for a global digital public infrastructure, is asserting itself as a tech-sovereign democracy, balancing innovation with regulation.

Food and Livelihood Security: In a world marked by climate shocks, displacement, and economic inequality, securing access to food, water, and sustainable livelihoods-particularly in climate-vulnerable and conflict-prone regions—is fundamental. India's efforts in agricultural resilience, food aid diplomacy, and south-south development cooperation illustrate its growing role as a provider of stability and sustenance.

This redefined paradigm shifts security policy from military deterrence to systemic resilience, and from state-centric protection to human-centered empowerment. For India, it is not only about defending its borders but about leading with responsibility, regional stability, and a global vision.

As India rises as a power to reckon with, its approach to security reflects a fusion of strategic autonomy and moral leadership, anchored in its civilizational ethos of Vasudhaiva Kutumbakam ("the world is one family") and focused on building a secure, sustainable, and inclusive global order.

5. The Battle of Narratives and the Soft Power Turn

In the 21st century, narrative warfare has become as decisive as kinetic conflict. The contest over ideas, identity, and legitimacy is now fought not just on battlefields, but across digital platforms, media ecosystems, international forums, and the collective memory of civilizations. In this struggle, soft power-rooted in history, values, and vision-has become a critical currency of global influence.

At the heart of this battle lies a fundamental set of questions:

What constitutes a legitimate global order?

Whose history, culture, and civilizational memory deserves prominence in shaping that order?

How should sovereignty and interdependence be reconciled in a multipolar, networked world?

Today, the world is shaped not by a singular ideology, but by a contest of grand narratives, each offering a different answer to these questions:

China's "peaceful rise" projects a narrative of benevolent authoritarianism and technocratic efficiency.

Russia's "sovereign civilization" emphasizes tradition, orthodoxy, and resistance to Western liberalism.

The West's "rules-based order" invokes post-war liberal internationalism and universal norms, though increasingly contested by the Global South.

Amidst this, India is asserting its distinct narrative: that of a "civilizational democracy." This framing bridges ancient philosophical traditions with modern democratic values, offering a vision of global order grounded in pluralism, dialogue, strategic autonomy, and non-coercive engagement. India's rise is not merely economic or diplomatic-it is cultural, epistemic, and increasingly strategic.

While India continues to shape global discourse through the global appeal of yoga, Ayurveda, cinema, diaspora diplomacy, and digital public goods, it has also sent an unmistakable message through the demonstration of hard power. The launch of Operation Sindoor-a swift, precise, and high-impact military operation conducted deep into hostile territory-was not only a tactical success but also a strategic statement. It showcased India's technological prowess, operational readiness, and political will to act decisively when its interests are threatened. The operation sent a chill down the spine of global observers and adversarial powers, firmly placing India among the few nations capable of integrating soft power with hard deterrence.

India's narrative now embodies:

Democracy without uniformity-a plural, federated model of governance.

Sovereignty with responsibility-respect for territorial integrity alongside humanitarian solidarity.

Strength with restraint-military capability guided by doctrine, not provocation.

Global leadership with humility-championing the aspirations of the Global South, while remaining non-aligned in bloc politics.

As strategic narratives increasingly define alliances, institutional frameworks, legal interpretations, and global legitimacy, India's civilizational-democratic-security narrative offers a unique alternative to both Western liberal hegemony and Eastern authoritarian centralism. In doing so, India not only speaks the language of tradition and culture but also backs it with credible power projection and strategic depth, shaping a multipolar order that reflects both identity and capability.

6. Global South:

The Global South is no longer a passive recipient of global agendas-it is emerging as a central force in shaping the normative, institutional, and strategic contours of the 21st-century world order. What was once considered peripheral is now pivotal, not only in terms of demographics and markets, but in ideational leadership, moral authority, and structural reform.

As explored in earlier chapters, the Global South's growing influence is reflected in:

Advocacy for climate justice, particularly through calls for loss-and-damage financing, equitable carbon budgets, and the recognition of historical emissions. These are no longer moral appeals—they are strategic demands, backed by economic leverage and diplomatic coordination.

Bold proposals for digital equity, data sovereignty, and technological co-development that challenge the monopolies of Silicon Valley and Beijing. India's leadership in promoting Digital Public Infrastructure (DPI), open-source innovation, and the Global Digital Public Goods Alliance has placed it at the forefront of shaping an inclusive tech governance framework.

Expansion of South–South cooperation platforms-from BRICS+ and IBSA to new minilateral forums like I2U2 and the India-led International Solar Alliance (ISA)-that deliberately bypass traditional Western power hierarchies, offering alternative pathways for development, energy transitions, and collective resilience.

As the world moves toward a more polycentric, fragmented, and contested order, the Global South will not just demand representation-it will be instrumental in norm-setting, institution-building, and agenda-framing.

Here, India stands as a first among equals-not only as the largest democracy and fastest-growing major economy of the South, but as a civilizational power, a security actor, and a moral voice. From hosting the G20 Presidency to shaping discourse on climate, trade, and debt relief, India is demonstrating that leadership from the Global South is not reactionary-it is visionary.

The transformation of the Global South from reactive to proactive, from recipient to architect, signals a fundamental shift in how global governance will be conceived and conducted in the decades ahead.

7. Conclusion - Architectures of Hope

The global order is not collapsing-it is being reimagined, recalibrated, and recontested. The objective is not to replace one hegemony with another, but to construct ecosystems of cooperation, accountability, and plural legitimacy that reflect the complexity of today's world.

From feminist foreign policies and green multilateralism, to indigenous diplomacy, AI ethics, and digital sovereignty, the contours of a new global order are emerging-unevenly, yet unmistakably. These shifts signal a departure from rigid, top-down governance toward models that are networked, decentralized, and deeply normative.

At the heart of this reimagination stands India-a rising civilizational power that brings to the table not just economic and military strength, but a philosophical worldview grounded in pluralism, strategic autonomy, and democratic resilience. India's approach to global politics is not hegemonic but harmonic, seeking to align power with justice, speed with deliberation, and sovereignty with solidarity.

As India bridges dialogues between North and South, East and West, it champions a future where leadership is earned through example, not imposition. Whether through its advocacy for Global South priorities, its contribution to Digital Public Goods, or its principled stance on multi-alignment and equitable multilateralism, India is shaping the architecture of hope for a fractured world.

In this emerging age of strategic pluralism, order will not arise from command but from consent. It will not be engineered from above, but cultivated from within-through dialogue, experimentation, mutual respect, and collective vision.

This is the unfinished task of global politics in the 21st century. And in this task, India is not a bystander-it is a builder.

Key References:

- Acharya, A. (2014). Constructing Global Order: Agency and Change in World Politics.
- Buzan, B., & Lawson, G. (2015). The Global Transformation: History, Modernity and the Making of International Relations.
- Mazarr, M. J. (2017). The Once and Future Order: What Comes After Hegemony?
- Stuenkel, O. (2016). Post-Western World: How Emerging Powers Are Remaking Global Order.
- Weiss, T. G., & Wilkinson, R. (2014). International Organization and Global Governance.
- Ikenberry, G. J. (2020). A World Safe for Democracy: Liberal Internationalism and the Crises of Global Order.
- United Nations. (2023). Our Common Agenda – Progress Report.

Author's Reflection

Conclusion: Navigating the Unfinished Architecture of Global Power

Architectures of hope are being etched across the fractured scaffolding of the international system. The global order is not in freefall-it is in flux. What we are witnessing is not the collapse of world order, but its reconstitution. Power is not vanishing; it is being redistributed, reshaped, and increasingly redefined by the interplay of diverse actors, normative frameworks, and transnational challenges.

In this evolving geopolitical landscape, the ambition is no longer to replace one hegemon with another. The emerging architecture aspires to something more enduring: ecosystems of cooperation rooted in accountability, inclusion, and plural legitimacy. From the institutionalization of climate justice and global health equity to the rising influence of digital sovereignty and data ethics, the framework of international relations is being stretched to accommodate new priorities and players.

These transformations are uneven and contested, but undeniably underway. Feminist foreign policies are reframing security beyond military calculus. Indigenous diplomacy is broadening the definitions of legitimacy and land. AI ethics and digital governance are forcing a reckoning with power beyond the state. Green multilateralism is reconfiguring diplomacy around planetary survival rather than national dominance.

And in this shifting order, the essential task is to reconcile competing imperatives: to align power with justice, to balance urgency with deliberation, and to ensure that sovereignty coexists with solidarity. It is a tall order-but a necessary one. Because legitimacy in this new era will not be secured through coercion or exclusion. It will emerge from dialogue, consent, and collaborative imagination.

The future of global power will not be defined by empire or ideology, but by the capacity to mediate difference and manage interdependence. It will not belong to those who dominate institutions, but to those who can renovate them to reflect a world more interconnected, more diverse, and more unequal than ever before.

India's rise, along with that of other strategically agile powers, signals a profound recalibration, where influence is earned through narrative, negotiation, and normative leadership, not merely through arms or alliances. As the old order recedes, a new architecture is under construction-not yet complete, not without fault lines, but full of possibility.

To navigate this unfinished architecture of global power is to embrace uncertainty, not as a threat, but as a space for innovation, cooperation, and ethical reinvention. In this sense, power in the 21st century is no longer about control-it is about coherence. And the states that understand this will not just survive in the new order-they will shape it.

India's Stand: Strategic Autonomy in a Multipolar World

India must enter this evolving geopolitical landscape not as a peripheral actor, but as a confident and consequential power. As the world moves steadily toward multipolarity, India, under the assertive leadership of Prime Minister Narendra Modi, must engage with realism, resilience, and resolve, recognizing that global influence today depends on both narrative and leverage.

While the United States remains a dominant force within India's media, technology, finance, and defense ecosystems, overdependence carries strategic risks. As India's economic ascent accelerates-likely surpassing Germany and challenging existing power hierarchies-pushback from entrenched powers is not a question of if, but when. This could manifest through regulatory pressures, sanctions, technology denial regimes, or financial recalibrations intended to preserve the status quo.

To mitigate these vulnerabilities, India must urgently advance its technological sovereignty and industrial depth. The 'Make in India' vision must evolve into a more holistic platform that includes domestic innovation in semiconductors, cloud infrastructure, digital platforms, and AI, reducing reliance on Western digital ecosystems and building the foundation for long-term strategic autonomy.

At the same time, India must retain the diplomatic dexterity to deepen historical partnerships-especially with Russia-and adopt a mature, interest-driven posture toward China. Much like how China once attracted Japanese and Western investment during its rise, India must pragmatically harness Chinese FDI in non-strategic sectors while carefully managing border tensions and geopolitical frictions.

What sets India apart is not just its scale, but its civilizational weight and strategic clarity. Under Modi, India's foreign policy is no longer reactive or risk-averse. It is bold, independent, and increasingly shaping the global narrative-from orchestrating Global South solidarity at the G20 to asserting sovereignty through operations like Operation Sindoor, India is demonstrating that it is not only capable of managing complexity, but of projecting coherence.

India's trajectory must remain anchored in strategic autonomy, economic self-reliance, and inclusive leadership. The objective is not to align blindly with any bloc, but to become a rule-maker in a system long dominated by rule-takers. To borrow from The Godfather, "Keep your friends close, and your enemies closer"-but for India, the core imperative is to keep its interests closest, always.

In the unfinished architecture of global politics, India is no longer just navigating the shifting terrain-it is poised to co-author the blueprint of a new global order.

Gratitude

THANK YOU FOR READING!!

www.ingramcontent.com/pod-product-compliance
Lightning Source LLC
Chambersburg PA
CBHW030429160726
47991CB00005B/1660
* 9 7 9 8 8 9 9 6 1 7 4 0 9 *